Berlitz HAND

M000074552

CHINA

Contents

FAMILY FRIENDLY SYMBOL 👪

This symbol is used throughout the Handbook to indicate a sight, hotel, restaurant or activity that is suitable for families with children.

Top **25** attractions

1 **The Great Wall** China's most famous sight is every bit as spectacular as you expect it to be *(see p.78)*

2 **The Li River, Guilin** The extraordinary limestone peaks of Guilin seem to defy geological possibility *(see p.173)*

Shanghai China's incredible megalopolis shows no signs of resting on its laurels. Prepare to be amazed *(see p.115)*

4 **Lijiang** Wonderfully preserved Old Town beneath awesome Jade Dragon Snow Mountain (see p.216)

5 **Local festivals** Witness exuberant Chinese culture at the dragon-boat races or other festivities (see p.14)

6 **The Terracotta Warriors** The mausoleum of a 3rd-century BC emperor is an unmissable sight (see p.99)

7 **The Forbidden City and Tiananmen Square** Chinese history on a grand, vivid scale (see p.61)

8 **The Silk Road** Travel across China's Wild West along the famous old trade route to Kashgar (see p.230)

9 **Xiamen** The romantic island of Gulangyu is the big draw, but the Old City has appeal, too *(see p.165)*

10 **West Lake, Hangzhou** Classic Chinese beauty spot, framed by pavilions and pagodas *(see p.133)*

12 **Fenghuang** Beautiful old riverside town tucked away in the wilds of western Hunan *(see p.153)*

11 **Hainan beaches** Year-round warmth and white-sand beaches – unique in China *(see p.170)*

13 **Xishuangbanna** Yunnan's tropical south feels closer to Southeast Asia than China *(see p.221)*

14 **Chengdu and environs** The capital of Sichuan is a great place to spend a few days, with a day trip to the giant Buddha at Leshan (see p.208)

15 **Yangzi cruise** The only way to appreciate the majesty of the Yangzi gorges (see p.23, 145)

16 **Guizhou province** A land of exotic minority groups and countless colourful festivals (see p.210)

17 **Hong Kong** Glittering, high-rise Hong Kong is like nowhere else on Earth (see p.183)

18 **Sacred peaks** These holy Buddhist and Taoist mountains offer spectral beauty and calm – if you can beat the crowds *(see p.34)*

19 **The Longmen caves** A superb, and extensive, ensemble of Buddhist statuary *(see p.103)*

20 **Longhsheng rice terraces** Gazing across this astonishing man-made landscape is an experience that will stay with you *(see p.175)*

21 **Pingyao** Probably the best-preserved Old Town in the north of China (see p.97)

22 **The Grand Canal and the water towns** Of 2,000-year vintage, this ancient waterway is lined with fascinating old towns (see p.24, 127)

23 **Train travel** Travelling overnight by train is a great way to see the 'real' China (see p.154)

24 **Dim sum in Guangzhou** There's no better place to sample delectable *yum cha* (see p.161)

25 **Dali** Splendid old walled town amid glorious scenery, blessed with a benign, sunny climate (see p.215)

China Fact File

China, the world's third-largest and most populous country, extends from the tropics to the sub-arctic, from desert to emerald green rice fields. The vast population is concentrated in the east of the country – where dozens of cities have in excess of 1 million inhabitants – in stark contrast to the wide open spaces in the west and far north, which are almost devoid of people.

 BASICS

Official name: People's Republic of China (Zhonghua Renmin Gongheguo)

Population: 1.35 billion (world's largest)

Area: 9,572,900 sq km/ 3,696,100 sq miles (third-largest in world)

Official language: Mandarin (putonghua). There are several regional dialects, including Cantonese spoken in the south and in Hong Kong. Minority groups, such as Tibetans and Uighurs, have their own languages, but Mandarin is increasingly spoken.

Religion: Buddhist, Daoist and Confucian elements are combined to varying degrees. There are significant Muslim, Tibetan Buddhist and Christian minorities.

Capital city: Beijing

Largest cities (urban areas): Shanghai (19 million); Beijing (17.5 million); Guangzhou (10 million); Chengdu (10 million); Wuhan (10 million); Shenzhen (8.6 million). There are some 45 cities across China with populations in excess of 1 million.

President: Hu Jintao

National anthem: March of the Volunteers (Yiyongjun Jinxingqu)

National symbol: Tiananmen Gate beneath five golden stars

Administrative divisions: China is made up of 21 provinces, 8 Autonomous Regions and 1 Special Administrative Region (Hong Kong).

CURRENCY
Renminbi ('the people's currency'),
abbreviated to Rmb. The unit of
currency is the yuan (colloquially
known as *kuai*). Hong Kong currency
is the Hong Kong dollar; Macau's
currency is the pataca.
The following figures are approximate:
£1 = Rmb 10.4
€1 = Rmb 8.7
US$1 = Rmb 6.7
HK$1 = Rmb 0.87

 TIME ZONE
All of China operates within the
same time zone, although Xinjiang,
far to the west of Beijing, has its own
unofficial local time (2 hours behind
Beijing)
GMT + 8 hrs
EST + 13 hours

In January:
    New York: 11pm (previous day)
        London: 4am
        Beijing: noon
        Sydney: 3pm
        Auckland: 3pm

In July:
        New York: midnight
        London: 5am
        Beijing: noon
        Sydney: 2pm
        Auckland: 4pm

KEY TELEPHONE NUMBERS
Country code: +86
(Hong Kong +852, Macau +853)
Police: 110
(Hong Kong and Macau 999)
Ambulance: 120
(Hong Kong and Macau 999)
Fire: 119
(Hong Kong and Macau 999)
Internet domain: cn

AGE RESTRICTIONS
Driving: 18
Drinking: 18
Age of consent: 14
(16 in Hong Kong and Macau)
Smoking: Banned in some public
places.

 ELECTRICITY
220 volts, 50 Hertz
(200 volts in Hong Kong and Macau)
3 flat-pin plug (2-pin round plug in
Hong Kong)

OPENING HOURS
• Banks and main post offices:
  Mon–Fri 8.30 or 9am until 5 or
  6pm. Some large branches are
  open every day, but always closed
  Sundays in Hong Kong and Macau.
• Shops: generally daily 8.30 or 9am
  until 8, 9 or even 10pm in cities.
• Museums: 9am–5 or 6pm; many
  are closed on Mondays.

Trip Planner

WHEN TO GO

Climate

China covers some 35 degrees of latitude, from tropical Hainan Island to the Siberian taiga of Heilongjiang province, and has an east–west span of some 5,200km (3,250 miles). Given this vast area, it is not surprising that the country encompasses a wide variety of climates. Essentially the east is wet, the west dry, everywhere (except high mountain areas) is warm or hot in summer, and only the far south (particularly the southwest) avoids cold weather in winter. All regions see most rain in the summer months.

Areas north of the Chang Jiang (Yangzi River) have cold, dry winters – particularly cold in the northeast where temperatures remain below freezing for months on end. Summers are warm or hot with variable humidity and some torrential rain.

In central China summers are long, hot and humid, with a great deal of rain. In low-lying regions around the Yangzi and along the coasts, winters are fairly mild but often damp: Shanghai is often grey and cool from December to March. The cities of Chongqing, Wuhan and Nanjing are notorious for their fierce summer heat and humidity.

Most of southern China has a sub-tropical climate, with long, hot summers and short, cool winters (even as far south as Hong Kong the temperature can sometimes drop below 10°C/50°F in winter). There are spells of heavy rain in the summer, and typhoons can affect the coasts between July and September. Upland areas inland tend to get a lot of rain throughout the year and can be cold in winter. The exception is Yunnan, which has warmer, drier winters. Southern Yunnan (Xishuangbanna) and Hainan Island have true tropical climates with year-round warmth.

In western China, the Tibet-Qinghai Plateau has moderately warm summers, while winters can get very cold; there is little rainfall throughout the year. Most of Xinjiang is arid and very hot in summer (Turpan is the hottest of all), but frigid in winter.

High/Low Season

The best times for travel are spring (Apr/May) and autumn (Sept/Oct, although the first week of October

Springtime on Huashan, Shaanxi province

Beijing has cold winters, although deep snow is unusual

can be busy – see below). For much of central and southern China, the autumn period in particular offers the best chance of pleasantly warm and dry weather. In northern and western China, visit in spring and autumn to avoid extreme temperatures.

The main exceptions are Yunnan and Hainan Island; the northwest of Yunnan (Dali and Lijiang) is a year-round destination, albeit with more rain in the high summer. The south of the province and Hainan Island are best between October and April.

Avoid travel during Chinese New Year, when the whole country is on the move and plane/train/bus tickets are hard to come by. The first week of October is also a holiday period and very busy.

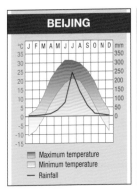

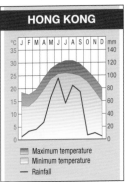

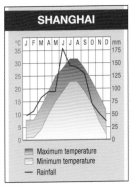

ESSENTIAL EVENTS

Lunar New Year at Beijing's Ditan Park

Official Public Holidays	
1 January	New Year
***mid-Jan/mid-Feb**	Lunar New Year (3–5 days' holiday)
4 or 5 April	Qingming (tomb-sweeping day)
1 May	International Labour Day
***mid-June/mid-July**	Dragon Boat Festival
***mid-Sept/early Oct**	Mid-Autumn Festival
1 October	National Day (3–5 days' holiday)

Traditional festivals, such as the Spring Festival (Lunar New Year), follow the lunar calendar and therefore dates vary annually (within a four-week range). Qingming, however, has a fixed date.

Hong Kong and Macau have their own public holidays.

Major Chinese Festivals (national)

The events listed below are traditional Chinese festivals, and provide great opportunities for visitors to experience Chinese culture. Other official public holidays are of modern invention and are fixed to set calendar dates.

Chinese New Year (*chunjie* – the Spring Festival). The year's most important festival, the Lunar New Year can occur at any time during the month that begins about 21 January. Public buildings are festooned with coloured lights, and people from all over China travel to reunite with family and friends. It is a time for buying new clothes, giving and receiving gifts, paying debts and eating well, and shops and offices close for 3–5 days, or longer. Temple fairs feature martial-arts demonstrations, stand-up comedy, home-made toys and, of course, food. The holiday ends with the Lantern Festival, a carnival of light and noise involving dragon dances, firecrackers and fireworks.

Dragon Boat Festival. On the fifth day of the fifth lunar month – usually in July – this celebration recalls the ancient poet and statesman Qu Yuan (340–278BC), who drowned in Hunan province in spite of efforts to save him by throwing rice cakes into the river to stop the fish devouring his body. Today sweet rice cakes made with dates or nuts are served. Many cities, including Hong Kong, organise highly competitive dragon-boat races.

Mid-Autumn Festival. The date depends on the full harvest moon – between mid-September and early October. Everyone turns out to toast the full moon and hope for a big harvest. The shops do great business in 'moon cakes' (pastries filled with gooey sesame paste, red-bean and walnut filling). In some places, notably Hong Kong, beautiful lantern parades also feature. It is now an official 1-day holiday.

Major Regional Festivals

Regional festivals are held all over China to honour various deities of particular local significance.

The **Matsu (Mazu) Festival** takes place on the 23rd day of the 3rd lunar month April/May) in southern coastal regions, in memory of the Fujianese girl who had a mystical premonition that her father was drowning in a storm and went out to rescue him. Known as Tin Hau in Hong Kong and A-Ma in Macau, she is regarded as the protector of all fishermen. The festival is full of colourful parades, ear-splitting firecrackers, song and dance.

Other festivities mark the the birthdays of **Confucius** (27th day of the 8th lunar month – most notably in Qufu, Shandong province) and **Guanyin**, the Buddhist/Taoist Goddess of Mercy (19th day of the 2nd lunar month).

China's **minority groups** are a rich source of festivals, from the exotic Miao and Dong knees-ups in Guizhou province (see pp.47–9) to the **Buddhist New Year** water-splashing events in southern Yunnan and the various Tibetan spectaculars including **Losar** (Tibetan New Year, usually in February), which leads into **Monlan** or 'Great Prayer' festival. One of the best places to witness this is Labrang Monastery in Xiahe (Gansu province), with pilgrims dressed in their finest clothes from all over the Tibetan-speaking world.

Around Chinese New Year, the amazing **Ice Lantern Festival** takes place in the frigid northern city of Harbin (see p.93).

Water splashing at Buddhist New Year

ITINERARIES

With China's places of interest often hundreds of miles apart, planning an itinerary is important if you want to make the most of your trip. Most people will want to see Beijing and/or Shanghai, as well as Hong Kong, and perhaps Xi'an, and a whistle-stop tour of these major attractions can be achieved in 1–2 weeks. The other area attracting short-stay visitors is the colourful southwest. To explore other parts of China, or anywhere in depth, requires significantly more time.

One Week: Classical China

Days 1–3: Beijing. Get the measure of China, exploring the Forbidden City, Temple of Heaven and the Great Wall.

Days 4–5: Shanghai. Take the overnight express train south to this amazing metropolis.

Day 5: Suzhou and the Grand Canal. Tour the romantic backwaters and classical gardens.

Day 6: Hangzhou. Visit West Lake, quintessential Chinese beauty spot.

Day 7: Hong Kong. Fly south from Shanghai to complete your tour.

Two Weeks: Southwest China

Day 1–2: Hong Kong. Acclimatise to the Far East in frenetic, glittering, unique Hong Kong.

Days 3–5: Guilin and Yangshuo. Marvel at the extraordinary scenery lining the banks of the serene Li River.

Day 7: Kunming. The capital of Yunnan province is known as the city of eternal spring.

Days 8–9: Dali. Unwind for two days in this delightful ancient town.

Days 10–11: Lijiang. A wonderfully atmospheric old town.

Dali, in northwestern Yunnan province, has a magnificent natural setting

Days 12–14: **Tiger Leaping Gorge and Zhongdian.** Awe-inspiring scenery before you head north to the Tibetan town of Zhongdian. Fly back to Hong Kong via Kunming.

Three Weeks: Beijing, Xi'an, Tibet, Sichuan, Guilin and Hong Kong

Days 1–3: **Beijing.** Three days to take in the city's highlights, including the Forbidden City and the Great Wall.
Days 4–5: **Xi'an.** Explore the sights of China's ancient capital including the famous Terracotta Warriors.
Days 5–6: **the train to Tibet.** A thrilling journey to the Land of Snows on the world's highest railway.
Days 7–11: **Lhasa.** Visit the Potala Palace, Jokhang and Ganden.
Days 12–14: **Chengdu and Leshan.** Fly to Sichuan's pleasant capital city, and take a day trip out to Leshan to see the giant buddha.
Days 15–17: **Guizhou.** Take the overnight train to Guiyang, then bus to Kaili, your base for exploring the fascinating minority villages.
Days 18–20: **Guilin and Yangshuo.** Journey by bus from Kaili to Guilin, stopping en route to admire the magnificent Longsheng rice terraces. Two days in Guilin or Yangshuo.
Day 21: **Hong Kong.**

Four Weeks: the Grand Tour

Days 1–3: **Beijing.**
Days 4–5: **Tai Shan.** Take the train south from Beijing to ascend the sacred peak of Tai Shan.
Days 6–7: **Shaolin and the Longmen Caves.** Continue to Zhengzhou to visit the nearby monastery at Shaolin before continuing east to the

Shaolin monastery, martial-arts centre

fabulous cave art at Longmen.
Days 8–9: **Xi'an and the Terracotta Warriors.**
Days 10–16: **Silk Road.** Travel by train from Xi'an to Jiayuguan, the end of the Great Wall, before proceeding to the oases of Dunhuang and Turpan. Bus to Ürümqi, with an excursion to ethereal Heaven Lake, before flying to Chongqing.
Days 17–20: **Yangzi cruise.** Chongqing to Yichang. Witness the majesty of the Yangzi gorges. Bus to Wuhan then fly to Shanghai.
Days 21–25: **Shanghai, Hangzhou and the Grand Canal.** Spend time in the amazing metropolis, with trips out to Suzhou and the Grand Canal, plus Hangzhou's West Lake.
Days 26–27: **Xiamen.** Explore this captivating old port and the charming island of Gulangyu.
Day 28: **Hong Kong.**

BEFORE YOU LEAVE

Visas and Entry Requirements
All foreigners except Japanese and Singaporeans must acquire an entry visa before arrival in China, although those visiting Hong Kong or Macau only do not usually require one. Individual travellers can apply at any Chinese embassy, and the process normally takes one week. If you are entering China from Hong Kong it is easier and quicker to get them there: the China Travel Service (CTS) office (tel: (852) 2853 3533) and the official visa office (tel: (852) 3413 2300) can issue visas in 1–3 days.

A 30-day single-entry visa usually costs US$30–50, but less if you obtain it in Hong Kong. Double- and multiple-entry visas up to six months are also available.

If your visa expires while you are in China, it can be extended by the local Public Security Bureau (police station). However, make sure you take action *before* it expires, because fines for overstaying can be steep.

Nowadays, most of the country

Nationality	Visa Required
UK	✓
US	✓
Canada	✓
Australia	✓
New Zealand	✓
Ireland	✓
Singapore	✗

is open to foreigners, except some border areas and military zones. A permit is still required for Tibet.

Embassies and Consulates
Australia: 15 Coronation Drive, Canberra; tel: (61-2) 6273 4780
Canada: 515 St Patrick St, Ottawa; tel: (613) 789 3434
New Zealand: 2–6 Glenmore St, Wellington; tel: (04) 472 1382
Singapore: 150 Tanglin Rd; tel: (65) 6471 2117
United Kingdom: 31 Portland Place, London; tel: (020) 7636 5637
United States: 2201 Wisconsin Ave NW, Washington DC; tel: (1-202) 337 1956

The bright lights of Hong Kong

Ticket office at Beijing's Summer Palace

Vaccinations

The only compulsory vaccination for visitors to China is yellow fever, and this is only required if you have visited an African or Latin American country within one week of arriving in China. However, it is recommended that you make sure your tetanus and hepatitis inoculations are up to date. If you plan to visit a malarial region, begin treatment before your trip and continue for a specified time after leaving.

Booking in Advance

It's a good idea to pre-book onward travel tickets in advance of your arrival in China. Train tickets can be bought online through www.chinatraintickets.net and www.china-train-ticket.com. For plane tickets, try http://chinatour.net/flight, and www.hotelscombined.com for advance hotel bookings. The http://english.ctrip.com/ site is good for flights, hotels and tours.

Tourist Information

Tourist Information Offices are hard to come by in China, and exist to sell tours rather than to provide information. The best sources of local information tend to be backpacker hostels.

China National Tourism Offices Overseas

Australia: Level 11/ 234 Georges St, Sydney; tel: (02) 9252 9838
Canada: 480 University Ave, Suite 806, Toronto; tel: (416)-599-6636
Singapore: 7 Temasek Blvd, 12-02 Suntec Tower One; tel: 337 2220
United Kingdom: 4 Glenworth St, London; tel: (020) 7935 9787
United States: 350 Fifth Ave, Suite 6413, New York; tel: (1-212) 760 9700

Books

Five recommendations for a richer understanding of China and its people.
The Good Earth, Pearl S. Buck
The Chinese, Jasper Becker
Mao: The Unknown Story, Jung Chang
The True Story of Ah Q, Lu Xun
The Search for Modern China, Jonathan Spence

Packing List

- plug adaptor
- mobile-phone charger
- torch
- earplugs
- high-factor sun block, sunglasses, hat
- pocket alarm
- universal sink plug
- small padlocks for securing luggage on overnight train journeys
- inflatable cushion for long bus rides
- spare credit/debit cards
- a fork (or chopsticks)

UNIQUE EXPERIENCES

Waterways

Rivers and lakes have always been central to the essence of China. The Chinese race evolved near the Yellow River and soon spread to the Yangzi, and 2,000 years later the Grand Canal anchored the empire. For visitors, a river cruise is the perfect way to connect to the country, its people and its history.

Some of the earliest images of China to emerge in the West were of its rivers. Marco Polo told of great cities filled with canals and half-moon bridges, and later came stories and photographs of coolies pulling boats up the Yangzi, of commerce on Shanghai's Bund waterfront, and of bat-wing junks plying the Pearl River near Hong Kong. Such watery images became emblematic of the Middle Kingdom, and the romance was further fuelled by brush paintings and poems that celebrated the smooth silent rivers, the deep gorges and the surrounding green mountains.

The mighty Yellow River, 'China's sorrow'

A Mixed Blessing

In a sense, the rivers (*jiang*) of China founded the country. Early emperors extended their domains and cemented their power by building dykes to tame the river floods, and constructing irrigation canals to supply the rice-based economy. When the Grand Canal opened in AD 600, it stretched 1,800km (1,100 miles) across the plains between Beijing and Hangzhou, linking the Yangzi and the Yellow (Huange He) rivers. It shifted China's centre of gravity to the south, and in the process forged an empire.

China's two dominant rivers, the 6,300km (3,900-mile) Yangzi, and the 5,460km (3,395-mile) Yellow, provide a very mixed blessing. They supply irrigation, transportation and good soil, but are both very prone to highly destructive flooding, bringing great loss of life. The Yellow River in particular, known as 'China's Sorrow,' frequently overflows its banks and changes course with disastrous consequences. Yet the Yangzi is now tamed by the Three Gorges Dam, a project that finally fulfils the flood-fixing promises made by the ancient dynasties.

The Pearl River, while not as important (or as flood-prone) as the Yellow or the Yangzi, is the key river in southern China, its delta region an important transport corridor between Hong Kong and Guangzhou. The Li, Han and other large rivers, while less well known, are no less central to the lives of the people who have lived on their banks since time immemorial.

The lakes (*hu*) of China are not as dramatic or dangerous as its rivers, but they are no less celebrated by the country's poets and painters. Hangzhou's beautiful West Lake (Xi Hu) was made famous by the highly cultured Southern Song dynasty; the concept of placid, mysterious, misted stretches of water has been central to the Chinese idea of natural beauty ever since, as a visit to a classical Chinese garden – nature in stylised form – reveals.

For visitors, travelling on the waterways of China can be a fascinating encounter with the country and its people. The riverbanks are alive with the ceaseless ebb and flow of 21st century commerce, yet they echo with sights and images from the country's distant past.

Cruising the Yangzi

For visitors to China, the key waterway experiences are the Grand Canal and the Yangzi, and of these, the Yangzi takes the crown as the top river trip in China, and one of the best on Earth.

It is possible to cruise the river between Chongqing and Shanghai, but most people choose the 'classic route' from Chongqing to Yichang, a small city just below the Three Gorges Dam. The trip usually takes three nights on a tourist cruise ship, with stops at the points of interest along the way.

The *Yangzi Explorer* (see p.159) is by far the most luxurious boat on the classic route. The five-star liner has just 62 cabins and carries only 124 passengers. It offers gourmet lunches and dinners, a spa, a beauty salon, a lounge bar with Filipino musicians, nightly entertainment, internet connection, and frequent presentations on Chinese history, culture, tea, embroidery and art, along with first-rate shore excursions and English-speaking guides. Of course, all this doesn't come cheap – the cost is around Rmb12,000

Kite-flying on the banks of the Yangzi at Yichang

(US$1,500) per person, depending on the berth and the season. All Yangzi cruises charge more during the peak seasons of May and October, and less during the hot summers, and many of the companies stop cruising altogether during the winter.

There are also many mid-range boats priced in the region of Rmb4,000–8,000 (US$500–1,000) for the Chongqing–Yichang route. *For listings, see p.159.* Local cruise boats, catering primarily to domestic tourists, can be arranged for as little as Rmb2,000 (US$250) for first-class cabins.

First-class cabins have two beds, a television and the all-important air conditioning. Second-class cabins have two to four beds and a private bathroom, while third and fourth classes have dorm rooms and shared bathrooms, and often don't offer access to the upper-level viewing decks.

Sailing through the Three Gorges

An alternative, faster and cheaper way of travelling along the Yangzi is to take a local passenger ferry (*ban chuan*), albeit with the major disadvantage of no exterior seating and no stops at the points of interest. Buy tickets – ideally at least a day in advance – from Chaotianmen ticket office in Chongqing. Hydrofoils cover the route from Wanzhou (three hours by bus from Chongqing) to Yichang in around seven hours.

The Grand Canal

The second-most popular waterway is the Grand Canal, the ancient link between north and central China. This busy, boat-filled expressway is still very much in use in its southern reaches (although the north has long fallen into disrepair), a feature that sets it apart from many other heritage sights in China, with a steady flow of ships, barges and ferries running along its length between Hangzhou and the Yangzi.

The best places to cruise the Grand Canal are Suzhou and Hangzhou, the garden cities so admired by Marco Polo. Four overnight ferries serve the Suzhou–Hangzhou route, and several also ply the longer route between Wuxi and Hangzhou. The Suzhou–Hangzhou ferries range in price from Rmb110 (US$14) per person for a twin-share to Rmb208 (US$28) per person. The trip to Suzhou takes 14 hours, while the return to Hangzhou is slightly shorter. The boat has air-conditioning but the overnight ferries are rather basic, making the route an under-utilised resource that is awaiting the launch of an upscale daytime

The ancient Grand Canal at Suzhou

cruise. For tickets, call the Suzhou Ship Transportation Co., tel: (0512) 6520 6681, or the Shanghai Tourist Hotline, tel: (021) 962288.

Short trips along the Grand Canal, and on the lakes that link it together, are another option. One particularly charming route is the section between the Unesco World Heritage water towns of Tongli and Zhouzhuang, a two-hour trip that can be arranged at either of the towns. Taxi drivers will deliver tourists to one town and pick them up at the other. Similar short excursions along key stretches of the canal are possible from Wuxi and Suzhou, while there is an array of departures from three wharfs in Hangzhou; ferries leave every half-hour from Gongchengqiao and Wulinmen wharfs, and make a third stop en route. These are commuter ferries, but they have viewing decks and cost just Rmb3 for a 30-minute trip.

In Suzhou, canal tours leave every few minutes from Nanmen wharf on Renmin Road, and ply the nearby canals. The bigger boats are cheaper, but they don't visit the smaller residential canal networks that radiate outwards from the Grand Canal. The hour-long Suzhou trip skirts the ancient walls of the Old City, and then slides past the residential waterfronts, where back doors open straight onto the water, and citizens wash clothes, brush teeth, bathe, and otherwise use the canal in time-honoured fashion. Prices are negotiable, and range from Rmb50 to Rmb100 (US$6–12), depending on the size of the boat and the mood of the operator.

City Cruises

Beyond the Grand Canal and the Yangzi, many other waterfront cities offer boat rides on their local rivers. Shanghai is a good example: a

Three Parallel Rivers

The Three Parallel Rivers of western Yunnan province are where the mighty Salween, Mekong and Yangzi run side by side for several hundred kilometres, surging through gorges separated by immense towering peaks on their journey from the Tibetan Plateau.

number of different trips leave from Shiliupu Dock, which opened in 2010 on the renovated Bund. The choices range from four-hour round-trip cruises to the mouth of the Yangzi, to one-hour up-and-down jaunts that take in the towers of Pudong and the historic buildings of the Bund, and prices range from Rmb80 to about Rmb500 for a luxury cruise that includes dinner. The boats run all day and in the evenings, and visitors who wish to do a short cruise can simply go to Shiliupu Dock and buy a ticket. The longer cruises to the Yangzi leave at 2pm every afternoon, while more extensive three-hour night-time cruises can be booked in advance at many travel agencies, such as www. worldtravelguide.net/tour/115/city_tours/Far-East-Asia/Shanghai.html.

In mid-2010, Shanghai began offering boat trips up and down Suzhou Creek, beginning from historic Waibaidu Bridge near the Huangpu to Changfeng, a 12km (7-mile), hourlong trip that costs Rmb45. Beyond that, if you are in any waterfront city and wish to take a boat ride, just ask. Chongqing, Nanjing, Guangzhou, Shantou and many other cities offer such excursions. In Hong Kong, the famous Star Ferries afford wonderful views of the harbour skyline for a bargain price, while in Beijing it is possible to journey by boat to the Summer Palace from the west of the city via a network of canals.

Li River

This is the place to come for magical river scenery – the famous karst landscapes around Guilin as captured in a million traditional Chinese scroll paintings. The must-do cruise on the Li is the five-hour trip between Guilin and Yangshuo; for passengers flying into Guilin, the switch to the ferry and the ride on the magical Li, with its signature karst limestone spires and emerald-green jungles, is a perfect introduction to the gentle charms of Yangshuo.

Cruising the Huangpu River, Shanghai

The Li River near Guilin

The boats depart from a tourist wharf in Guilin in the mornings, and some packages include a bus trip back to the starting point. Spring and summer are best, as low water levels often close part of the route during the winter.

Other options on the river and its tributaries include bamboo rafting, floating and kayaking. The Li is admired for its crystal-clear water, said to be the cleanest in China. Trips on powered bamboo rafts have long been popular; these leave and return from Yangshuo. Bamboo rafting on the Yulong, a tributary, is also becoming more popular; one-hour, two-hour and four-hour trips are available. Most operators also offer kayak trips of varying lengths, and will meet boaters downstream. Unpowered float trips on the nearby Long Jing River have recently surged in popularity, as the soundless rafts provide a serene trip through some of the finest scenery in Asia.

Water Towns

Tucked away on some of the country's backwaters are picturesque old river towns. Fenghuang (*see p.153*) in western Hunan province is a prime example, but there are many others – including the beautiful Dong village of Zhaoxing in Guizhou province, and the villages along the Mekong in south and southwest Yunnan.

Dragon Boats

The time-honoured relationship between the Chinese and their rivers and lakes is illustrated by the Dragon Boat Festival, which takes place on the fifth day of the fifth lunar month, usually in late June. Dragon-boat races, swimming and other water-based pastimes highlight the celebration. Races are fiercely competitive. Two of the major gatherings are in Hong Kong (*see p.203*), and Yueyang in Hunan province – close to Dongting Lake, from where the legend of Qu Yuan originates. The story relates how the famous poet (Qu Yuan) drowned himself so as to avoid witnessing his kingdom's imminent defeat. Locals leapt into their boats to try and save his life – but to no avail. Pork and *zongzi* (sticky rice wrapped in leaves) were then thrown into the river to placate Qu's spirit.

Eating Out in China

Restaurants are where the Chinese socialise, have fun and let their hair down with good food and friends, wine and beer, in an atmosphere that is relaxed, happy and loud. For visitors, eating out offers insight into Chinese culture, and a chance to enjoy some excellent food as well.

Chinese cuisine provides an easy entry point into the country's culture, and a visit to a neighbourhood restaurant is a great way to experience China more deeply. Visitors will sometimes be forced to grapple with menus in Chinese, and waiters who don't speak English. Their table might be visited by cheerful fellow diners drinking *huang jiu* (yellow rice wine) and proposing toasts. Or perhaps a Chinese fellow diner will grab the bill, forcing a round of ritual protests about who pays the tab, or maybe he will insist that a guest sit in a certain seat, igniting a conversation about Chinese concepts of hierarchy.

Despite a certain Western perception of a universal 'Chinese' food (based on the experience of Chinese takeaways in Europe and America), China remains a regional country, and its diversity is reflected in the food: there is no true national cuisine. In Guangdong, for example, seafood is common and fuel is scarce, and flash-frying is the most popular cooking style. In Sichuan, far from the oceans, the cuisine is dominated by hot spicy preparations and pickled preserves, the better to mask the lack of freshness and preserve the flavour. In the Muslim west, lamb and mutton are more common and pork is absent,

Shopping mall dining, Hong Kong

while in Beijing, land of the imperial cuisines, roasting is common and wheat largely replaces rice. For more on regional cuisine, *see pp. 284–7.*

Ordering and the Philosophy of Food

Ordering food in China is more art than science. In a perfect world, you will end up with a handsome selection of dishes that complement each other in flavour, colour and cooking style.

Some easy guidelines will help you through the process. Remember that variety is the key to a well-composed Chinese meal: a number of different ingredients and cooking methods, a nice display of colours, some big chunks and some small pieces, and a range of flavours from spicy to sweet to mild. The Chinese phrase is *se xiang wei ju quan*, which means 'colour, fragrance and taste in complete harmony'.

Another concept that provides balance is the idea that certain foods have either 'hot' or 'cold' properties. People in the south, and older folks, believe that these hot and cold properties should be balanced to avoid indigestion and other ailments. The properties have nothing to do with temperature; instead they are related to the concepts of *yin* (cold) and *yang* (hot). These in turn are related to the dryness of the food, with watery vegetables such as bean sprouts, cabbage, carrots, watercress and cucumber on the 'cold' list, and dry items, especially spices and meats including beef, chicken, ginger, mushrooms, and sesame oil, on the 'hot' list.

The general diversity of ingredients makes it easy to order a variety of dishes. Even a small restaurant will offer four or five vegetables, several egg dishes, some different kinds of tofu, and lots of pork and chicken. Most will also have beef and maybe

A selection of healthy Shanghai dishes

lamb, and several types of fish and shellfish. Menus are usually divided into chicken, fish, meat, vegetables, tofu and appetisers.

Flavours and strengths should be balanced, especially when eating a spicy cuisine like Hunanese or Sichuan. In a Sichuan restaurant, a sweet dish like home-style tofu, or a mild soup or vegetable or noodle dish, can relieve the pervasive presence of garlic, chilli and Sichuan peppercorns. In a Cantonese restaurant, crispy chicken dipped in salt and pepper balances the sweet-sour combinations that are the hallmark of southern cooking. In Shanghai, a mild snow-pea and chicken dish can provide pea-popping relief from the satisfying fattiness of *dong po rou* (stewed pork belly).

A good general rule is to order one dish for every diner, plus one extra. Select maybe one chicken dish, one beef or pork, a couple of vegetables, an

Early Doors

The Chinese tend to eat early, and lunch is often served from 11am. Away from the big cities, dinner starts at 6pm, and you won't easily find a meal after 8.30pm.

egg or tofu dish, and possibly a fish or shellfish dish, depending on the restaurant. Always order an appetiser, and, especially if Chinese are present, a soup.

Etiquette

Listening to Chinese diners emit happy sated belches, and watching them talk with their mouths full and smoke cigarettes between bites, a visitor might be tempted to conclude that they have no table manners at all. They do, it's just that the issues are different. Chinese guidelines govern social interplay and hygiene, rather than the physical act of eating.

A spilled glass is not a catastrophe; more often, it indicates a fun-loving, free-spirited event. Chinese diners cherish a lively, boisterous atmosphere, filled with toasts and jokes and conversation, rather than the formal tones of top Western restaurants, with their sedate atmospheres and their emphasis on table manners.

Despite all of this, certain formalities remain important. One example is the seating ritual, which illustrates Chinese notions of hierarchy. Getting everyone to sit down can take some time, as guests refuse the honour of a prestigious seat, arguing that they are not worthy, and that the higher seat surely must belong to someone else. The best approach for visitors is to stand for a few moments as the Chinese sort themselves out, and wait for a cue. Spouses always sit together.

Some of the rules are hygiene-related, although they are often ignored. For example, communal dishes come with a serving spoon or serving chopsticks; use these to put food on your own plate or bowl, and then return the spoon to the common dish. Also, it is not polite to 'troll' through common dishes with your personal chopsticks, looking for the best nuggets.

Beyond that, there are a few other courtesy tips. If you want tea, pour a cup for your neighbours first. Chopsticks should be placed on the chopstick rest when you are drinking or talking – they should not be waved around, and should never be used to point. When serving yourself, take the portion of food nearest to you, and never, ever stick your chopsticks

Dim sum in Guangzhou

Xiao long bao, a Shanghai speciality

straight into the rice. This is a funeral arrangement, and is very bad luck.

Highlights: Dim Sum

Nothing captures the loud and lively essence of Chinese dining as completely as a dim-sum brunch. Its most vibrant incarnation is in Hong Kong and Guangzhou, where at weekends, and especially on Sundays, the best establishments are identified by long, loud queues at the doors, while the interiors resound with the boisterous rattle and clatter of dim-sum carts and the din of hundreds of people talking and shouting at the same time. An archetypal Cantonese treat, dim sum is becoming popular throughout China, especially in upscale restaurants and five-star hotels.

Dim sum is the Cantonese word for *dian xin*, which is variously translated as little hearts, touch the heart, tiny morsel or even order to your heart's content. It is also called *yum cha*. The dim-sum carts, pushed about by harried, no-nonsense waitresses, offer some standard specialities, including translucent steamed dumplings containing combinations of pork, shrimp and vegetables; steamed buns with barbecue pork; pork and chicken congee; pan-fried potstickers; wet, hard-to-hold rice

---

Reading the Menu

Chinese menus are more easily navigated if you know a few simple words *(see also Phrasebook, p.297)*

Preparations

song: minced into tiny squares.

si: shredded. literally, it means threads.

ding: cut into chunks.

kuai: cut in larger pieces, often with bones.

Cooking styles

chao: to stir-fry quickly in an open wok, with a little oil.

jian: to pan-fry slowly.

zheng: to steam in a covered bamboo basket.

kao: to dry-cook. Ovens are rare in China, so *kao* often means barbecue.

zha: to deep-fry.

shao: to braise in a rich broth, and serve with the resulting gravy.

Ingredients

ji: chicken

zhu rou: pork

niu rou: beef

yu: fish

yang rou: lamb or mutton

baifan: boiled rice

chaofan: fried rice

miantiao: noodles

Highly prized: the Kunshan hairy crab

noodle rolls with pork fillings; savoury fried cakes made from radish or taro root; meatballs and steamed spareribs; chicken and goose feet, and many more choices besides. The delicate treats are invariably washed down by near-endless pots of jasmine or pu'er tea.

Highlights: Peking Duck

The top dish in the northern repertoire is Peking duck. Once the exclusive dish of Mandarins, roast duck has spread like wildfire throughout the country, and is now available at reasonable prices virtually everywhere; it is even making its way into street stalls and night-market stands, though the quality is much better at upscale establishments.

Ubiquitous though it is, the dish isn't easy to make. Super-fat, force-fed ducks are slaughtered and rinsed, then blown up like balloons, a process that separates the skin from the flesh and guarantees super-crispy slices of succulent skin. The ducks are then painted in sugary syrup and roasted for 30 to 40 minutes. Because of the long roasting time, ducks are often ordered in advance. Sometimes a showy chef will slice the duck at the table, with

Shanghai Hairy Crab

The most remarkable seasonal food in China, and an annual food craze that has no parallel anywhere else on Earth, is the Shanghai Hairy Crab season in Kunshan, a small town an hour's drive from Shanghai. Every weekend from mid-October until the end of December, the highway from Shanghai is bumper-to-bumper with crab-crazed diners driving to Yangcheng Lake, where hundreds of hairy-crab restaurants stand on stilts over the water, all of them filled with crab-lovers eating the humble 10cm (3in) crustacean.

Other places produce hairy crab – Tai Lake near Suzhou, for one – but the Kunshan crab has a unique sweet flavour that is unmatched. All Kunshan crabs come from Yangcheng Lake, where the clean water imparts a one-of-a-kind flavour, what the French would call *terroir*. Powerboats are prohibited on Yangcheng Lake, because they would pollute the water and bother the crabs.

The Kunshan hairy crabs have a velvety, buttery texture and mild, sweet flavour that is enhanced by a dip of vinegar, ginger and sugar, and normally washed down by a glass of *huang jiu*. Such exotic flavours don't come cheap: a pair of crabs – male and female – can start at Rmb160 to 180, and go on up to Rmb400. But price is no object, and the annual ritual becomes more popular with each passing year.

the best slicers achieving 108 perfect pieces of duck. The meat is served in tiny delicate pancakes, accompanied by fresh scallions, and dipped in a sweet sauce made from fermented bean. The skin should be crisp and fresh and never oily, the spring onion mild and sweet, and the pancakes fresh and never sticky. In some places, the duck bones are boiled and served as soup at the end of the meal.

Street Food and Markets

Street food in China caters to the poor, with greasy squid, fatty sausages, deep-fried meat, stir-fried cabbage and tofu, boiled tripe and other cheap and cheerful offerings that comprise a quick meal for Rmb5 or less. Hygiene is suspect, and many of the vendors are illegal 'wild chickens' that set up shop after dark, with a wokful of boiling oil and a bagful of doubtful ingredients. But happily, some street foods are both safe and delicious. Heading the list are the ever-popular steamed buns, or *baozi*. Marked by puffs of steam and coils of bamboo steamers, these shops purvey pork, vegetable, sweet-sesame and red-bean buns, all of them cheap (usually one kuai or less) and satisfying. Another reliable option is the breakfast pancake, or *you bing*. These fried dough pancakes, often containing scallion and sometimes an egg, are a morning staple throughout China. Muslim Uighur stands, which serve so-so skewers of fatty lamb, flatbread and rich, doughy dumplings filled with savoury lamb filling, also provide a quick pick-me-up for undemanding diners.

Street food at Donghuamen night market in Beijing

Sacred Mountains

The sacred mountains of China are steeped in mysticism, rich in lore and history, and studded with pagodas and temples. They are visited by legions of pilgrims, sightseers and tourists, who are attracted by the religious aspects and stunning natural beauty of the peaks.

Climbing one of China's sacred mountains propels the visitor away from the born-again capitalism of its modern, money-mad cities, and into its earliest, Neolithic beginnings. The sacred peaks hark back to an older domain, when Mother Nature ruled, ghosts were legion and man insignificant. Joining the pilgrims on an ascent is a wonderful way to connect with the country's enduring spirituality – although you'll need to time your visit carefully to avoid the tourist hordes.

In ancient times, these misted heights were steeped in legend, haunted by dragons, witches, immortals, spirits and other supernatural beings. As pillars connecting Heaven to Earth, they had magical powers, and legendary sages and philosophers travelled great distances to spend time lost in contemplation on their slopes. Way back in the past, animists worshipped the mountains even before Daoists, and later Buddhists, began to attach their own spiritual significance to them.

There are nine holy mountains scattered across China: five Daoist and four Buddhist. The **Daoist mountains** are arrayed in four directions like a cross, with 1,440m (4,720ft) **Song Shan**, in Henan province, in the middle. The easternmost peak is 1,545m (5,070ft) **Tai Shan**, in Shandong, while to the

Tai Shan, high above the North China plain

west is 2,160m (7,090ft) **Hua Shan**, in Shanxi. Also in Shanxi province, is 2,017m (6,620ft) **Heng Shan**, while hundreds of miles to the south is its 1,290m (4,232ft) namesake in Hunan. Hua Shan and Tai Shan are most deeply associated with Daoism, while the others cling more tightly to their mystical roots.

The pre-eminent **Buddhist mountain** is 3,099m (10,167ft) **Emei Shan**, in Sichuan province, which attracts enormous numbers of pilgrims and tourists. The others are the lofty 3,058m (10,032ft) **Wutai Shan**, in Shanxi province, 1,342m (4,403ft) Jiuhua Shan, in Anhui; and much smaller 284m (930ft) Putuo Shan, an island off the coast of Zhejiang province.

Before you Ascend

To climb a sacred mountain, you won't need much beyond a good pair of shoes and a warm, waterproof jacket, as stone steps and guardrails line most of the routes, and hostels, vendors and restaurants are plentiful. Expect admission charges of up to Rmb200, with associated temples and other sites also charging admission.

Seekers of solitude will be disappointed, however, for the majority of the year: sacred though they may be, the mountains have become major tourist attractions. Cable cars whisk those with little time or desire for contemplation up to the summits, and litter and noise are big problems. Overall, spring and autumn are the best times to visit,

Buddhist monastery at Wutai Shan

although you can expect crowded trails, especially at weekends. One way to beat at least partially the crowds is to overnight at a monastery on the mountain, then set off at (or before) dawn to climb the remainder of the trail.

Versatile Gods

The deities worshipped in China are not jealous gods: Buddhism and Daoism mix easily and often, and most of the sacred peaks share both religions, while local folk religions are also popular on the mountains. The odd man out is Confucius: China's Confucian tradition, dealing as it did with the world of strict ritual and human relations, had no place in the mystic mountains – hence the absence of sacred Confucian mountains. Yet there has been a steady evolution, from animist to Daoist to Buddhist, as the four Buddhist peaks began as Daoist preserves, before becoming associated with Buddhism, which came much later.

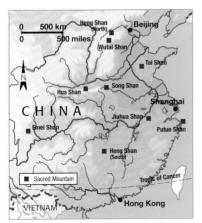

Daoist Mountains

Song Shan

Located on the south bank of the Yellow River in Henan province, Song Shan (Rmb10–100, depending on area) is a 60km (40-mile) long range, rather than a single mountain, that extends from Luoyang to Zhengzhou. Those two cities are the entry points for a visit, and tours can be arranged from either city. Dengfeng, a smaller town that lies between Luoyang and Zhengzhou, is the best base for explorations of its trail and temple network.

The mountain attracts huge crowds, largely because 1,500-year-old **Shaolin Temple** *(see p.103)* lies on its slopes. World-famous as the epicentre of Chinese kung fu and the birthplace of Zen Buddhism, the martial-arts shows are a big attraction.

Tai Shan

As the Daoist peak that greets the dawn, Tai Shan (Rmb100 winter/125 summer) is the mother mountain of birth and renewal, and spiritually it is the most powerful Daoist peak. It is also one of the most-climbed on earth, attracting nearly 10 million visitors per year. Its 'stairway to heaven' is one of the most famous sights in China, while the Immortal Bridge, a natural bridge of tightly wedged rocks, and **Tai Miao Temple** (daily 7.30am–6.30pm; Rmb20) a vast, palace-style temple honouring the god of the mountain, are also popular. Tai Miao was the venue for elaborate sacrifices and provided quarters for the emperor before he ascended Tai Shan.

Two routes lead to the summit. The famous east route, with its iconic stairway to heaven, a broad steep path of more than 7,000 steps that is filled with pilgrims, has two dozen temples, hundreds of inscriptions and many ruins. The west route is less crowded, though it has fewer religious attractions. Tourists who wish to avoid these arduous climbs (allow a full day from base to summit and back again) can do so; buses carry visitors part-way up, while a cable car (daily 8.30am–5pm; Rmb80 one-way, 140 round-trip) takes visitors to just below

Contemplation on the slopes of Song Shan

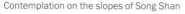

A shrine on Hua Shan

South Peak to North Peak. These planks, suspended from the cliff face, require a harness (Rmb40), and are scary indeed. Hostels, restaurants and vendors dot the popular routes. Hua Shan lies 120km (75 miles) east of Xi'an; frequent buses take two hours.

Heng Shan (Hunan)

Two of the five Daoist mountains are named Heng Shan. The southern incarnation (Rmb100), in Hunan province, is a range rather than a peak, with some 70 relatively gentle hilltops lined up on a 150km (95-mile) ridge. The chief peak is 1,290m (4,232ft) Wishing for Harmony Peak (Zhurong Feng), an eight-hour round trip hike from the village of Nanyue, 120km (75 miles) from the provincial capital Changsha. Lacking the natural drama of Hua Shan, or the temple-strewn history of Tai Shan, it is one of the least visited of the nine peaks.

The **Heng Shan Grand Temple** (daily 8am–5pm; Rmb40) is a large palace-style complex that sits on a 1,300-year-old site; largely destroyed in the Cultural Revolution, much of what you see is a reconstruction.

Sacred Mountains

the summit. Both road and stairs are lined with vendors, inns, restaurants and shops. The starting point for tourists is the town of Tai'an, around an hour by bus from the provincial capital, Jinan.

Hua Shan

Hua Shan (Rmb60/100), the westernmost of the Daoist mountains, is also one of the most beautiful, with an array of jagged peaks that lie in a semicircle, like the petals of a flower (Hua Shan means 'Flower Mountain'). The range has many summits: Tai Hua Shan remains the goal of most visitors, although East Peak, which has four 'summits' and peaks to the south and west, is also popular. As with the other peaks, Hua Shan features an abundance of temples and religious sites.

Hua Shan is most famous for its dangerous trails carved into cliff faces, especially the 'plank walk' trail from

---

Sunrise

Getting to the top of a mountain before sunrise, a deep-rooted Chinese tradition, was originally established to avoid vertigo. The dark and unseen cliffs, it was thought, would not be so frightening, and at the same time, fewer pilgrims would jostle for space on the thin trails. Dawn is also the source of rebirth and renewal, and is the best time to view the 'sea of clouds' phenomenon.

Heng Shan (Shanxi)

Remote and hard to reach, the northern Heng Shan (daily 6.30am–7pm; Rmb55) in Shanxi province is not as popular or significant as Song Shan, Tai Shan or Hua Shan. Yet it does have one of the most famous sights in China: the gravity-defying **Xuankong Si** (Hanging Monastery,;daily 6.30am–7pm; Rmb130/152). *For more on the monastery, see p.97.*

Heng Shan's most popular summit is 2,017m (6,617ft) Tianfeng Peak, which is served by cable cars as well as trails. The point of departure for the monastery is the village of Hunyuan, 63km (40 miles) south of Datong city.

Buddhist Mountains
Emei Shan

The most famous Buddhist peak is **Emei Shan** (daily 6am–5pm; Rmb90/150), in Sichuan province. This was China's first Buddhist holy site, as the religion spread from west to east. The mountain is strewn with more than 70 monasteries, many from the Ming and Qing eras, and it is also famous for its 'sea of clouds' phenomenon, as cottony clouds fill the deep valleys at dawn.

It is possible to leave the provincial capital of Chengdu before dawn, travel 150km (95 miles) to the mountain, take a bus and a cable car (daily 5.30am–6pm; Rmb50/120) to the two temples at Jinding, make the short hike from there to the summit, and return to Chengdu in the same day. But Emei Shan is large – its main hiking path is more than 50km (31 miles) long, and visitors who wish to explore further can stay in one of the many lodges and monasteries that offer accommodation. Beautiful scenery abounds, and the protected forests shelter rare animal and bird species, as well as an abundance of butterflies.

Wutai Shan

Deep in the backwaters of north China, **Wutai Shan** (Rmb218, includes transportation) was spared from the vandalism of the Cultural Revolution by its sheer remoteness, and as a result it features superb, original temple architecture. Its five peaks – at 3,058m (10,032ft), the loftiest point in northern China – are strewn with more than 50 monasteries, many of them in fine condition. These include **Nanchan Temple** (Rmb10), the oldest wooden building in China.

Wutai Shan is located halfway between Taiyuan and Datong, a

Burning incense at an Emei Shan temple

five-hour bus trip from either city. A large concentration of temples can be found in the tourist village of **Taihuai**, nestled in a valley encircled by the mountains, as well as several small hotels, and restaurants.

Jiuhua Shan

Jiuhua Shan (Rmb190), in Anhui province, features hundreds of temples spread over an area of some 120 sq km (39 sq miles). A land of rolling, rounded hills rather than dramatic peaks, the main attraction is **Tiantai Temple** (daily 7am–6pm; included in main ticket), a rambling, five-storey structure that sits like a castle atop precipitous Tiantai Peak, while **Huacheng Temple** (daily 7am–6pm; included in main ticket), originally built 2,000 years ago, though renovated since, is the most famous temple on the mountain.

Jiuhua Shan exudes a quiet beauty. The area is filled with waterfalls, caves, and groves of pine and bamboo. Tourists base themselves in Jiuhua Street, a small strip of hotels, shops, restaurants and other amenities on the lower slopes of the mountain.

Putuo Shan

Few would call modest **Putuo Shan** (Rmb140/200) a mountain – it is just 284m (930ft) tall – but its religious significance is very real, and it attracts pilgrims from all over China. The island which it dominates is dotted with monasteries big and small, but its most famous attractions are a 33m (108ft) statue of Guanyin at Zizhulin, and its two holiest sites, Puji and Fayu temples, are impressive.

Tiantai Temple, Jiuhua Shan

The 'mountain' also boasts a pair of beaches – Hundred-Step and Thousand-Step – both with admission charges and modest amenities.

Boats to Putuo Shan leave from Ningbo, in Zhejiang province, and Shanghai, while the island's tourist sights are served by minibuses.

Huang Shan

Huang Shan, just south of Jiuhua Shan in Anhui province, is not considered sacred in the same way as the other peaks, yet deserves a mention as this is, above all, the mountain that is immortalised in countless Chinese scroll paintings. Together with Tai Shan, it is the peak that most Chinese aspire to climb, and the scenery is utterly spellbinding – all twisted pines on towering cliffs above a sea of clouds. It is accessed easily by bus (to the foot of the mountain) from Nanjing, Shanghai, Hangzhou and Hefei.

Wilderness China

Most China tours focus on big cities and iconic sights, such as Beijing and the Great Wall, Shanghai and the Bund, and Xian and the Terracotta Warriors. But the country also has vast tracts of wilderness where determined visitors can see rare animals, observe minority lifestyles and trek into untrammelled wilds amid stupendous natural beauty.

Perceptions of China tend to revolve around the huge numbers of inhabitants: vast, teeming cities, crowded transport, densely populated countryside, abundant cheap labour, and other visions of a people-packed place. Those images have a firm basis in fact, as anyone knows who has visited one of China's super-crowded cities, or taken a train across its town-and-factory-filled plains and gazed at the endless residential blocks, villages, roads, warehouses, retail stores, and other endless urban-sprawl developments.

But this, the world's third-largest country, also encompasses large swathes of remote wilderness, into which few people ever venture. The vast majority of China's 1.3 billion people live in the coastal flatlands, an area that has precious few pockets of genuine wilderness, while at the other extreme, the high mountains and plateaux have tiny populations and vast tracts of empty land.

This sharply divided demographic is a result of geography, as China is split into distinct regions: coastal flatlands, central steppes and the high mountains of the far west. As the land rises ever higher in the west, the land gets more forbidding and the climate ever fiercer. As conditions become increasingly extreme – drier, colder or hotter, depending on the season – the population dwindles dramatically.

The most epic wilderness begins in the far perimeters of China, a ring of territory that includes the Helan Mountains in north-central China, the Taklimakan and Gobi deserts in the northwest, the Tibetan Plateau and Himalayan peaks in the west, and the jungle-covered mountains of southwestern Yunnan and Guizhou provinces.

Geography aside, the overwhelming emptiness of far western China also

The Helan Mountains in the bleak Mongolian borderlands

The Tibetan plateau is one of the least populated places on the planet

has cultural roots: generally speaking, the Han Chinese don't like empty spaces, and most prefer to live in cities and towns surrounded by fellow citizens. Few Chinese would choose to live in remote areas unless they must, nor do they visit the wilderness areas in great numbers. As a result, visitors who take the time and effort – and large amounts of both are required – can experience unique wild areas that are rich in wildlife, filled with fascinating minority tribes and overflowing with rare natural beauty.

Unless you are willing to make arrangements (you'll need lots of time to do this, particularly if you don't speak Chinese), it is advisable to book a package tour into the remote wilderness, where public transport is lacking, hotels and restaurants widely scattered and English largely nonexistent. In most cases the key hurdle will be making arrangements rather than travelling to the sites, as China's

steadily improving roads, rails and airports have made many of the remote areas much easier to reach. There are exceptions, such as the distant hinterlands of Tibet and northwest Yunnan province, which are filled with high mountains and pierced by just a few bone-jarringly rough dirt roads.

Tibet

One of the most obvious, and exciting, destinations for any wilderness-seeking visitor is Tibet. The vast autonomous region is almost entirely comprised of wilderness, mostly high-elevation grassland plateaux and rocky snow-capped mountains. The inspiring scenery is enhanced by the presence of the Tibetans, as even the most distant patches of grassland are often dotted with yurts, lonely monasteries and herds of yaks and goats and other livestock.

Most travellers begin their Tibet experience by taking the train from Beijing or elsewhere. The epic journey gives fine views of the Tibetan wilderness, with antelopes, yaks, birds and remote mountain lakes and glaciers all looming outside the large picture windows.

Several companies offer well-supported treks into the Tibetan outback, including China Hiking Adventure Inc. (www.china-hiking.com/tibet/itinerary.html). The company's five-day hikes begin at 600-year-old Ganden Monastery, a two-hour drive from Lhasa, and then traverse the grassy steppes and superlative scenery of the high plateau, with its up-close views of the snow-capped Himalayas, and its Tibetan Buddhist pagodas, stupas, monasteries and ancient ruins.

Yaks carry essential belongings, and trekkers stay in yurts like the nomads themselves, and have ample opportunities to meet Tibetans and experience their spartan way of life. The trek proceeds at an easy pace, but it isn't for the out-of-shape, as it begins at 3,800 m (12,500ft) and then winds its way over the top of a 4,940m (16,200ft) pass, before ending at the monastery of Samye.

The Qinling Mountains

Another first-rate wilderness tour, this one in the remote and little-known Qinling mountains of Shaanxi province, takes visitors through rugged mountains in search of the iconic emblem of China, the giant panda. This is a more challenging, and rewarding, experience than the more commonly made trip to the panda sanctuary at Wolong in western Sichuan. Animal-lovers join a small group

Giant pandas can be seen in the wild in the Qinling Mountains south of Xi'an

of fellow aficionados led by Indri Tours (www.indritours.com) and trek into some of the wildest and wettest terrain in China, in search of the elusive wild pandas. The week-long journey requires long hikes over rugged forested terrain, in order to reach the animals' preferred habitat. Accommodation is basic but comfortable as the small groups visit the Changqing and Foping nature reserves, which are reached via Xi'an. The temperate broadleaved and coniferous forests are filled with other wildlife as well, including Golden Takin antelopes, Golden snub-nosed monkeys, Red-and-white giant flying squirrels, while Golden pheasants, Golden eagles, Red-billed blue magpies and other bird species also haunt the misty forests.

Tiger Leaping Gorge is one of the highlights of northwest Yunnan

Yunnan

Nowhere else in China offers such a variety of lifestyles and landscapes as the southwestern province of Yunnan, from the tropical jungles of the south along the border with Thailand and Burma to the snow-capped peaks of the northwest, where Tibetan culture reigns supreme.

Yunnan is widely known as the land of flowers and in the past has attracted legendary plant-collectors from around the globe, including Joseph Rock and George Forrest. Several companies, including Greentours (www.greentours.co.uk) follow in the footsteps of the legendary botanists.

The Greentours itinerary begins in Lijiang and proceeds north through Tiger Leaping Gorge to Zhongdian (called Shangri-La by the government), and on to Weixi, Deqing and Baima Xueshan. Along the way, visitors take day-hikes of up to eight hours, visiting remote hillsides at 4,000m (13,100ft) or more and observing large numbers of the province's 15,000 plant species, along with birds and other wildlife.

If birds and flowers are a perhaps a bit too contemplative, Yunnan also offers a more hair-raising wilderness experience: whitewater river rafting on the upper reaches of the Yangzi and Salween rivers in the remote Three Parallel Gorges region close to the Burmese border. Rafting tourism in Yunnan is in its infancy, and the area is remote and the rivers challenging, but several companies, including Last Descents River Expeditions (www.last-descents.com/schedule.html) are beginning to solve the logistical hurdles, and are selling guided tours to the rivers. The rewards are breathtaking, as both rivers flow through virgin landscapes filled with minority villages, terraced fields and stunning natural beauty.

The tropical south of Yunnan is another wilderness area that lures nature-seeking travellers. Navo (www.navo-tour.com), a purveyor of dozens of exotic treks in China and elsewhere, offers a five-day trekking trip through the jungles of Xishuangbanna. Among the tour destinations are Monkey Mountain, villages that are home to different minorities and a number of temples. Interactions with the minority tribes that live in the area, including the Dai and the Hani, are highlights of the excursion.

Several operators, including Navo (*see above*) offer walking trips through neighbouring Guangxi, and Guizhou, similarly filled with ethnic tribes and

Tropical jungle scenery in southern Yunnan

hillside scenery. The tours usually include home-stays in local minority villages, and up-close looks at local lifestyles.

The Northeast

Within relatively easy reach of Beijing, there are some fascinating wilderness areas in China's far northeast. The mountains and highland lakes of Changbai Shan (*see p.92*), close to the North Korean border, are rich in wildlife and spectacular scenery: several companies, including China Holidays (www.chinaholidays.com), operate trekking tours of the area.

Further north, close to the Russian border, are the boreal forests of northern Heilongjiang province. Here in 'China's Siberia', where winter temperatures plummet to –50°C (–60°F), the pine forests are home to rare birds and other wildlife, and a few surviving Siberian tigers. Tangwanghe National Park protects a large area against logging. Tour operators include Muztagh (www.muztagh.com). The marshes northwest of Harbin are protected as part of the large Zhalong Nature Reserve, a major attraction for birdwatchers.

Inner Mongolia is another sizeable area of wilderness, much of it grassland, but trending towards desert to the west. Tours can be arranged in Hohhot (*see p.93*), or through numerous online companies.

Xinjiang

China is home to some of the driest, hottest deserts on earth, in particular the Taklimakan, the blazing desert that presented such peril to traders on the ancient Silk Road. The classic route through the desert is between Ürümqi and Dunhuang, site of the Mogao Caves, Whistling Sand Mountain and the vanishing Crescent Moon Lake.

Several companies, including China Adventure Tours (www.cnadventure. com), offer camel rides into the deep desert, one of the remotest areas on Earth. Also on the itinerary are the blazing-hot depression of Turpan, the provincial capital Ürümqi, and Kashgar, site of the famous Sunday market. As its grand finale, the tour visits Lake Karakul, a jewel of a lake that sits at 3,770m (12,368ft), and is dyed a permanent turquoise-blue by the silt from the glaciers of nearby Mount Muztagh Ata.

Lake Karakul, high in the Pamir mountains south of Kashgar

Wilderness China

Conservation in China

The concept of conservation is still very new in China, and in a country that is pursuing headlong development, preservation of species and habitat all too often takes a back seat to the business of making money. Throughout China, massive infrastructure investment is creating dams, roads and bridges at a rate that is historically unprecedented, while conservation efforts are hampered by widespread beliefs in the efficacy of medicines based on tiger bones, rhino horns, turtle blood and parts from other endangered animals – and the lucrative black-market trade which goes with it.

One of the most beleaguered species is the Siberian tiger, found in the forests of the Russian Far East, the Korean peninsula and northeastern China; the surviving population is thought to be about 450, with perhaps no more than 30 remaining in China. Even rarer is the South China tiger; a few individuals may survive in the hills of southern Hunan and northern Guangdong. Another endangered species, but one with a brighter future, is the giant panda. Fewer than 2,500 remain alive in the wild, but there are now more than 50 panda reserves, and nearly half of the panda's habitat is now under protection. Many others hover on the extreme edge of extinction, including the Chinese sturgeon, Black-necked crane, dugong, Yangzi soft-shelled turtle, and Chinese alligator. The Yangzi river dolphin is now considered extinct.

Conservation awareness is growing, but slowly, and despite assurances and 'commitments' by various government and corporate bodies, the relentless growth of China's economy makes the prospects for many species appear bleak.

Minorities of the Southwest

China's Han nationality constitutes around 92 percent of the population and dominates the heartland of the country. Yet, primarily in the west and southwest, there are no fewer than 55 separate ethnic minority groups with their own languages, cultures and costume.

The best places to experience China's ethnic minorities are the southwestern provinces of Yunnan and Guizhou. Cut off from the rest of China by high mountain ranges, both have been historically isolated from the influence of Beijing. Yunnan, for example, was only fully incorporated into the empire under the Yuan dynasty (1271–1368), and minority nationalities still make up almost 40 percent of the

Miao dancers in elaborate costume at a *lusheng* festival

population. Guizhou's final absorption was yet more recent, and today minority people account for more than one in three inhabitants. By way of comparison, eastern provinces such as Jiangsu and Zhejiang are more than 99.5 percent Han.

By Chinese standards, **Guizhou** province is a remote and relatively undeveloped backwater. Almost 95 percent of the land is mountainous. Han Chinese first invaded the region during the Tang dynasty, but it proved too isolated, impoverished and intractable to assimilate, and it would remain outside the Chinese polity until the Ming conquest hundreds of years later. Even then, the indigenous population rebelled frequently and bloodily against their Chinese overlords, most notably during the Miao Rebellion of 1854–73.

Over the years, Han Chinese settled in the region's fertile lowland valleys, forcing the indigenous population into the less productive uplands, where they remained, essentially beyond the reach and influence of mainstream Chinese culture until recent times. Consequently, many groups were able to maintain a distinct cultural identity and even some degree of political independence until the mid-20th century. As a result, minority groups are still very visible and assertive.

Fertile, mountainous and immensely colourful, neighbouring **Yunnan** is home to more than 30 percent of all China's ethnic groups, including 25 distinct national minorities. The best known are the Naxi of Lijiang and the colourfully clad Bai in and around Dali, while the Dai of tropical Xishuangbanna are close kin of the Thais. All display sophisticated cultures, colourful ethnic clothing and fascinating festivals and rituals that share little with each other and even less with the Han Chinese. A visit to any of these areas is a most rewarding experience, particularly if your trip coincides with a festival (see p.51).

Visiting the Minorities: Guizhou

Most visitors to Guizhou will fly into the provincial capital, Guiyang, but it is best to move on swiftly from this unremarkable industrial centre to the more convenient hub of Kaili, easily accessible from Guiyang by bus or train. From Kaili, take a tour or travel independently by bus to the outlying Miao villages in the east of the province. Similarly, to visit the Dong people, take a bus from Guiyang to the Dong cultural centre at Zhaoxing, a good base for visiting the surrounding communities, several of which are within walking distance for the reasonably fit – though local tour agencies will be more than pleased to arrange a guide and transport. If possible, try to time your visit to catch a local festival (see p.51).

Mosuo women, northwest Yunnan

The Dong

The Dong predominate in southeast Guizhou and neighbouring northern Guangxi. They are famous for their covered bridges, known as 'wind and rain Bridges', elaborate drum towers and also for their unique polyphonic choral singing. The Dong 'capital' at **Zhaoxing** is a wonderful little town of traditional three-storey wooden

Miao Silver

The Miao are famous for their elaborate headdresses and costumes. The spectacular silver ornamentation may be worn as collars, earrings, belts and in a variety of elaborate headdresses. Silver represents wealth and status, with some heavy silver jewellery weighing as much as 15kg (33 lbs). Girls and unmarried women usually wear traditionally dyed indigo, while married women wear black clothes and indigo waistbands. Great attention is paid to the design, colour and style of each costume, which identifies them within their own group.

Dong woman, southeastern Guizhou

houses, narrow streets and colourfully-clad people, for the Dong – especially the women – favour traditional garb, including indigo robes, heavy silver necklaces and elaborate headdresses. They are famous for their carpentry skills, and Zhaoxing boasts five elaborate drum towers, as well as an equal number of covered bridges. Animals are kept in the open space beneath their dwellings, and head out each day to work in the visually stunning terraced rice paddies that define the hills beyond Zhaoxing and the neighbouring villages.

Getting to Zhaoxing can be rather complicated and time-consuming. There are buses from Kaili by way of Congjiang (seven to eight hours, then another two hours by local bus from Congjiang to Zhaoxing); it's also possible to travel by bus from Sanjiang in neighbouring Guangxi province, a journey of about four hours. Sanjiang is nine hours by bus from Guilin, and three hours from Longsheng and its celebrated rice terraces. It is simpler (but more expensive) to arrange a visit with a local tour agency in Guiyang, Kaili or Guilin.

One of the best ways to visit the Dong villages is to follow a 4km (2½-mile) trail starting at Zhaoxing Middle School in the northwest part of town. The well-established route heads up into the rice-terraced hills to Pingshan village, offering wonderful views across the neighbouring valley, then through the larger village of Tangan with a fine drum tower and covered bridge, before curving back through Shage and its three drum towers, and back to Zhaoxing – a pleasant and rewarding half-day stroll. For those with plenty of time, it's easy to find accommodation in Zhaoxing and to spend several days exploring the neighbouring area. Note, however, that not all the villages are as well off as those in the vicinity of Zhaoxing – the further you go into the mountains, the harder the life of the local Dong people becomes.

The Miao

More numerous than the Dong, and still more spectacular in their costume, are the **Miao** ethnic minority. Nearly 4 million Miao, or about half the national total, live in Guizhou and comprise several sub-groups – from the Small Flowery Miao to the Long-Horned Miao, all readily distinguished by the elaborate costume worn by the women.

Their ethnic heartlands are centred around **Kaili**, 195km (120 miles) due east of Guiyang. Kaili is neither terribly interesting nor overwhelmingly

Miao. In fact, it's a rather ordinary Chinese city, but it makes a great base for visiting the surrounding counties and villages, with the best accommodation and choice of restaurants in the area. Guided tours are easily arranged through the numerous agencies here.

The Miao are closely related to the Hmong of Vietnam, Laos and northern Thailand, and are similarly famous for the elaborate costume of their womenfolk, their tenacious self-sufficiency and independence, and their single-minded refusal to assimilate into larger cultural groups. Fortunately, this has paid off, as the Miao in China are now actively encouraged to embrace their traditional culture, and tourism – overwhelmingly Han Chinese – is now bringing some prosperity to this inherently poor people.

Though the Miao have various names for themselves, the Han have long classified them by the style of dress of their women. In Guizhou there are several groups, including the Black Miao of the southeast, the Flowery Miao of the northwest and the White, Green and Blue Miao of the west. The Miao women around Kaili are particularly noted for their elaborate headdresses and heavy silver jewellery. Especially famous are the Long-Horned Miao, a small but spectacular sub-group who live in a group of 12 villages in Zhijin county, 95km (60 miles) north of Anshun, in the west of Guizhou.

Visiting the Minorities: Yunnan

Various minority groups are scattered around the length and breadth of the province, although most tourists will make a beeline for the beautiful old towns of Dali and Lijiang, home to the Bai, Naxi and Yi groups, amongst others. The tropical southern region is also rich in minorities. Tibetans dominate in the far northwest.

Terraced hillsides around a Dai minority village in southern Yunnan

The Naxi

The delightful Old Town of Lijiang, in the lee of the imposing Jade Dragon Snow Mountain is a Unesco World Heritage Site in its own right, and not to be missed, but the sight of colourfully clad Naxi, Yi and Tibetan minorities mingling in its narrow cobbled streets and busy markets adds immeasurably to the experience of visiting. The **Naxi**, a Tibeto-Burman people whose women favour distinctive blue and purple gowns accompanied by jackets and long trousers, have their own script and religious beliefs – a mixture of shamanism, Tibetan Buddhism and Daoism – and are famous for their Yuan-dynasty music. Lijiang is their spiritual and cultural capital, and a visit to the Old City's famous Naxi Orchestra is not to be missed. There

Lijiang's venerable Naxi orchestra

are daily performances at the Naxi Music Hall every evening at 8pm.

The Yi

The **Yi**, by comparison, are more rural. Like the Naxi, they are a Tibeto-Burman people who may have originally migrated from the northwest. They are readily visible in and around Lijiang, especially in the outlying villages. Yi women generally wear a colourful long-sleeved blouse and vest over long skirts, pleated from the knees. Headgear varies according to marital status, with unmarried girls favouring an elaborately multicoloured headdress decorated with cowries heels or glass beads, while older married women wear a more sombre black hat. The Yi are great dancers, especially at festival times, notably the celebrated Torch festival *(see opposite)*.

The Bai

The **Bai** live south of the Yi, and are very visible in and around the old walled city of Dali. They live in close proximity to the local Yunnanese Hui Muslims, with whom they enjoy excellent relations, but they practise a mixture of Buddhism and animism. Bai women traditionally wear a white coat trimmed with a black or purple collar over loose blue trousers and skilfully embroidered shoes. The ethnic Bai village of Zhoucheng lies by the shore of Er Hai Lake about 15km (9 miles) north of Dali, and has a museum of Bai culture and folklore.

The Dai

The **Dai** are closely related to the nearby Lao and Thai people. Their lush, tropical homeland lies in south-ernmost Yunnan (Xishuangbanna), astride the Mekong River. They are pious Theravada Buddhists, following the traditional Tai calendar and festivals – notably the water-throwing festival of Songkran at their traditional New Year in April.

The capital of Xishuangbanna, Jinghong, is now very much a Chinese town, with Han forming the majority of the population. All around, however, are more traditional Dai villages, with colourful, elaborate Theravada Buddhist temples reminiscent of northern Thailand. Visitors are most welcome, but remember to remove your shoes in sacred areas, dress politely, and women should refrain from touching monks. The most interesting towns to visit in the vicinity of Jinghong are Damenglong, about 70km (43 miles) to the south and close to the Myanmar (Burma) frontier, Menghan, about 85km (53 miles) to the southeast and close to the Lao frontier, and Mengyang, about 35km (22 miles) northeast of Jinghong on

A Bai festival in Dali

the road to Simao. All are easily accessible by bus from Jinghong No. 2 bus station, with departures every 20–30 minutes between 6am and 6pm.

Minority Festivals

In Guizhou practically every Miao and Dong minority village celebrates a *lusheng festival* at some point between late October and April. Traditionally a courtship ritual, young girls don the spectacular Miao costume and dance to the *lusheng* pipes. Bullfights also feature. **Miao and Dong New Year festivals** take place after the autumn harvest, around the 10th lunar month (late Nov/early Dec). The Miao **Sister's Meal Festival**, in villages northeast of Kaili, takes place in the middle of the 3rd lunar month and features the symbolic exchange of gifts between prospective partners. In Yunnan the **Dai Water Festival** (Buddhist New Year/Songkran) in mid-April, the **Naxi Torch Festival** in early July (Lijiang) and the **Bai March Fair** (Dali) are all worth seeking out. Local tour agencies (notably CITS in Kaili) are by far the best source of information on when and where to visit. You could also try http://www.chinahighlights.com/festivals/ for details of upcoming events.

Shopping in China

With its low prices, custom-made goods of all kinds, occasional antique gems, ubiquitous luxury brands and abundant knock-offs of almost every item imaginable, China can be a great place for shoppers. But it doesn't yield its bargains easily; shopkeepers are shrewd, quality is suspect and a 'buyer beware' ethos prevails.

Every citizen in China, it seems, wants to open a shop and sell some wares, whatever those wares may be. For sheer number and variety of retail choices, from street markets and sidewalk stands to boutique outlets and high-end malls, no country on Earth can match the Middle Kingdom.

China also has a long tradition of hand-crafted and cottage industries, which has fuelled a thriving business in custom-made goods. Here again, the range is enormous, and shoes, suits, hand-knitted cashmere sweaters, paintings, jewellery, lamps, leather belts and handbags, furniture and many other items can be made to order at bargain prices.

Visitors to the far-flung provinces of China can still find one-of-a-kind items such as handmade carpets from Tibet and Xinjiang, silver and copper jewellery from Yunnan, high-quality 'purple sand' teapots from Jiangsu, embroidery and brocade from Sichuan, woven bamboo mats from Anhui, cashmere sweaters from inner Mongolia, and other purchases unavailable anywhere else.

Problems and Pitfalls

Shopping in China can, however, be extremely hard work. Plenty of legwork is involved: as factory to the

Shanghai has more shops and more choice than anywhere else in the country

world, the country produces a staggering number of cheap items, much of which clogs up the retail outlets and makes genuine high-quality goods hard to find.

The bargaining process is another hurdle. As practised in China, bargaining is a bare-knuckle sport. One common piece of advice – never make an offer unless you intend to buy at that price – is nonsense, because making an offer is the best way to determine the vendor's price point. You may get yelled at if you walk away after a vendor has agreed to your price, but refusing to buy is – of course – your prerogative, and you will be respected for your savvy. In a street market, the best approach is to offer a very low price, and then make concessions towards the middle ground. Often, if you walk away in the middle of a negotiation, the vendor will chase after you with an unbelievably low offer.

Yet another hurdle is the 'buyer beware' ethos that prevails throughout China. Is it real silver, or real jade, or real cashmere? Are those antiques genuine? Is that an authentic Armani? If you are in a street market, or knock-off market, or temporary tourist market, the answer is probably 'no'. If you are in a branded shop, or an air-conditioned mall, the answer is probably 'yes'. But in the end, the only protection is knowledge; buyers who know their jade and silver and cashmere and antiques can determine the authenticity, while other shoppers should just assume the item is fake, unless they are in a high-end mall or exclusive branded outlet.

Fakes and Bargains

Most cities in China, especially if they attract foreign tourists, have a 'fashion and gift' market (*fangming paihuo shichang*); in other words, a market selling fakes of well-known brands. The latest vogue brands are readily available, at prices that are too good to be true, and these markets are massively popular with foreign

A traditional Chinese tea set makes a stylish souvenir

visitors. The knock-offs range from overt fakes to factory seconds to semi-genuine items that are made at the same factory that produces authentic brand-name goods, albeit during a clandestine 'midnight' shift. The 'fashion and gift' markets are not hard to find, as the crowds of touts shouting 'watch bag DVD' will become ever thicker as the shopper approaches. Beware of pickpockets and keep an eye on your valuables at all times – tourist markets tend to attract thieves, whose audacity makes up for a comical lack of skill.

DVDs are another favourite purchase. Upon walking into a shop, it may appear that only Chinese movies are for sale, but often, a sliding wall or hidden door will reveal a big room full of Western movies and music. Prices range from Rmb6–15 for a movie, and Rmb8–10 for a music CD, with boxed editions more expensive. Buyers should make sure

Beijing's most famous shopping street, Wangfujing

the movie is 'clear' – that is, a factory-quality fake, not a movie shot on a video camera in a theatre.

Custom-Made

One of the pleasures of shopping in China is the widespread availability of high-quality bespoke goods. Hand-knitted sweaters, hardwood furniture, sofas and lamps, semi-precious jewellery, leather belts and handbags and shoes, and of course, custom-tailored clothing, are among the items that can be made to order.

Labour is inexpensive, so buyers should invest their money in quality material, and they should make it clear from the beginning that workmanship is of the greatest importance. Bring a photo or sample of the desired piece, be very specific about

the details, and allow additional time for adjustments if the final result is not as expected. Most establishments will require a deposit; the amount is usually about one-fifth of the total price. Be sure to check for flaws and fit before paying the balance.

A number of studios specialise in leather items, especially shoes; the cobbler will measure the customer's feet and then stitch handmade shoes to order. Depending on the complexity of the design, completion usually takes about seven to 10 days, and some studios will also make handbags and belts to specifications.

By far the most popular bespoke item is clothing, because it can be made quickly and well. Two general types of outlets specialise in custom clothing: fabric markets and custom tailor shops. The fabric markets feature scores of vendors selling silk, wool, linen, cashmere, cotton and many other kinds of cloth, with tailors on hand to cut and sew. Tailoring tends to take three to five days, and it helps enormously to bring favourite items of clothing to be copied. Try to leave extra time, in case the first fitting proves unsuccessful. The fabric markets are highly recommended – they can deliver superb bargains and good workmanship, along with an intimate local shopping experience.

The custom tailor shops that dot the streets of Hong Kong, Shanghai, Beijing and many other cities are more expensive, but more consistently reliable. Superb wool suits, silk dresses, shirts and skirts made from quality fabric and sharply tailored in the latest fashions can be bought at a

Antiques

In general, Shanghai and Hong Kong are the best places in China to buy antiques, because traders from throughout the country bring their wares to those cities, where asking prices are higher. Beijing's sprawling Panjiayuan market can throw up the occasional gem.

Period-piece Art Deco lamps and furniture are popular purchases, and prices have increased sharply in recent years. Shanghai is the capital of Art Deco, and the lanes and shops surrounding Dongtai Lu market feature many hidden gems. Most tourists prefer to buy more portable items, such as table lamps and ceiling lamps.

Prices start at about Rmb1,500, but better pieces cost up to Rmb5,000. Because Art Deco is such a niche market, there are fewer fakes, and intrepid buyers can end up with a unique souvenir. In Hong Kong, most of the antique shops are clustered along Hollywood Road in Central District.

Antique items that are more than 200 years old are not permitted to leave the country, but few items in antique markets are actually that old. Beware of new items made to look old, because what looks like a centuries-old patina of graceful age is often just a handful of mud rubbed on a couple of weeks ago.

---

considerable discount to off-the-rack clothing of similar quality. The quality of fabric is critical, and buyers should allow time for at least two fittings, which usually takes three or four days. Many tailor shops will deliver finished items to hotels, and some will also ship overseas. Buyers usually get what

they pay for, and should beware the 24-hour suit, for obvious reasons.

In Beijing try the tailors at Yashow Market (58 Gongti Beilu) or, for higher quality/prices, Lisa's at 3006, 3/F, 3.3 Shopping Center, 33 Sanlitun Beijie (tel: (139) 1079 8183). In Shanghai, the South Bund Fabric Market at 399 Lujiabang Road has a huge range of fabrics and tailors. For top quality, go to Dave's Tailor at Lane 288, Wuyuan Road. In Hong Kong try Sam's Tailor (94 Nathan Road, Tsim Sha Tsui; tel: 2367 9423) or Taipan Tailor (1/F, Tower 1, Admiralty Centre; tel: 2529 8861).

Visitors interested in buying expensive watches, jewellery and designer clothes should know that in China, luxury taxes raise the prices by more than 30 percent. The tax does not apply in Hong Kong and Macau.

Chinese silk can be a good buy, but choose carefully

PLACES

Getting Your Bearings

China divides into five principal regions – the north, centre, south, southwest and west. For the purposes of this book we have added extra regions for the cities and environs of Beijing, Shanghai and Hong Kong.

Beijing lies at the edge of the northern plains, beyond which steppe and grasslands of Inner Mongolia and Dongbei extend to Siberia. To the south and west of the capital are the loess lands around the Yellow River, the heartlands of ancient Chinese civilisation. Further south, the interior is dominated by the Yangzi River which empties into the East China Sea close to Shanghai. The subtropical south is anchored by the cities of Guangzhou and Hong Kong, with the large tropical island of Hainan close to the Vietnam border. Southwest China is a colourful, highland region of great interest, while much of the west is a gigantic expanse of deserts and high mountains, its emptiness in stark contrast to the teeming cities and densely populated farmland of the east.

For easy reference when using this guide, each of the eight regions has a whole chapter dedicated to its exploration, colour coded for quick navigation. Detailed regional maps are included within each chapter. A listing index is located at the end of each section identifying the best hotels, restaurants and activities. The listings cater to all budgets, from shoestring travel to high-end luxury.

Distances between regions in China can be great and journeys long, which is why it makes sense to plan your route in detail before setting off.

MONGOLIA

Xinjiang
KUNLUN SHAN
Xizang

SILK ROAD AND TIBET
Pages 230 – 245

Qaidam Pendi
Golmud
Qinghai
Xining
Lanzhou

Zhangye
Qilian Shan
Gansu
Yinch

CHINA
Sichuan
Chengdu
Chongqing

SOUTHWEST CHINA
Pages 204 – 229

Guizhou
Dali
Guiy
Kunming
Yunnan
Gejiu

BURMA (MYANMAR)

VIETNAM

LAOS

THAILAND

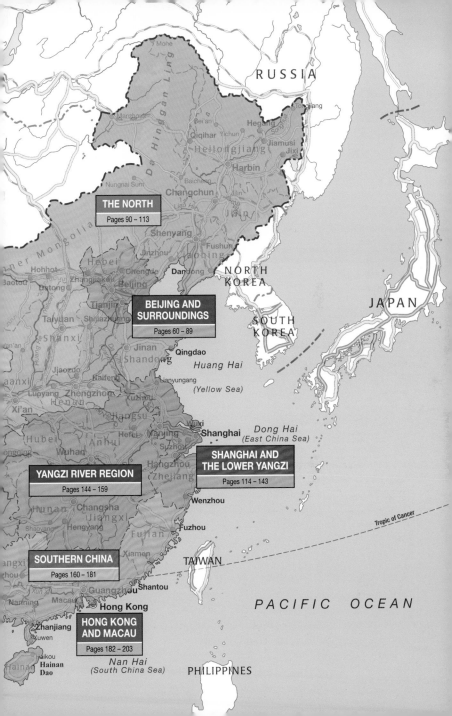

RUSSIA

Mohe

Manzhouli

Tongjiang

Bei'an

Hegang

Qiqihar

Yichun

Jiamusi

Heilongjiang

Jixi

Harbin

Baicheng

Nungnai Sum

Changchun

Jilin

Jilin

Liao He

THE NORTH
Pages 90 – 113

Shenyang

Jinzhou

Fushun

Liaoning

Dandong

Inner Mongolia

Hohhot

Hebei

Chengde

**NORTH
KOREA**

JAPAN

Baotou

Zhangjiakou

Datong

Beijing

Taiyuan

Tianjin

Shijiazhuang

**SOUTH
KOREA**

Shanxi

Xi'an

Jinan

Shandong

Qingdao

Huang Hai

Jiaozuo

Luoyang

Zhengzhou

Lianyungang

(Yellow Sea)

Xi'an

Henan

Xuzhou

Hubei

Jiangsu

Wuxi

Shanghai

Dong Hai

Chongqing

Wuhan

Anhui

Hefei

Nanjing

Suzhou

(East China Sea)

YANGZI RIVER REGION
Pages 144 – 159

Hangzhou

Zhejiang

**SHANGHAI AND
THE LOWER YANGZI**
Pages 114 – 143

Hunan

Changsha

Jiangxi

Wenzhou

Shaoyang

Hengyang

Fujian

Fuzhou

Tropic of Cancer

SOUTHERN CHINA
Pages 160 – 181

Xiamen

TAIWAN

Guangxi

Guizhou

Guangzhou

Shantou

Nanning

Macau

Hong Kong

PACIFIC OCEAN

Zhanjiang

Xuwen

**HONG KONG
AND MACAU**
Pages 182 – 203

Haikou

**Hainan
Dao**

*Nan Hai
(South China Sea)*

PHILIPPINES

Beijing and Surroundings

This great city has had a long and eventful past. Home to the magnificent Ming-era Imperial Palace and several other must-see sights, it has witnessed the fall of empire, the rise of the People's Republic and – in recent years – an unprecedented economic boom.

Beijing

Population: 17.5 million (urban area)

Local dialling code: 010

Local tourist office: Beijing Tourist Information Centre, 11–12 Gongti Beilu, Chaoyang District; tel: 6417 6627; **english.visitbeijing. com.cn**

Local newspapers/listings magazines: *Time Out*; www.timeout. com/cn/en/beijing *The Beijinger*; www.thebeijinger.com

Main post office: Beijing International Post & Telecommunications Office. Jianguomenwai Dajie, Dongcheng District

China's capital has a long and eventful past. Lying at the northern edge of the empire – where the very different cultures of the settled farmers and the nomads of the steppes collided – the city became the prey of each victorious faction in turn, a fact reflected by the many changes to its name throughout the centuries.

The area has been inhabited for millennia, but first rose to prominence in the Warring States period (5th–3rd century BC) when, as Jicheng, it became the capital of the Kingdom of Yan. The 10th-century Liao dynasty renamed it Yanjing, while two centuries later the Jin knew it as Zhongdu ('Central Capital'). The Mongol armies of Genghis Khan levelled the city in the 13th century, then rebuilt it under yet another name, Dadu ('Great Capital'). By now one of the largest cities on Earth, it was described by Marco Polo as containing 'unbelievable numbers of people and houses'.

The Ming emperors transferred most of the imperial pomp south to Nanjing in the 14th century, when Dadu received yet another name, Beiping ('Northern Peace'). In 1403, Emperor Yongle re-established the imperial court in the north and the city was named Beijing ('Northern Capital'). Many of the magnificent temples and palaces, including the vast Imperial Palace (Forbidden City), date from this period.

It was Yongle who set out the city according to geomantic principles which can still be clearly seen to this day: the grid of north–south and east–west streets at the heart of which lay the Forbidden City, surrounded by high walls. To the south of Qianmen Gate was the Inner City, where the commoners lived.

A long, slow decline from *c.*1800 culminated in the Boxer Rebellion of 1900, when European armies wrought havoc in the city. The Qing Empire fell in 1911. In 1949, Communist victory saw Beijing become the capital of the People's Republic of China.

Modern Beijing is a vast, sprawling mass of tower blocks, gargantuan flyovers and expressways. The Olympic Games in 2008 prompted a rapid and

The Olympic Stadium

exhaustive makeover of the ancient city. Old buildings and picturesque *hutong* (lanes) were ruthlessly torn down in many districts, new subway lines snaked and bifurcated into the city's furthest suburbs and the skyline became a playground for the whim of foreign architects. But despite the rapid modernisation, there remains a great deal to see, including the unmissable Forbidden City and some of China's most spectacular temples and palaces.

Tiananmen and Surroundings

Tiananmen Square

The largest city square on Earth, **Tiananmen Square ❶** covers 40 hectares (100 acres) in the very centre of Beijing. The square is breathtaking in its scale – it can hold up to a million people – and despite the brash Communist architecture, affords a pleasant panorama.

On 1 October 1949, Mao Zedong proclaimed the founding of the People's Republic of China from the balcony of the iconic **Tiananmen Gate** (Gate of Heavenly Peace; daily

Tiananmen Square

8.30am–4.30pm; charge to climb the tower) at the northern end of the square. The present structure dates from 1651, and was preceded by a wooden gate built in the early 15th century. Mao's giant portrait gazes across the square from the gate.

The low, squat building close to the southern end of the square is the **Chairman Mao Zedong Memorial Hall** (Mao Zhuxi Jinian Tang; Tue–Sun 8–11.30am), housing the embalmed body of the man who led the People's Republic for its first 27 years.

On the western side of the square, the **Great Hall of the People** (Renmin Dahuitang), erected in 1959, is the grandiose meeting place of the National People's Congress. Behind it stands the titanium-and-glass dome of the National Grand Theatre. Across the plaza to the east is the **National Museum of China** (Zhongguo Guojia Bowuguan), which actually consists of two museums – the Museum of Chinese History and the

Museum of the Chinese Revolution, which house photographs, paintings, documents and relics from the period of the Communist Revolution. Both have been closed for renovation for several years, but are expected to reopen in 2011.

Forbidden City

First stop for most visitors is the **Forbidden City** ❷ (daily 8.30am–5pm summer, 8.30am–4.30pm winter; charge; www.dpm.org.cn), which is quite simply one of the most outstanding historical sights on Earth. Here you will find more than 72 hectares (175 acres) of wonderfully preserved grandeur, with palaces, courtyards and gardens.

The Forbidden City, so described because it was off-limits to ordinary people for nearly 500 years, is now called the **Imperial Palace Museum** (Gugong). Built between 1406 and 1420, the palace was the residence of 24 emperors, their families and their

The Hall of Preserving Harmony in the Forbidden City

Mao's portrait on Tiananmen Gate

enormous retinues for nearly seven centuries. Designed to contain the auspicious number of 9,999 rooms, its scale is overwhelming, and hiring an audio guide from a ticket booth is advisable.

Most tourists enter the Forbidden City complex from Tiananmen Gate, from where it is a few minutes' walk north to the ticket booths at the Meridian Gate (Wumen). It is also possible to enter from Shenwumen Gate at the northern end of the complex.

Beyond the Meridian Gate is a large courtyard, bisected by the **Golden Water River** (Jinshahe), crossed by five marble bridges. Across this first courtyard to the north is the **Gate of Supreme Harmony** (Taihemen),

Beijing Transport

 Airport: Beijing Capital International Airport (**en.bcia.com.cn**) is around 30km (18 miles) northeast of the city centre. The Airport Express light rail links it to Dongzhimen subway station, on subway lines 2 and 13. The journey takes about 20 minutes. The service currently runs from Terminal 3 from 6.21am–10.51pm and from Terminal 2 from 6.35am–11.10pm. Cost is Rmb25 one-way. Air China runs coach services from all airport terminals to major stops in the city centre every 15–30 minutes. Tickets cost Rmb16 one-way.

A taxi journey to the city centre by taxi takes about 30 to 40 minutes, longer at peak hours. The fare will be between Rmb80 and 120; always ensure the meter is used.

 Metro: Beijing currently has nine subway lines. The network was expanded for the 2008 Olympics, and is projected to be the world's largest metro system by 2020.

Trains run from 5am–11pm and leave every five minutes or so. Tickets cost Rmb2 regardless of distance. Single-journey ticket cards are bought from ticket-office windows or automatic machines at each station.

 Buses: Beijing's bus network is extensive, reaching every corner of the city and outskirts. Most services run from 5.30am–8.30pm or 11pm, leaving every five to 10 minutes. Tickets start at Rmb1 and can be bought from conductors.

Taxis: Beijing's taxis are cheap, with flagfall at Rmb10 for the first 3km (2 miles), with an additional Rmb2 for each additional kilometre. All are metered, and drivers are generally reliable at using them.

Dazhalan street stall

rebuilt in 1890. Inside it there is a large map of the palace. Beyond this gate is the largest courtyard of all, the magnificent **Court of the Imperial Palace** (also known as the Outer Court; Waichao), where the imperial shops selling silk and porcelain were situated.

Continue north to the **Hall of Supreme Harmony** Ⓑ (Taihe Dian), which housed the Dragon Throne. For hundreds of years this was the tallest building in all Beijing; by law no house could rise higher. Only the emperor could enter the hall by walking up the ramp adorned with dragon motifs. On the platform in front of the hall are two symbols – a grain measure on the left and a sundial to the right – representing imperial justice and agriculture. Also present are bronze figures of cranes and tortoises – symbols of good luck and longevity.

The roof of the hall is supported by 72 pillars, with the inner six adorned by dragons. The roofs of the Imperial Palace symbolised the highest degree of power through their colour, construction and material. Their breathtaking beauty makes it worth taking the time to see them again and again from different perspectives.

Proceed north to the smaller, golden-roofed **Hall of Complete Harmony** Ⓒ (Zhonghe Dian) and the **Hall of Preserving Harmony** Ⓓ (Baohe Dian), where the palace examinations – the world's first civil-service tests – took place. Beyond is a ramp comprised of sculptured dragons carved from a single slab of marble. The stairway was reserved for the passage of the emperor's sedan chair.

From here to the north, the density of structures in the Forbidden City increases markedly as one passes from the Outer Court (where official business was conducted) to the halls and pavilions of the Inner Court, where the emperor, the imperial family and court members lived. Many of the old palaces and halls are now used to display the artwork and other posses-sions of the emperors. The **Hall of Clocks** and **Imperial Treasury**, col-lections of gifts to the emperors, are worth a detour to the right, as is the magnificent **Nine Dragon Screen** ❺ (Jiulongbi), carved in 1775. The rear (northern) section ends at the **Impe-rial Garden** (Yuhuayuan), with mag-nificent stone rockeries.

Southern Beijing

The old neighbourhood south of Qianmen Gate, centred on Qianmen Dajie, has undergone a controversial transformation as part of Beijing's modernising facelift. What was once a traditional and characterful collection of restaurants, opera houses and shops dating back to the Ming dynasty has become a modern retail development of more than 300 shops with faux 1930s facades, hawking international brands such as Adidas and Apple.

Dazhalan is a long *hutong* (lane) heading west off Qianmen Dajie, famous for its old shops and businesses that now draw mostly tourist custom. It was completely renovated (and pedes-trianised) before the Olympic Games.

Nearby **Liulichang** ❸ owes its name to a Yuan-dynasty workshop that produced the distinctive glazed tiles for the city's palaces and temples. It is now a renovated 'culture street', featuring numerous shops for art supplies, calligraphy, trinkets and antiques, mostly reproductions, as well as a large amount of kitsch. It's still a good point from which to explore the maze of surrounding *hutong*.

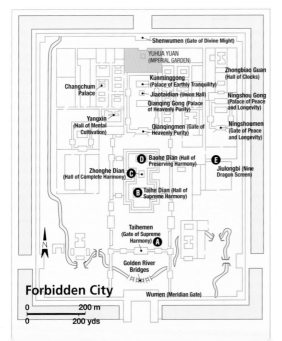

Imperial and Communist icons at Tiananmen Gate

Temple of Heaven Park

Around 2km (1¼ miles) southeast of the Qianmen area is **Tiantan Park**, known to foreigners as the **Temple of Heaven Park** ❹ (daily 6am–9pm; charge ). The largest of Beijing's parks, it is celebrated for its assembly of thrilling 15th-century architecture. The highlight is the circular, blue tile-roofed **Hall of Prayer for Good Harvests** (Qiniandian). This marvel of geometry, art and engineering, built of wood without a single nail, measures 37.5m (123ft) to the gilded orb on its topmost roof. The park is the best place in Beijing to observe practitioners of t'ai chi at their (very early) morning exercise. It is also a favourite hangout of musicians – mostly elderly locals playing traditional instruments.

The Hall of Prayer for Good Harvests

The southern group of buildings includes a white, circular marble terrace, **Yuanqiu** (Altar of Heaven), the most spectacular of the city's imperial altars, consisting of a stone terrace of three levels surrounded by two walls. The lowest level symbolises the Earth, the second, the world of human beings, and the last, Heaven. The nearby **Echo Wall** is famous for its acoustics – sound is transmitted along its length with remarkable clarity.

North of the Forbidden City

Jingshan Park (Coal Hill)

Immediately north of the Forbidden City complex is **Jingshan Park** ❺ (Jingshan Gongyuan; daily 6am–8pm; charge). The highest point of Old Beijing, the hill was created from earth that was originally removed to form the moat system around the Forbidden City. Each of the five artificial peaks was provided with a romantically designed pavilion. The three-tiered Pavilion of Ten Thousand Springs (Wanchunting), on the middle peak, offers an inspiring view over the glistening rooftops of the Imperial City.

Beihai Park

Beihai Park ❻ (Beihai Gongyuan; daily 6am–10pm summer, 6.30am–7pm winter; charge), has been a beauty spot for many hundreds of years. Its lake, which young couples now explore in rented rowing boats, was created in the 12th century. The graceful **Bridge of Eternal Peace** (Yonganqiao) leads to an artificial island 1.5km (1 mile) in circumference with a long covered corridor

Boats on Houhai Lake

that sweeps along the northern shore. On a hill in the centre of the isle is situated a Tibetan-style stupa, the **White Dagoba** (Bai Ta), built in 1651 to commemorate the first visit of the Dalai Lama to Beijing.

The Back Lakes and around

Snaking north from Beihai Park are three man-made lakes – **Qianhai**, **Xihai** and **Houhai** – which once served as the terminus of the city's canal network. The area was a gentrified locale during the Yuan dynasty and boasts some impressive courtyard houses and former residences. As tourists flock to the decreasing number of traditional *hutong* in the area – collectively known simply as 'Houhai' – and Beijingers' thirst for nightlife grows, so it has exploded into a frenetic, and profitable, free-for-all. Nonetheless, it remains an attractive, leafy area.

The picturesque little **Silver Ingot Bridge** (Yindingqiao), at the eastern end of Houhai, once marked the terminus of China's Grand Canal – the main artery between north and south. Here traders from as far as Hangzhou would unload huge shipments of grain for trading.

For a more casual stroll, **Nanluoguxiang**, around 10 minutes' walk east of Houhai, is a long renovated

Beijing and Surroundings

Activities around Houhai

- Pedicab drivers hawk their 'tours' enthusiastically to tourists around Houhai.
- Many hostels in this area rent bicycles for a more leisurely exploration of the winding back alleyways.
- The lakes are not considered clean enough for swimming, though many locals still jump in for a dip. In winter they are popular ice-skating spots.
- Boating on the lakes is inexpensive, and would-be sailors can take their own food and drinks aboard.

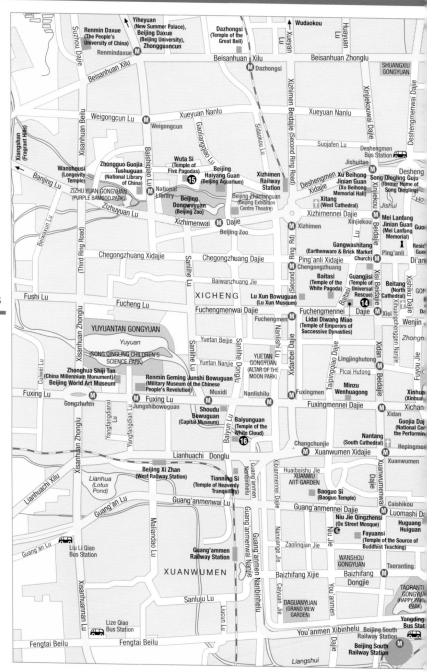

Yiheyuan
(New Summer Palace),
Beijing Daxue
(Beijing University),
Zhongguancun

Wudaokou

Dazhongsi
(Temple of the
Great Bell)

Renmin Daxue
(The People's
University of China)

Renmindaxue

SHUANGXIU
GONGYUAN

Beisanhuan Xilu

Beisanhuan Zhonglu

Dazhongsi

Suzhou Dajie

Beisanhuan Beilu

Xizhimen Beidajie (Second Ring Road)

Xueyan Lu

Huayan Lu

Deshengmenwai Dajie

Weigongcun Lu

Xueyuan Nanlu

Xueyuan Nanlu

Xinjiekouwai Dajie

Weigongcun

Xiangshan
(Fragrant Hills)

Suojafen Lu

Deshengmen
Bus Station

Jishuitan

Banjing Lu

Wanshousi
(Longevity
Temple)

Zhongguo Guojia
Tushuguan
(National Library
of China)

Wuta Si
(Temple of
Five Pagodas)
15

Beijing
Haiyang Guan
(Beijing Aquarium)

Xizhimen
Railway
Station

Xu Beihong
Jinian Guan
(Xu Beihong
Memorial Hall)

Song Qingling Guju
(former Home of
Song Qingling)

Desheng

ZIZHU YUAN GONGYUAN
(PURPLE BAMBOO PARK)

National
Library

Beijing
Dongwuyuan
(Beijing Zoo)

Deshengmen
Xidajie

Xitang
(West Cathedral)

Xinjiekou Beidajie

Jishui

Ho

Zizhuyuan Lu

Beijing zhanlanguan
(Beijing Exhibition
Centre Theatre)

Xizhimennei Dajie

Mei Lanfang
Jinian Guan
(Mei Lanfang
Memorial)

Guo

Xisanhuan Beilu

Xizhimenwai

Dajie

Xinjiekou

Xishiku Dajie

Beihuan Lu

(Third Ring Road)

Beijing Zoo

Xizhimen

Gangwashitang
(Earthenware & Brick Market
Church)

Ping'anli

Resid
Guo

Di'an

Chegongzhuang Xidajie

Chegongzhuang Dajie

Ping'anli Xidajie

Chengongzhuang

XICHENG

Baitasi
(Temple of the
White Pagoda)

Guangjisi
(Temple of
Universal
Rescue)
14

Beitang
(North
Cathedral)

Sanlihe Lu

Baiwanzhuang Jie

Baitasi

Xisi Beidajie

Fushi Lu

Fucheng Lu

Fuchengmennei Dajie

Lu Xun Bowuguan
(Lu Xun Museum)

Fuchengmennei

Dajie

Xisi

Xihuangchengen Nanjie

Xisanhuan Zhonglu

YUYUANTAN GONGYUAN

Fuchengmen

Lidai Diwang Miao
(Temple of Emperors of
Successive Dynasties)

Wenjin

Yuyuan
(SONG QINGLING CHILDREN'S
SCIENCE PARK)

Yuetan Beijie

Lingjinghutong

Zhongn

Sanlihe Lu

Yuetan Nanjie

Picai Hutong

Fuyou Jie

Xidanbei Dajie

Xindan

Zhonghua Shiji Tan
(China Millennium Monument)/
Beijing World Art Museum

Renmin Geming Junshi Bowuguan
(Military Museum of the Chinese
People's Revolution)

YUETAN
GONGYUAN
(ALTAR OF THE
MOON PARK)

Minzu
Wenhuagong

Xinhua
(Xinhua

Fuxing Lu

Muxidi

Xichan

Yangfangdianx
Lu

Yangfangdian

Nanlishilu

Fuxingmennei Dajie

Xidan

Gongzhufen

Fuxing Lu

Jungshibowuguan

Fuxingmen

Guojia Da
(National Cer
the Performin

Shoudu
Bowuguan
(Capital Museum)

Baiyunguan
(Temple of the
White Cloud)
16

Hepingme

Baiyu

Lianhuachi Donglu

Changchunjie

Nantang
(South Cathedral)

Lianhua
(Lotus
Pond)

Beijing Xi Zhan
(West Railway Station)

Tianning Si
(Temple of Heavenly
Tranquillity)

Xuanwumen
(South Cathedral)

Xuanwumen Xidajie

Xuanwumen

Xuanwumenwai
Dajie

Liu Li Qiao
Bus Station

Huaibaishu Jie
XUANWU
ART GARDEN

Guang'anmennei Dajie

Caishikou

Luomashi Da

Guang'ammen
Railway Station

Guang'an Lu

Guang'anmennei Lu

Mailiandao Lu

Guang'anmen Nanbinlu

Baoguo Si
(Baoguo Temple)

Niu Jie Qingzhensi
(Ox Street Mosque)

Niu Jie

Fayuansi
(Temple of the Source of
Buddhist Teaching)

Huguang
Huiguan

XUANWUMEN

Sanluju Lu

Baizhifang Xijie

Baizhifang
Dongjie

WANSHOU
GONGYUAN

Taoranting

TAORANTI
GONGYUA
(HAPPY PAVI
PARK)

Guang'anmenwai Nanjie

Namxiange Jie

Zaolinqian Jie

You'anmen

Xisanhuannan Lu

Lize Qiao
Bus Station

DAGUANYUAN
(GRAND VIEW
GARDEN)

Caiyuan
Jie

Lucun Lu

You'anmen Xibinhelu

Beijing South
Railway Station

Yongding
Bus Stat

Fengtai Beilu

Fengtai Beilu

Liangshui

Beijing South
Railway Station

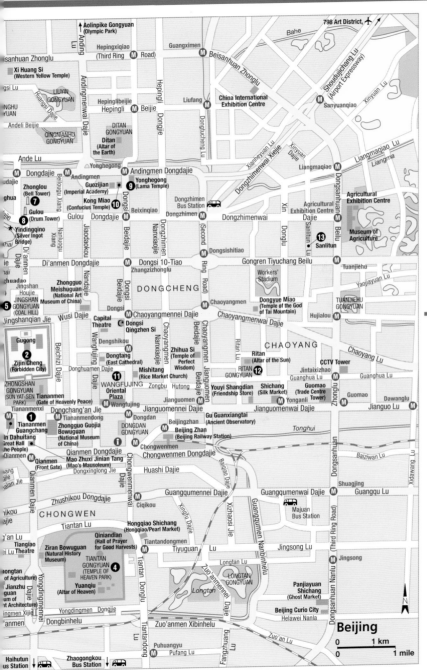

Beijing and Surroundings

Beijing

0   1 km
0   1 mile

N

hutong packed with cafés, restaurants, backpacker hostels and some quirky – and implausibly small – shops.

The Drum and Bell Towers

On the east side of the Back Lakes area are two towers dating from the rule of Kublai Khan – **the Bell Tower ❼** (Zhonglou) and **Drum Tower ❽** (Gulou; daily 9am–5.30pm; charge). They once marked the northern edge of Beijing, but were in the centre of the Yuan-dynasty city. Last rebuilt in 1747, the Bell Tower stands 33m (108ft) high. The Drum Tower once held 24 giant drums that were struck to mark the closing of the city gates and the passing of the night watches. There is a great view from the top over the surrounding area of traditional *siheyuan* courtyard houses.

The Lama Temple

Beijing's most popular temple is a 17th-century Lamasery, **Yonghegong ❾**, popularly known as the Lama Temple (daily 9am–4pm; charge) and most easily reached by taking the subway to the Yonghegong stop (lines 2 and 5). It was originally the palace of the prince who became the emperor Yongzheng. The stately complex of wooden buildings, containing nearly 1,000 rooms, has been painstakingly restored. The temple recalls 18th-century efforts to unify China, Mongolia and Tibet.

Confucius Temple

Across the street and down a narrow lane from the Lama Temple is Beijing's most serene place of worship, the **Temple of Confucius and Imperial Academy ❿** (Kong Miao Guozijian; daily 9am–4.30pm; charge), with statues and stone tablets honouring the ancient sage. This was where emperors came to offer sacrifices to Confucius for guidance in ruling the empire.

Built in 1306, it is the second-largest Confucian temple in China, after the one in Confucius' hometown, Qufu. The adjoining Imperial Academy, where Ming-dynasty scholars studied Confucian texts, is set in a pleasant campus. In 2010, a ceremony to mark

The Confucius Temple

the sage's birthday was the first to take place here since the 1940s.

Olympic Sites

In the far north of the city, out beyond the fourth ring road, are the impressive stadia created for the 2008 Olympics – *see pp. 74–5*.

Eastern Beijing

Wangfujing and around

About 1km (⅔ mile) east of Tiananmen lies **Wangfujing** ⓫, Beijing's premier shopping district, crowned by the vast retail complex Oriental Plaza. Partly pedestrianised, the street has a commercial history of several hundred years, and many long-standing brands can still be found such as Quanjude roast duck, Yongantang traditional medicine and Wuyutai tea. Set back off the northern part of Wangfujing is the **East Cathedral** (Dongtang, or St Joseph's; Mon–Sat 6.30am–8pm, Sun 9am), rebuilt after a fire in 1900, and one of the city's most prominent churches. Nearby on Donghuamen Dajie is **Donghuamen Night Market**, a good place to try street food including such outlandish items as fried locusts, scorpions and silkworms.

Jianguomennei, Jianguomenwai and Ritan Park

At the junction of Jianguomennei Dajie – a popular shopping street, home to the Silk Market – and the second ring road, is the **Ancient Observatory** (Gu Guanxiangtai; daily 9am–4pm; charge). Originally constructed in 1279 north of its present-day site, the observatory you see today

A side-street off Wangfujing

was built in the mid-15th century and sits atop a watchtower that was once a part of the city walls. It served both the Ming and Qing dynasties in making predictions based on astrology, as well as helping navigators who were about to go to sea.

Northeast of the observatory is **Ritan Park** ⓬ (daily 6am–9pm; charge), housing one of the eight altars which, along with the Temple of Heaven, played a great role in the ritual life of the Ming and Qing emperors. The rebuilt altar still stands,

Beijing and Surroundings

Land of Plenty

According to a 2010 report, Beijing is home to more of China's rich than anywhere else, with 151,000 people amassing a fortune in excess of Rmb10 million (around US$1.3 million). Guangdong province occupies second position, Shanghai is third, Zhejiang province fourth. There are around 875,000 such millionaires in China.

and is sometimes used for alternative art exhibitions. The park itself is a pleasant place for a stroll if you are in the neighbourhood – with rocks, ponds, meandering paths, flower beds and a lakeside café that resembles a Qing-dynasty boat.

Sanlitun Nightlife

Once known only as Beijing's main embassy district, **Sanlitun** ⑬ has for years been the city's throbbing heart of nightlife and bacchanalia. The main strip is lined with (often mediocre) bars, while the Nali Patio and Tongli Studio area a few minutes north harbours the favourite spots of many long-term residents. On the corner of Sanlitun Lu and the Worker's Stadium North Road is the unrepentantly conspicuous all-in-one entertainment district Sanlitun Village, greeting

Silk Street Market

Beijing's legendary shopping destination at 8 Xiushui Dongjie is packed with up to 20,000 shoppers a day bargaining furiously for shirts, silk ties, jackets, shoes and countless other items. It is regularly targeted for intellectual property violation, though the vast profits to be made from counterfeit designer goods keep the vendors one step ahead of the authorities. The popularity of the superstore with foreign buyers guarantees the availability of clothing and shoes in larger sizes than most other stores, and also ensures that ruthless haggling is absolutely essential.

passers-by with the curved metallic facade of the world's largest Adidas store. Cafés, restaurants and shops sit side by side in this ambitious, international project – architects from Britain, Hong Kong, New York and Japan each designed sections – though much of the merchandise on sale can be bought at home for similar prices.

798 Art District

In the far northeast of Beijing, beyond the fourth ring road and also known as just '798' after the German-built former arms factory-turned-gallery that serves as its symbolic heart, the **Dashanzi Art District** (Dashanzi Yishu Qu; most galleries Tue–Sun

10am–5pm) is a thriving community of contemporary artists, shops, studios and galleries great and small. Under the threat of demolition for years, the district's future now seems secure as a government-sanctioned cultural zone. Though somewhat commercialised and a stopping point for tourist coaches, Dashanzi remains a collective of grass-roots talents who still have the ability to surprise and even shock. The easiest way to get here is to take a taxi to Jiuxianqiao.

Western Beijing

About 1km (⅔ mile) west of the Back Lakes is **Guangjisi** ⓮ (Temple of Universal Rescue; daily 8am–4pm), a well-used and atmospheric Buddhist temple. In the third hall is a thousand-armed statue of the goddess of mercy, Guanyin.

West past the second ring road is **Beijing Zoo** (Beijing Dongwuyuan; daily 7.30am–6pm; charge). Be warned that standards are not up to those of most Western zoos. The main attraction is the giant pandas, whose quarters are right by the entrance. Also within the zoo complex is the **Beijing Aquarium** (same hours as zoo, separate charge).

Just behind the zoo is **Wuta Si** ⓯ (Temple of Five Pagodas; daily 9am–4.30pm; charge), dating back to the 15th-century reign of the Ming emperor Yongle. The building, with five small pagodas standing on a massive square base, is quite different from other temples in Beijing. Look out for the bas-reliefs on the outside, which depict Buddha figures, symbolic animals and other Buddhist symbols.

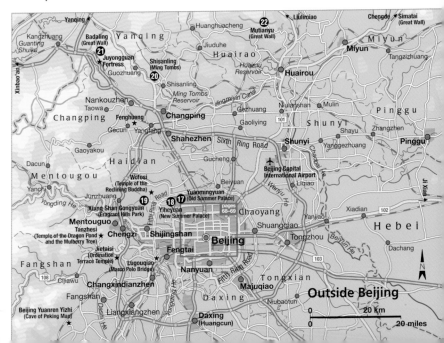

⏃ OLYMPIC PARK TOUR

This tour brings you half a day – or a more casual full day – of taking in the awe-inspiring facilities built for the 2008 Olympic Games, an ancient city wall and the Chinese Ethnic Culture Park.

Take the northwest exit out of Anzhenmen subway station to arrive at the 4.8km (3-mile) long **Tucheng Park** (Tucheng Gongyuan), your first stop and once part of the city wall of Dadu, as the city was known during the Yuan dynasty. The wall was originally made of earth (*tucheng* means 'earthen wall'); only a few shapeless mounds remain, but the city moat, called Little Moon River (Xiaoyuehe), still exists.

Stroll westwards through the park,

then turn north on Beichen Lu. The **Chinese Ethnic Culture Park** is on the left. It showcases the different architecture and lifestyles of the 56 officially recognised ethnic groups of China, including the majority Han. Typical dwellings of various ethnic minorities – from the Tibetans' inward-sloping forts to the slate-piled houses of the Bouyei – have been transported here from their native areas. Members of the various ethnicities have also been hired to represent their people in traditional dress. In this sense, visitors can gain a crash course in the various groups through their crafts, customs and beliefs – albeit in a rather ersatz fashion.

There are some choices for lunch here. Between the northern and southern sections of the park are a few

Performance at the Ethnic Culture Park

Nearby Attractions

- To extend your tour to a full day, the huge Olympic Forest Park offers numerous winding paths and picnic spots to explore.
- Bicycles are not allowed in the Olympic Forest Park, but tricycles and small electric vehicles can be rented here.
- Regular song-and-dance routines are a staple of the Chinese Ethnic Culture Park. Check the performance timetable displayed at the entrance and take in the 'authentic' cultural shows with a pinch of salt.
- The National Aquatics Centre is now open to the public as a swimming facility, water park and performance area.

The Olympic stadium under construction

restaurants serving ethnic food. Among them, Caixianggen serves authentic cuisine from Hunan – Chairman Mao's place of birth.

Along with the opportunity of hosting the 2008 Olympics, Beijing also won a chance to give itself a complete makeover with some world-class architectural projects. Head north from the Ethnic Culture Park and you come to the Rmb3.5 billion **National Stadium** (Guojia Tiyuchang; also known as the Bird's Nest). Its main feature is the 'nest' of girders that function as both structure and facade – the building is essentially a steel network completely open to the elements.

The **National Aquatics Centre** (Guojia Youyong Zhongxin) was inspired by the work of physicists on the structure of soap bubbles. Its walls are made of steel girders draped with a teflon-like material, which is inflated with pumps. The transparent walls trap most of the energy from sunlight, providing a natural source of heating for the pools.

The **Olympic Park** (Aolinpike Gongyuan), north of the sports facilities, is the city's largest green space. Positioned on the same north–south axis that runs through the Forbidden City and the Drum Tower, the 12.2-sq km

(5-sq mile) park is envisioned as the green heart of a new Beijing suburb. Solar power runs many of the lighting and heating facilities, and carefully designed gutters and canals maximise the benefits of rainfall. One of the best-designed parks in the city, it is well worth a couple of hours' exploration.

Despite being acclaimed, even iconic structures, some of the Olympic venues face an uncertain future – none more so than the National Stadium; it is supposed to host sporting events, but sky-high running costs may be an obstacle.

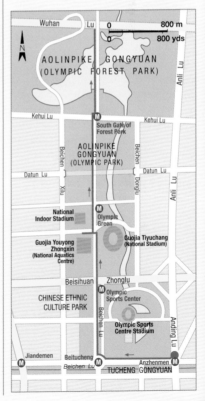

Looking across Kunming Lake to Yiheyuan, the New Summer Palace complex, Beijing

Around 5km (3 miles) south is the serene **Baiyunguan** ⑯ (White Cloud Temple; daily 8.30am–4.30pm; charge), once the greatest Daoist centre of northern China. Today a small group of monks lives here, and Beijingers of all ages crowd in to pray for good fortune.

Tianning Si (Temple of Heavenly Tranquillity; daily 9am–4pm), thought to be the oldest building in Beijing, lies just to the south. All that remains of the original building is the magnificent 58m (190ft) hexagonal pagoda.

Outside Beijing

Many pleasant day trips can be enjoyed away from the frenetic energy of the city to take in mountains, lakes and grasslands, imperial tombs, and of course the world-famous Great Wall.

Summer Palaces

The great aesthete Emperor Qian-long (r.1736–95) fashioned a huge masterpiece of landscaping and architecture 16km (10 miles) northwest of the city centre: **Yuan-mingyuan** ⑰ (7am–7pm summer, 7am–5.30pm winter; charge 🏫), known as the **Old Summer Palace**. Construction followed the most lavish European styles, such as that of the palace at Versailles. But it didn't last long: during the Second Opium War (1856–60), British and French troops pillaged the palace and reduced it to rubble. Amidst the picturesque ruins, set in expansive grounds, is a restored brick maze with a central pavilion.

A replacement, **Yiheyuan** ⑱ (6.30am–8.30pm summer, 7am–7pm winter; charge 🏫) – the **New**

Summer Palace – was built nearby by the notorious Empress Dowager Cixi, for whom it fulfilled a wonderful, if rather expensive, dream. As in every classical Chinese garden, water and mountains (usually represented by rocks) determine the landscape. **Kunming Lake** covers three-quarters of the total area; on its shore is **Wanshou Shan** (Hill of Longevity). Of light wooden construction and decorated with scenes from Chinese mythology, the impressive 784m (2,572ft) **Changlang** (Long Corridor) runs parallel to the northern shore of the lake, linking the scattered palace buildings. It ends near the Marble Boat, a treasury-draining folly in which Cixi took tea.

A stone dragon at the Ming tombs

Xiang Shan (Fragrant Hills)

One of the most popular destinations for Beijing's day-trippers, particularly when splashed with brilliant autumn colours, is **Xiang Shan Gongyuan** ⑲ (Fragrant Hill Parks; daily 6am–7pm summer, 6am–6pm winter; charge 🎟️), 8km (5 miles) west of the Summer Palace. Clamber up the steps or jump aboard the cable car for views from the summit of Incense Burner Peak. **Biyun Si** (Temple of the Azure Clouds), near the North Gate, is also worth a visit.

The Ming Tombs

On the way to the Great Wall is the peaceful valley the Ming emperors chose as their burial ground. In 1407 the emperor Yongle ordered a search for a suitable burial place with auspicious 'wind and water' conditions, as well as appropriate grandeur. This site proved so perfect that all but three of the succeeding Ming rulers were entombed in the same valley.

The route to the 13 **Ming Tombs** ⑳ (Shisanling; generally 8.30am–5pm; charge) begins at a great marble gateway, beyond which the **Sacred Way** (Shendao), flanked by 36 enormous stone guardians both human and animal, leads 7km (4 miles) through the complex.

The largest tomb, **Changling**, belonged to Yongle himself and lies at the end of the Sacred Way. Its Hall of Eminent Favours (Lingendian) is Beijing's largest wooden structure remaining from ancient times.

Ninety-one steps lead down below ground level to **Dingling** (the tomb of the Emperor Wanli, r.1573–1620). It took 30,000 workers six years to build

Beijing and Surroundings

this underground palace. Most of the regalia and artefacts on display, including the wooden coffin containers, are copies of items excavated in the 1950s.

The Great Wall

The Great Wall is the single greatest tourist attraction in China, and one of the greatest in all the world. It has excited fascination and wonder among Westerners ever since tales of its immensity and scale began trickling back to Europe in the 17th and 18th centuries. Its popularity as a tourist attraction among Chinese is more of a 20th-century phenomenon, one given a considerable boost by Chairman Mao's comment, 'He who has not been to the Great Wall is not a real man.'

The most accessible section of the Wall – and consequently the most crowded – is at **Badaling** ㉑, 60km (38 miles) northwest of Beijing (daily 7am–7pm; charge 🏛). It is easily reached by tourist buses 1 from Qianmen or 2 from Beijing Railway Station. Despite the hordes of sightseers, avoidable in the early mornings and more generally in the colder months, Badaling has great scenery, restored forts and exhibitions to see.

The Wall here was strategically important and heavily fortified by the Ming emperors. The towers are solidly built, with high arrow slits. The way up on both sides of the valley leads to high beacon towers, from which you can see the northern plain and the Wall snaking across faraway hills. The western side is a steeper climb.

If you walk far enough west, you reach dilapidated and unrestored sections of the Wall that trail off into the distance.

The Great Wall is an unmissable sight

Flags on the Great Wall at Badaling

it best to take a tour. You can either take a cable car to a point 20–30 minutes' walk below the Wall, or make a longer excursion on foot.

Chengde

A five-hour train ride 250km (150 miles) northeast of the capital, the summer residence of the Qing emperors at Chengde offers perfect respite from the noise and summer heat of Beijing. The **main palace complex** (Bishu Shanzhuang; daily, park: 5.30am–6pm, buildings: 8am–5pm; charge), has spacious grounds studded with elegant pagodas, halls and pavilions. To the north and east, the **Eight Outer Temples** (Waiba Miao; 8.30am–5.30pm; charge) feature some spectacular architecture, none more so than at the **Little Potala Temple** (Putuozongsheng miao), modelled on the Potala Palace in Lhasa.

Some 90km (55 miles) northeast of Beijing, **Mutianyu** ㉒ (daily 6.30am–6.30pm; charge) is equally spectacular but much less crowded than Badaling. It can be accessed by tourist bus 6 from Xuanwumen (west of Qianmen in the city centre) A long section of restored Wall follows a high ridge, giving views over wooded ravines. The nearest point on the Wall is a steep one-hour climb from the car park. A cable car offers a breathtaking alternative and a luge-like slide, a quick way down. Mutianyu was not part of the main Wall but a barrier wall shielding passes to the north towards Zhangjiakou.

A favoured section of Wall for hikers, **Simatai** (daily 8am–6pm; charge) shows the unrestored Wall at its most majestic, crowning a narrow ridge and sharp pinnacles. The site is quite remote, 115km (70 miles) northeast of Beijing, and many visitors find

Beijing and Surroundings

Rambling on the Ramparts

- Walking is mostly on the Wall itself, so it's difficult to get lost, but the going is often slow. Take great care on steep, crumbling sections. In some places, you may have no alternative but to leave and rejoin the Wall; in others, rickety piles of fallen bricks may be your only climbing aid.
- Jinshanling and Simatai are two of the more popular hiking stretches, the last being the most challenging if you traverse the whole ridge. Camping is not officially allowed on the Wall but, while numbers remain small, it seems to be tolerated.

★ BEIJING PERFORMING ARTS

China's performing arts have a rich and fascinating history, with the most refined and stylised – Beijing Opera – its quintessential cultural showpiece. Drama, dance, songs and symphonies have entertained the masses and served political designs for thousands of years. Though China's theatre is still rather elitist, its doors are always open to the curious and well-heeled visitor.

Although Chinese theatre in the form of skits, vaudeville, puppet shows and shadow plays has existed since the Tang dynasty (618–907), formal music-drama had its origins in the Yuan period (1279–1368), when scholars who were displaced from their government positions by the foreign Mongols turned to writing dramas in which songs often alternated with dialogue. Since then, opera has evolved into one of the most popular forms of mass entertainment in China, with more than 300 different styles. Plots are based on legends or folklore with which audiences are familiar, and performances are a composite of different art forms – such as song, dance and mime. Costumes and make-up are symbolic, helping the audience to understand the various roles.

By far the most popular Chinese opera is the highly stylised *jingxi* (Beijing or Peking Opera), which dates from the 1800s. It is considered one of the world's most conventionalised forms of

Beijing Opera is a colourful spectacle

theatre and requires years of training to master.

Spoken drama was first introduced to China by Chinese students studying in Japan around the turn of the 20th century. It was seen as modern and progressive because it differed from traditional Chinese drama – which was always sung and accompanied by music – and because it frequently dealt with social issues. Works such as Lao She's *Teahouse* have become classics.

Foreign influence also led to the creation of orchestras of traditional Chinese instruments during the 1950s. Because these were not intended to be played in huge ensembles, many technical changes had to be made and new instruments invented. Some purists still scoff at the whole idea.

Most of China's 56 official minority groups have strong folk-dance traditions, and dance has been a part of ordinary people's entertainment in China since antiquity. It played a key role at the imperial court during the cosmopolitan Tang dynasty – some scholars believe that foot-binding first developed because fashionable women began to imitate the way Tang court dancers wrapped their feet.

Acrobatics also has a long history in China – close to 3,000 years. During the Cultural Revolution, leftist revolutionaries considered it to be a respectable 'proletarian' art form. Today there are about 80 professional acrobatics troupes in China. Beijing's troupe is one of the best, and the city is also home to an acrobatics school that trains young acrobats from around the world.

Acrobatics has a long history in China, but its popularity has declined in recent years

The make-up used in Beijing Opera indicates the role of the character

ACCOMMODATION

Beijing has many spectacular new or refurbished five-star hotels, as well as a number of lower-end hotels and youth hostels. Many of Beijing's luxury hotels are in the business district of Chaoyang, with several along Jianguomenwai Dajie. Less expensive hotels are found all over the city,

with a concentration in central tourist areas, particularly south of the Forbidden City. There are a growing number of budget options in and around Sanlitun, in northeastern Beijing. For people wanting something more traditional, courtyard hotels such as the Lusongyuan can be found in the *hutong* in the Drum and Bell towers area and elsewhere.

Beijing

Beijing Bamboo Garden Hotel
24 Xiaoshiqiao Hutong, Jiugulou Dajie
Tel: (010) 6403 2229
www.bbgh.com.cn
Simple, clean rooms open onto a classical Chinese garden, with a great location close to the Drum Tower. What it lacks in facilities is more than made up for in atmosphere. **$$$**

Leo Hostel
52 Dazhilan Xijie
Tel: (010) 6303 1595
www.leohostel.com
Friendly, bustling hostel on Dazhalan Street offering various tour bookings for travellers including a popular trip to a 'secret' section of the Great Wall. **$-$$**

The Lusongyuan Hotel offers a pleasingly old-fashioned experience

Lusongyuan Hotel
22 Banchang Hutong, Dongcheng District
Tel: (010) 6401 1116
This delightful courtyard hotel occupies a former Qing-dynasty residence. Rooms are very attractive with period furnishings, and it has a good location south of the Bell and Drum towers. Dorms available. **$$$**

Opposite House
11 Sanlitun Lu, Chaoyang District
Tel: (010) 6417 6688
www.theoppositehouse.com
This impossibly fashionable Japanese-designed hotel is one of the most stylish spots in town. The lobby seems more like a work of art, and the rooms are a minimalist's dream. Two bars and three restaurants. **$$$**

Red Capital Residence
9 Dongsi Liutiao
Tel: (010) 8403 5308
www.redcapitalclub.com.cn
This exclusive boutique hotel is within a Qing-dynasty courtyard house northeast of Wangfujing (past the Dongsi Mosque). Its rooms are furnished with period antiques and each has a different theme. **$$$$**

Saga Youth Hostel
Shijia Hutong, Dongcheng District
Tel: (010) 6527 2773
Popular with budget travellers, this hotel offers double rooms and dorms, tour

booking and bike rental. Discounts for Hostelling International members. **$$**

St Regis Hotel
21 Jianguomenwai Dajie
Tel: (010) 6460 6688
www.stregis.com
Matching Chinese tradition with modern furniture, this luxurious hotel opened in late 1997 in a prime Chaoyang location. The hotel's Press Club Bar is a favourite of the foreign business community. **$$$$**

Outer Beijing
Fragrant Hills Mountain Yoga Retreat
6 Gonfuzhen, Fragrant Hills, Haidian District
Tel: (010) 8259 5335
www.mountainyoga.cn
An idyllic retreat for yoga enthusiasts or others seeking a unique experience. All rooms are beautifully appointed. Meals are vegetarian, and yoga classes are offered each morning, including one on the Great Wall. **$$$**

Xijiao Hotel
18 Wangzhuang Lu, Haidian District
Tel: (010) 6232 2288
www.xijiao-hotel.com.cn
In the middle of the university district, convenient for the Summer Palaces, Wudaokou's nightlife and Zhongguancun. **$$**

Five-star luxury at the St Regis Hotel

Great Wall
Commune by the Great Wall
Badaling Highway
Tel: (010) 5869 6668
www.commune.com.cn
Twelve spectacular villas designed by Asia's top architects. Each is furnished by renowned designers and comes with a personal butler. **$$$**

Further Afield
Qianwanglou Hotel
Bifengmen Lu, Chengde
Tel: (0314) 202 4385
For atmosphere alone this is the best option in Chengde. The small, exquisitely refurbished hotel occupies a Qing-dynasty mansion set just inside the grounds of the Imperial Resort. **$$**

83

Listings

RESTAURANTS

Wherever you are in Beijing, you will never be far from one of the city's countless restaurants, cafés, kebab stands and snack shops. While five-star hotels boast excellent restaurants, they often focus on Western food for those with generous expense accounts. The embassy and nightlife area Sanlitun showcases an invasion of global cuisines at competitive prices. The university district Haidian offers minority restaurants catering to students from around China and throngs of inquisitive diners. Traditional Beijing food is not ubiquitous, but a collection of time-honoured local food stalls can be enjoyed at Jiumen Xiaochi by Houhai Lake.

Restaurant Price Categories
Prices are for a full meal per person, with one drink

$ = below Rmb50 (below US$7.50)
$$ = Rmb50–100 (US$7.50–15)
$$$ = Rmb100–150 (US$15–22.50)
$$$$ = over Rmb150 (over US$22.50)

Beijing

Da Dong Roast Duck 大董烤鸭店
Nanxincang International Plaza, A22
Dongsishitiao
Tel: (010) 5169 0328
Classy Peking duck and swish service.
Located next to a restored imperial granary.
$$$

Golden Peacock Dai Ethnic Flavour 金孔
雀傣家酒楼
2 Minzu Daxue Bei Lu, Haidian District
Tel: (010) 6893 2030
Popular eatery near Beijing's Minorities
University featuring the sweet, spicy food of
Yunnan. Pork cooked in bamboo segments,
fried potato balls and pineapple rice are
common favourites. **$$**

Jiumen Xiaochi 九门小吃
1 Xiaoyou Hutong, Houhai
Tel: (010) 6402 5858
A collection of traditional Beijing snack stalls
recreated in a large courtyard. Try flash-
boiled tripe, hand-pulled noodles, bean juice
and many other unlikely delights. **$**

Pure Lotus 净心莲
Inside Zhongguo Wenlianyuan, 12
Nongzhanguan Nanlu
Tel: (010) 6592 3627

Da Dong Roast Duck restaurant

Buddhist monks serve up the best and most
creative vegetarian dishes in town. **$$$**

Three Guizhou Men 三个贵州人
West Gate of the Worker's Stadium (above
Coco Banana)
Tel: (010) 6551 851
Hip, spacious restaurant offering authentic,
spicy Guizhou food of reliable quality 24
hours a day. Full picture menu offers favour-
ites such as 'sour soup' fish, wild-grown
vegetables and lip-smacking milk teas. **$$**

Outer Beijing

Bai Family Mansion 白家大院
15 Suzhou Jie, Haidian District
Tel: (010) 6265 4186
Based on imperial cuisine, Bai dishes would
have even kept the notoriously irascible
Empress Dowager Cixi happy. The Qing-style
ornamentation of the interior and waitresses
creates an impressive regal atmosphere. **$$$**

Songlin Restaurant 松林餐厅
Xiangshan Villa, East Gate of Fragrant
Hills Park
Tel: (010) 6259 1296
This is a massive restaurant specialising
in home-style cooking from Shandong pro-
vince. There is the option of 'fast food' ser-
vice or full restaurant facilities. **$$**

Tingliguan Restaurant 听鹂館
Inside Summer Palace (Yiheyuan)
Tel: (010) 6288 1955
www.tingliguan.com
Imperial-style restaurant serving more
than 300 dishes that were popular at court
in Ming and Qing times. Fish caught from
Kunming Lake is a house speciality. **$$$**

Great Wall

Badaling Restaurant 八达岭饭店
Badaling Great Wall
Tel: (010) 6912 1486
This is the main, state-owned restaurant at
Badaling, the only one tourism officials will
promote to groups – it can hold up to 1,000
people, serves Sichuan and Jiangsu food, in
clean surroundings. **$$$**

Peking duck involves a lengthy and meticulous preparation

Further Afield
Shangke Tang 上客堂
West side of Puning Temple, Chengde
Tel: (0314) 205 8888
A hall built for Buddhist monks visiting Chengde, this impressive hotel and restaurant serves a variety of food including vegetarian cuisine. **$$**

NIGHTLIFE

Beijing's original Bar Street is located next to the Sanlitun area. It's packed full of mediocre bars and untrained staff, so choose a reliable spot before you head out. Sanlitun's bars and clubs spill over into the Worker's Stadium area. For a more local experience, once-tranquil lake park Houhai has become a neon-lit free-for-all with a few nice spots. Nearby Nanluoguxiang is a backpacker-friendly *hutong* currently being transformed into another bar street.

Beijing
Destination
Opposite Worker's Stadium West Gate
Tel: (010) 6551 5138
Destination is currently the city's only dedicated gay bar, with a clientele that is 90 percent male. It's a popular spot for dancing and cruising.

No Name Bar
3 Qianhai Dongyan, Houhai
Tel: (010) 6401 8541
Tasteful decor and lakes views make this one of Houhai's best bars-cum-coffee houses.

Passby Bar
108 Nanluoguxiang
Tel: (010) 8403 8004
Nanluoguxiang's original bar. Has an outside courtyard to enjoy food and drinks as well as a library of travel books.

The Tree
43 Sanlitun Beijie, behind Poachers Inn
Tel: (010) 6415 1954
A cosy pub atmosphere, Belgian beers and

an authentic pizza oven make this one of Sanlitun's most popular spots for those in the know.

Vics
Inside Worker's Stadium North Gate
Tel: (010) 5293 0333
Vics is the largest nightclub in the Worker's Stadium North Gate section. Expect crowds of fashionable young people and loud volumes.

Vineyard Café
31 Wudaoying Hutong
Tel: (010) 6402 7961
www.vineyardcafe.cn
Located on a trendy café-and-craftshop *hutong*, Vineyard Café is well-known to locals for its brunches and decent wine list.

Yugong Yishan
3 Zhangxizhong Lu, Dongcheng District
Tel: (010) 6404 2711
One of the hottest spots for local live music in Beijing and one of the few venues successful in regularly attracting foreign talent.

ENTERTAINMENT

Ticket prices at major theatres in Beijing are still out of reach of ordinary people, making the entertainment scene rather dominated by tourists and wealthy locals. Things are changing, however, and grass-roots performances now take place in areas that attract arty types – such as the Danshanzi Art District. Meanwhile, time-honoured cultural shows such as Beijing Opera and acrobatics can be enjoyed in several world-class facilities.

Theatre

Capital Theatre
22 Wangfujing Dajie
Tel: (010) 6524 9847
www.bjry.com
This large, Soviet-style building is Beijing's premier venue for Chinese-language theatre and occasional performance space for visiting troupes from abroad.

National Grand Theatre
Chang'an Avenue
Tel: (010) 6655 0000
www.chncpa.org
Otherwise known as the National Centre for the Performing Arts or 'The Egg', this extravagant venue encompasses four theatre spaces for drama, concerts, lavish performances and even children's theatre. 🎭

Dance

Beijing Modern Dance Company
46 Fangjia Hutong, Dongcheng District
Tel: (010) 6402 9627
www.bmdc.com.cn
Beijing's best-known modern dance group have toured the world and recently established an arts centre and theatre on Fangjia *hutong* near the Lama Temple.

Concert Halls

The Poly Theatre
Poly Plaza, 14 Dongzhimen Nandajie, Chaoyang District
Tel: (010) 6500 1188
www.polytheatre.com
Another large theatre with a reputation for high-quality and varied performances. The China Philharmonic Orchestra generally performs here.

Cultural Shows

Acrobatics
Chaoyang Theatre
36 Dongsanhuan Beilu, Hujialou
Tel: (010) 6507 2421
www.bjcyjc.com
Regular, and extremely flashy, acrobatics shows are held in this spacious, modern theatre. 🎭

Opera

Laoshe Teahouse
3 Qianmen Xidajie
Tel: (010) 6303 6830
www.laosheteahouse.com
This old favourite aims to give patrons a taste of Old Beijing with nightly performances, traditional snacks and pricey cups of tea poured by servers bedecked in flowing gowns. It's all for the tourists, of course, but certainly entertaining.

Zhengyici Theatre
220 Xiheyan Dajie, Xuanwu District
Tel: (010) 8315 1649
The only surviving Beijing Opera theatre built entirely of wood, the Zhengyici Theatre preserves the traditional intimate layout of a roofed stage surrounded on three sides by tea tables. Ticket prices here are significantly higher than elsewhere. Performances every night.

Film

Hart Centre of Arts
4 Jiuxianqiao Lu, Dashanzi Art District
Tel: (010) 6435 3570
www.hart.com.cn
Screens Chinese art movies and foreign documentaries as well as providing a salon atmosphere.

SPORTS AND ACTIVITIES

As an Olympic host city, Beijing's sports facilities have improved enormously in recent years. Olympic venues such as the National Aquatics Centre have opened to the public, private gyms have popped up all over the city, and some residents make use of excellent, but unadvertised, facilities at nearby universities.

Biking

Cycle China
12 Jingshan Dongjie, Dongcheng District
Tel: (010) 6402 5653
www.cyclechina.com
Rents bicycles and organises tours of Beijing's *hutong* and the Great Wall.

Golf

Beijing International Golf Club
North of the Ming Tombs Reservoir, Changping District
Tel: (010) 6076 2288
An 18-hole, 72-par international-standard golf course with views of the Ming Tombs Reservoir. Non-members pay Rmb800 for weekdays – not a budget option.

Horse Riding

Equuleus International Riding Club
91 Sunbai Lu, Sunhe Town, Chaoyang District
Tel: (010) 6432 4947
www.equriding.com
Accredited riding club offering bilingual lessons in an outdoor or indoor arena, competitions and other events.

Martial Arts

Beijing Milun School of Traditional Kung Fu
33 Xitangzi Hutong, near Wangfujing
Tel: (138) 1170 6568
www.kungfuinchina.com
Teaches a variety of traditional fighting styles, including t'ai chi and Shaolin boxing. Pay per class for group classes and private lessons or complete a full course.

Skiing

Nanshan Ski Village
Shengshuitou Village, Henanzhai Town, Miyun County

Tel: (010) 8909 1909
www.nanshanski.com
Though some 60km (37 miles) out of central Beijing, Nanshan Ski Village is on the best resorts around. Includes snowboard park and water- and grass-skiing facilities in summer.

Sports Centres

National Olympics Sports Centre
Tel: (010) 6497 2393
www.nosc.net.cn
The former Olympic venue has facilities for various sports including badminton, basketball, diving, rock-climbing, football, swimming, tennis, tae kwon do and track running.

Swimming

National Aquatics Centre (Water Cube)
11 Taincheng Donglu
Tel: (010) 8437 1588
www.water-cube.com
The eye-popping Olympic swimming venue is now open to the public for swimming or enjoying the onsite water park.

National Aquatics Centre

TOURS

Hundreds of tour operators eagerly seek out tourist money in a largely unregulated market, so pick your tour carefully and bear in mind that many sights in and around Beijing can be reached easily by public transport. The better hotels and hostels will often provide tours to sights such as the Great Wall and Ming Tombs that offer convenience and value for money.

Beijing Xinhua International Tours
2001-1-1, Nanxiaojie, Guangqumen,
Chongwen District
Tel: (010) 6716 0201
www.tour-beijing.com
Offers numerous packages to various sections of the Great Wall, as well as theme tours: martial arts, cooking, birdwatching, etc.

Bespoke Beijing
38 Baofang Hutong, Dongcheng District
Tel: (010) 6528 6603
www.bespoke-beijing.com
Tailor-made tours and translation service from local experts. They can even provide a mobile phone pre-programmed with useful numbers.

C-Trip
Tel: (400) 619 9999
English.ctrip.com
Popular private travel agency running literally dozens of tours in and around Beijing and other cities around China. Its well-organised website provides hotel and flight-booking options.

China Culture Centre
A101 Kent Centre, 29 Liangmaqiao Road,
Chaoyang District
Tel: (010) 6432 9341
www.chinaculturecenter.org
Long-standing cultural education agency offering classes, special events and tours of Beijing and beyond.

A range of different Great Walls tours are available

FESTIVALS AND EVENTS

As Beijingers' disposable income grows, so too does their appetite for public celebration. Traditional festival dates will usually be celebrated with displays and performances in public spaces such as parks. A nascent music-festival scene has even emerged, though the whims of bureaucracy make these events hard to predict.

January/February

Chinese New Year or Spring Festival falls between mid-January and mid-February, and at this time many Beijing parks and temples hold fairs where you can still see performances such as dragon dances, Yang Ge dances and Beijing Opera. The oldest and best known is Changdian Temple Fair. Festivities last for a week.

Changdian Temple Fair

Liulichang Jie, Xuanwu District
Part of the lunar New Year celebrations. Stalls hawk calligraphy, antiques, kites and other traditional crafts while acrobats and opera singers provide the entertainment.

Lantern Festival

The Lantern Festival falls in January or February, and in recent years Beijing has started promoting Qing-style processions, including musicians, lion dancers, Yang Ge groups and banners with pictures of deities. Chaoyang Park usually has the biggest display of paper lantern and colourful light displays.

May

Midi Music Festival

1–4 May
Haidian Park
www.midifestival.com
China's longest-running outdoor rock festival attracts enthusiastic, if not world-famous, bands and musical performers each year.

Affordable Art Fair

Usually in May
Tel: (010) 6407 5314
www.affordableartchina.com
The Affordable Art Fair has been running since 2006 for art-lovers and investors to pick up original, contemporary art for a maximum of Rmb10,000 per piece.

October

National Day

1 Oct
Tiananmen Square
The founding of the People's Republic of China sees Beijing's central square decorated with extravagant floral displays and portraits of revered leaders.

Beijing International Music Festival

Performances held at various theatres
Tel: (010) 6593 0250
www.bmf.org.cn
A month-long celebration of classical music that sees Chinese and foreign virtuosos take to stages around Beijing. Recent years have seen a more eclectic mix of performances.

The Lantern festival follows on from Chinese New Year

The North

Anchored by the great imperial cities of Beijing and Xi'an and bisected by the Great Wall, this vast swathe of land stretches for thousands of miles across the wide open spaces of the northeast and Inner Mongolia to the dusty heartlands of ancient China around the Huang He (Yellow River). HIghlights include the Terracotta Warriors, the beautiful old town of Pingyao and the Longmen Caves.

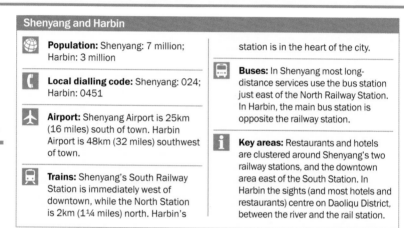

Shenyang and Harbin

Population: Shenyang: 7 million; Harbin: 3 million

Local dialling code: Shenyang: 024; Harbin: 0451

Airport: Shenyang Airport is 25km (16 miles) south of town. Harbin Airport is 48km (32 miles) southwest of town.

Trains: Shenyang's South Railway Station is immediately west of downtown, while the North Station is 2km (1¼ miles) north. Harbin's station is in the heart of the city.

Buses: In Shenyang most long-distance services use the bus station just east of the North Railway Station. In Harbin, the main bus station is opposite the railway station.

Key areas: Restaurants and hotels are clustered around Shenyang's two railway stations, and the downtown area east of the South Station. In Harbin the sights (and most hotels and restaurants) centre on Daoliqu District, between the river and the rail station.

To the north of the ancient capital of Beijing and its protecting wall is Dongbei, better known to the world as Manchuria, with its own unique customs and traditions. Russian-influenced Harbin draws visitors with its intriguing architecture and dazzling Ice Lantern Festival. Reaching all the way west to Gansu and the Silk Road are the vast empty grasslands and deserts of Inner Mongolia, where pockets of traditional Mongolian life still flourish. To the southwest of Beijing around the flood plain of the Huang He (Yellow River) and its tributaries are the regions where Chinese civilisation first

flowered, the setting for the ancient capital, Xi'an, famous for the Army of Terracotta Warriors discovered nearby. Further east are the awesome Longmen caves near Luoyang, and globally renowned Shaolin Temple.

The Northeast: Dongbei

The three provinces of Liaoning, Jilin and Heilongjiang are collectively known as Dongbei, literally 'East-North'. The old name of Manchuria is a reminder of the fact that this was once the territory of the Manchu rulers of the Qing dynasty. With a blend of Chinese, Korean and Russian influences, this far-flung region has an unusual cultural identity.

Shenyang

A busy transport junction and the capital of Liaoning province, **Shenyang** ❶ is one of the most important industrial cities in China. More likely to be a place you'll pass through than travel to see, the principal attraction is the impressive **Imperial Palace** (Shenyang Gugong; daily 8am–5pm; charge), China's largest and most complete palace complex after the Forbidden City in Beijing. It was built in 1625, after the Manchu had declared the city as their capital, and contains more than 300 well-preserved buildings.

Dalian

An economic success story dubbed the 'Hong Kong of the North' and one of the more attractive cities in

The extraordinary ice festival at Harbin

north China, **Dalian** ❷ is a thriving port and popular domestic tourist destination. The city is renowned for its extensive sandy beaches, mild climate and seafood restaurants. Sections of the coastline offer dizzy views of plunging cliffs, especially at Laohu Tan (Tiger Beach). There is a pleasant sandy beach at Bangchuidao Scenic Area (Bangchuidao Jingqu; charge), 5km (3 miles) southeast of the city centre.

Korean borderlands

Northeast from Dalian is the city of Dandong and the mountainous vistas of the **Dagu Shan** range, right on the North Korean border. Boats carry visitors to within only a few metres of the North Korean side on the Yalu Jiang (Yalu River). Alternatively you can walk along the original bridge that linked China with North Korea until you reach the twisted wreckage created by American bombers and carefully preserved since by Chinese authorities.

Ji'an, once the capital of the Korean kingdom of Koguryo, also lies on the Chinese-Korean border. The Yalu

Shenyang's Imperial Palace

Jiang is only 30m (100ft) wide here, and in the summer months children from both sides swim in it.

Between Tonghua and Yanji, the provincial capital, the **Changbai Shan Nature Reserve** ❸ (Changbai Shan Ziran Baohu Qu) follows the mountains along the Korean border, one of the most diverse mountain-forest ecosystems in Asia and sanctuary for many endangered animals, including a few leopards and Siberian tigers. The easiest way to explore is to head to the **Changbai Shan Scenic Area** (Changbai Shan Fengjing Qu; daily 7am–4.30pm; charge), or arrange a tour through CITS or a major hotel in Jilin.

Jilin

Jilin city, in central Jilin province, is most famous for its winter display of ice-rimmed trees along the banks of the Songhua River. Other sights include the impressive **Catholic Church** (Mon–Fri from 5am, Sat–Sun from 8am) and the **Wen Miao** (Mon–Fri 8.30am–4pm, Sat–Sun 9am–4pm; charge), a temple built for imperial examination hopefuls to pay homage to Confucius.

The city of **Changchun** ❹ is best known for being the HQ of the Japanese puppet state of Manchukuo in the 1930s, with China's last emperor, Pu Yi, at its helm. At the **Weihuang Gong** (Puppet Emperor's Palace; daily 8.30am–4.30pm; charge), you can peruse Pu Yi's living quarters and mementoes from his bizarre and tragic life.

Heilongjiang: the far north

From Changchun, the journey continues north to **Harbin** ❺, the capital

each year and lasts for one month (though frozen sculptures often remain longer) centred on **Zhaolin Park** (Zhaolin Gongyuan; 5am–6.30pm; charge), which becomes home to dozens of extraordinary ice sculptures lit up from inside by coloured lights.

Several **ski resorts** can be reached by bus from Harbin, including **Yabuli**, China's best-equipped and largest ski centre, 200km (120 miles) southeast of the city.

In the summer months it is possible to journey north into 'Chinese Siberia', a remote region of birch and pine forests extending to the Heilong Jiang (Amur River). An area of forest – threatened by loggers – is protected within **Tangwanghe National Park**.

Inner Mongolia

Extending in a huge crescent across a vast swathe of northern China from the Siberian borderlands to the Gobi Desert, Inner Mongolia (Nei Monggol) is one of the world's emptiest places, a continuation of the boundless grasslands and deserts of the independent Republic of Mongolia to the north.

Hohhot

Most visitors use **Hohhot ❻**, the regional capital, for organising summer trips to the grasslands and to make contact with Mongolian traditions. It's largely a Han Chinese conurbation, although there is a palpable Mongolian presence in the old quarter in the southwest of town, with a cluster of Buddhist lamaseries, heavily Tibetan in both style and substance, and clear

of Heilongjiang province, situated almost 1,400km (900 miles), and 13 hours by train, from Beijing. The city lies along the Songhua Jiang, which joins the Heilong Jiang, the river that defines China's border with Russia to the north.

Russians first arrived in Harbin at the end of the 19th century with the railway, which passed through the city on its way from Vladivostok to Dalian, and the city has retained something of the feel of a Siberian outpost. The central Daoliqu District features Russian restaurants and onion-domed churches culminating in the restored **Cathedral**, formerly known as St Sofia's (9.30am–5.30pm; charge). The unmissable **Ice Lantern Festival** starts on 5 January

93

The North

reminders of the historic importance of Lamaist Buddhism to Mongolia.

The largest and most active temple is the Ming-dynasty **Dazhao** (daily 8am–6pm; charge), tucked away on the west side of Danan Jie. First built in 1579, the original temple was itself a symbol of Mongolia's acceptance of Lamaist Buddhism.

Baotou

The industrial town of **Baotou**, shrouded in smog from its numerous furnaces, lies two hours by train to the west of Hohhot. Though there is little to see in the city itself, it is the staging point for excursions to the handful of nearby attractions. The area's most historically significant sight is the captivating Tibetan-style lamasery of **Wudangzhao** (daily 8am–5.30pm; charge), some 70km (44 miles) to the northeast. The largest and best-preserved lamasery in Inner Mongolia, the complex of white-washed temples and prayer halls stretches up the side of a hill and still houses numerous lamas.

Genghis Khan Mausoleum

The **Genghis Khan Mausoleum** ❼ (Chengjisihan Lingyuan; daily 8am–5.30pm; charge), outside the coal-stained city of Dongsheng, 110km (68 miles) south of Baotou, is very much revered by Mongolians from Inner and Outer Mongolia alike. Within the three distinctive cement buildings, constructed by the Chinese in the 1950s and representing Mongolian yurts, lie what are reputedly artefacts from the 13th century. While most experts do not believe the Great Khan was ever actually interred here, this does not deter thousands of ethnic Mongolians from converging on the grounds during the impressive sacrificial ceremonies that are held on the grounds four times each year.

Resonant Sand Bay

Encroaching on the steppe about 45km (28 miles) south of Baotou is the spectacular **Resonant Sand Bay** (Xiangshawan), a sprawling sea of shifting sand dunes on the northern fringe of the Kubuqi Desert. The golden dunes, the highest of which are 110m (360ft), are an arresting sight, swallowing whole the surrounding patches of sparse grassland.

The Grasslands

The most memorable aspect of a visit to Hohhot is likely to be an excursion to the grasslands, across the desolate Daqing Mountains, where horseback

Buddhist stupa, Hohhot

Children outside the Genghis Khan Mausoleum

riding is a way of life among Mongolians. A good paved road eases the strain of the zigzag climb that continues up approximately 2,000m (6,500ft) above sea level.

Most visitors end up at either **Xila-muren** or **Gegentala**, a three-hour drive from Hohhot. At these tourist camps, guests sleep in wool-felt yurts with quilts, hot-water flasks and electric lights. Daily activities can include archery, Mongolian wrestling, visits to local villages and horse- riding.

Shanxi

Extending from the edge of the Mongolian grasslands to the Yellow River valley, Shanxi – not to be confused with its near-namesake neighbour, Shaanxi – is often neglected by tourists, but has more than its fair share of interest.

Datong and around

In the far north of Shanxi, a seven-hour train ride west of Beijing, the industrial sprawl of **Datong** is home to a diverse array of ancient religious structures and statuary left over from the succession of non-Han Chinese peoples who made it the seat of their dynasties.

Visiting the Grasslands

- The best time to visit the grasslands is from July to September.
- Travel agents aggressively sell grassland tours to tourists. Not all are reliable, and hard bargaining is usually necessary.
- When enjoying the hospitality of a Mongolian, allow your host to choose cuts of meat for you. Don't help yourself.
- You may be offered milk-tea, or vodka. Refusal is seen as impolite – taking even a small sip will usually save face.

Yungang Shiku near Datong

Within Datong itself the most significant sight is the two temples that comprise the **Huayan Si** (both daily 8.30am–5pm; separate charges), among the oldest remnants of the Mongol Khitan people's Liao dynasty which made the city its capital in 907. The more architecturally impressive Upper Huayan Si, first built in 1062, is distinguished by the soaring roof of its main hall.

The main reason to visit Datong, however, is to see the sublime cave sculptures at nearby **Yungang Shiku** ❽ (Cloud Ridge Grottoes; daily 8am–6pm; charge), China's oldest and best-preserved collection of Buddhist cave carvings. This series of several dozen man-made caves have been forged into the side of a sandstone cliff, 16km (10 miles) west of Datong, stretching for about 1km (⅔ mile). The caves were constructed from AD453–525 by tens of thousands of labourers and artisans.

Heng Shan and Xuankong Si

Heng Shan ❾, 70km (45 miles) south of Datong, is the most northerly of China's five sacred Daoist mountains

(see pp.36–8). The hilly area is dotted with historic temples, hinting at its importance as a spiritual retreat as long as 2,000 years ago. Though devout Daoists still flock here to worship at the temples and climb the highest peak, the vast majority of visitors come to see the gravity-defying **Xuankong Si** (Hanging Temple; daily 8am–6pm; charge), a former monastery perched high on a cliff face and supported only by wooden beams embedded into the rock. A Buddhist site built in 491, and restored during the Ming and Qing dynasties, it has had religious/mystic significance for more than 2,000 years.

Wutai Shan

South of Heng Shan, and a five-hour bus ride from Datong, lies **Wutai Shan ❿** (Five Terrace Mountain;

overall charge, plus charge for each temple), one of China's four sacred Buddhist mountains and a major point of pilgrimage for Chinese and Tibetan Buddhists, who come in droves to worship at the three dozen or so temples that dot the hillsides. *For more on Wutai Shan, see p.38.*

Pingyao

On the Beijing–Xi'an railway line around 100km (62 miles) south of Taiyuan, the idyllic town of **Pingyao ⓫** is perhaps China's best-preserved ancient walled city and a highlight of many tourists' visit to the country. Although it has a 1,200-year history, Pingyao is mostly renowned for its largely intact Ming- and Qing-dynasty architecture, a result of its prominence as one of China's first banking centres. A Unesco World Heritage

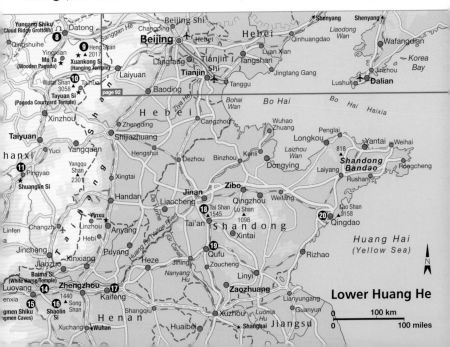

Site, the town is surrounded by a 6km (4-mile) Ming-dynasty city wall (which you can walk around) complete with gates, enclosing the quaint streets in a grid-like pattern. Though the entire town is filled with surprises, some of the best-kept architecture lies on Mingqing Jie (Mingqing Street) and Nan Dajie (South Avenue), both filled with souvenir shops, restaurants and hotels. Many of the old buildings have been converted into atmospheric guesthouses with lovely courtyards and period furnishings.

Xi'an and Shaanxi

Shaanxi's brilliant past has bequeathed some truly spectacular sights. The dusty plains surrounding Xi'an – capital of China when Beijing was but a mere remote trading post – are covered with imperial tombs, foremost among them that of Qin Shi Huangdi with its underground Army of Terracotta Warriors.

Xi'an

Xi'an ⑫, capital of Shaanxi province, lies in the valley of the Wei River, some 160km (100 miles) west

of its confluence with the Huang He. It was from this irrigated valley that the emperor Qin Shi Huangdi unified China for the first time. Xi'an served as the capital for more than 1,100 years and 13 imperial dynasties; during the Tang years (618–907) it was the largest city in the world. Chang'an (Everlasting Peace), as it was called back then, was the destination of thousands of foreign Silk Road traders and enjoyed unsurpassed prestige.

Although the city walls built during the Tang dynasty no longer exist, 14km (9 miles) of the **Ming city wall** still surround the centre, and much of their length has been restored (*see opposite*). In places such as Nanmen (South Gate), it is possible to climb on top of these 12-m (40ft) thick ramparts.

At the heart of the city within the walls are the prominent landmarks of the **Bell Tower** Ⓐ (Zhonglou; 8.30am–9.30pm, closes 6pm in winter; charge) and **Drum Tower** Ⓑ (Gulou; same hours; charge). Both date from the 14th century, were rebuilt in the 17th century, and offer views across the

Xi'an

🌐 **Population:** 4.4 million

📞 **Local dialling code:** 029

✈️ **Airport:** Xianyang Airport is some 40km (26 miles) northwest of town.

🚆 **Trains:** The main station is at the northern end of Jiefang Lu, close to the northeastern corner of the city walls.

🚌 **Buses:** Xi'an has several bus stations, but the largest is opposite the railway station. The east and west bus stations are around 2km (1¼ miles) beyond the old city walls.

ℹ️ **Key areas:** Xi'an is easy to navigate, with most of the hotels, restaurants and bars clustered within the old city walls in the vicinity of the Bell Tower. The Terracotta Warriors are located some 30km (20 miles) to the east of the city.

The Terracotta warriors

Bowuguan; Tue–Sun late Oct–Mar 9am–5.30pm, Apr–late Oct 8.30am–6pm; charge). More than 3,000 historic artefacts are displayed here in chronological order and labelled in English. The collection ranges from tools and pottery from Palaeolithic and Neolithic times to bronze cooking vessels from the Shang and Zhou dynasties right on through to Ming- and Qing-dynasty ceramics.

Terracotta Warriors

A highlight of any visit to China is Xi'an's most popular site: the **Terracotta Warriors** ❸ (Bingmayong; daily 8.30am–5.30pm; charge; www.bmy.com.cn 🖼). This vast treasure, vying with the Great Wall and Forbidden City as China's most famous monument, lies 30km (20 miles) east of Xi'an and was stumbled upon in 1974 by peasants digging a well.

city. To the north of the Drum Tower is the main Muslim district.

About 3km (2 miles) to the southeast is the 64m (210ft) high, seven-storey **Great Wild Goose Pagoda** ❸ (Dayan Ta; daily 8am–6.30pm; charge), anchoring the southern end of Yanta Lu. One of Xi'an's most recognisable structures, it was built in AD652, at the beginning of the Tang dynasty, and was used to store Buddhist scriptures brought back to China in AD645 by the eminent monk Xuan Zang. Xuan's adventures are recorded in the Chinese classic *Journey to the West*.

Just northwest is one of the city's foremost attractions: the **Shaanxi History Museum** ❹ (Shaanxi Lishi

Xi'an's City Walls

The rectangular Ming-dynasty city wall, the most intact major city wall in China, was built on a classic Chinese grid pattern. The roadway on top is wide for two-way chariot traffic and can still be accessed from gates at any of the compass points. There are ramparts every 120m (395ft), to allow archers stationed there to cover the entire length of the wall. Currently, the whole wall cannot be circumnavigated, although in 2010 a multibillion-yuan restoration plan was drawn up to recreate the complete defence system – and illuminate it with huge LED panels.

Fenghuangshan Revolutionary HQ, Yan'an

Long before his eventual death in 210BC, the first Qin emperor, Qinshi Huangdi, conscripted hundreds of thousands of his subjects to construct a suitably impressive tomb. An escort into the afterlife was prepared in the form of more 8,000 clay soldiers – as well as cavalry, chariots and assorted hangers-on – all standing in battle formation.

An arched structure resembling an aircraft hangar has been built to protect the exposed soldiers and horses in Vault 1 from the weather. Walkways permit tourists a bird's-eye survey of the site, revealing the deployment of the troops, 6,000 of them reassembled and back in their original ranks. Each warrior is an individual, with his own headdress, moustache or beard and unique expression. Vault 2 contains the imperial cavalry: 900 soldiers, 116 saddled horses and 356 horses hitched to 89 chariots.

Other sights around Xi'an

History and natural beauty mingle easily at **Huaqing Hot Springs** (Huaqing Chi; daily 8am–7pm; charge), a popular side trip for tourists on the way to or from the Terracotta Warriors. The spa's hot, mineral-rich waters and its situation on Black Horse Mountain (Lishan) attracted a series of royal patrons as far back as the 8th century BC.

The **Banpo Museum** F (Banpo Bowuguan; daily 8am–6.30pm; charge), in the city's eastern suburbs, is dedicated to the Neolithic settlement that has been partially excavated near here. Relics, including ceramics, weapons and infant burial jars from the matriarchal Yangshao culture are on display.

On the north bank of the Wei River west of Xi'an, **Xianyang** G was the capital during the reign of Qin Shi Huangdi, although few traces of the palaces said to have been built here remain. The **Xianyang Musuem** (Xianyang Bowuguan; daily 8am–5.30pm; charge), situated in a former Confucian temple, contains a fabulous terracotta army of its own: some 3,000 small figures of soldiers and horses dataing from the early Qin dynasty.

Further to the northwest is **Qian Ling ⑪** (Qian Tomb; daily 8am–5pm; charge), the joint burial place of the Tang emperor Gaozong and his wife, the empress Wu Zetian who succeeded him to the throne, becoming China's only female ruler in the process. The approach to the tomb – itself unopened – is guarded by a 'spirit way' of large stone sculptures of animals and dignitaries.

Yan'an

The time-warped town of **Yan'an ⑬**, 270km (170 miles) north of Xi'an in the bleak loess hills of northern Shaanxi, functioned as the Communist Party headquarters in the 1930s and 1940s. It was here that Mao Zedong's epic Long March finally

came to an end in October 1935. During the Cultural Revolution and through the 1970s, Yan'an was, and to some extent remains, a national centre of pilgrimage. It still attracts large numbers of patriotic domestic tourists.

The main attractions are the three former Communist Party headquarters sites, each simply maintained as if the revolutionaries themselves were still living there. The most popular of the three is the **Yangjialing Revolutionary Headquarters** site (Yangjialing Geming Jiuzhi; daily 8am–5.30pm; charge), about 3km (2 miles) northwest of the town centre. Here is the meeting hall where the first Central Committee meeting was held. The other two sites are **Wangjiaping** and **Fenghuangshan** (both daily 8am–5.30pm; charge for each). Mao's austere wooden bed and

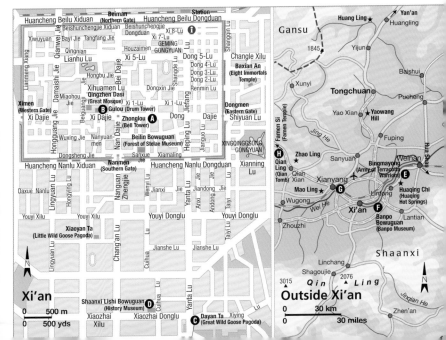

desk, letters and photographs are all on view.

Yellow River Heartlands

Together with neighbouring southern Shaanxi, Henan province forms the heartlands of early Chinese civilisation, germinated by the waters of the Huang He, which nourished the soil and encouraged the settlements to which the Han Chinese trace their roots. Religion flourished here, and the area was a major portal in the spread of Buddhism throughout China. Henan has many of the country's oldest Buddhist sites, including the world-renowned Shaolin Temple.

Luoyang

A five-hour train journey east of Xi'an, **Luoyang** was one of China's greatest ancient capitals, serving as the seat of power for numerous dynasties dating back to the Zhou, who made it their main capital in 770BC. Heavy industrialisation has taken its toll on the modern city, and within its current confines there is little to suggest its former glory. Not far outside the city, however, are two of China's most important Buddhist shrines: Baima Si and the exquisite rock carvings of the Longmen Caves. Some visitors also use Luoyang as a base for day trips to nearby Song Shan and Shaolin.

Within the city itself, the only attraction worth visiting is the **Luoyang Museum** (Luoyang Bowuguan; daily 8am–5pm; charge), which houses four special collections of bronzeware, jadeware, ceramics and gold and silver artefacts, offering an overview of the area's development from the Neolithic period to the Song dynasty.

Some 13km (8 miles) east of downtown Luoyang is the venerable **Baima Si** ⑭ (White Horse Temple;

Seeking good fortune, Baima Si

latter period of the Northern Wei, the Sui and the Tang. There are said to be more than 2,300 grottoes and niches containing over 40 pagodas, some 2,800 inscriptions and over 100,000 statues and images. Regrettably, many of the most intricate sculptures were stolen or beheaded by collectors around the start of the 20th century. Another round of destruction took place during the state-sanctioned vandalism of the Cultural Revolution.

Shaolin

Known worldwide for its pivotal role in the development of Chinese martial arts, **Shaolin Si** ⑯ (Monastery of the Mount Shaoshi Forest; daily 8am–6.30pm; charge) is one of northern China's foremost tourist attractions. Located about 80km (50 miles) southeast of Luoyang, the monastery can be visited on a day trip from either city, or explored at a more leisurely pace from the nearby town of Dengfeng.

Shaolin was first built in the 5th century AD but has been burnt down several times over the ages. Tradition holds that the Indian monk Bodhidharma lived here with the blessing of the emperor and introduced Chan (Zen) Buddhism to the resident Chinese monks. Once a remote and romantic retreat where the wisdom of the ages passed from master to novice, it is now a major tourist area as well as a place of pilgrimage for monks and lay Buddhists alike.

A short walk to the northwest of the monastery is **Talin** (Stupa Forest),

daily 8.30am–5pm; charge), founded in AD68 and considered China's first Buddhist temple. Now an active monastery, the name of the temple reflects the story of how its two founding monks brought saddlebags of Buddhist scriptures to China on the backs of white horses.

The Longmen Caves

The awe-inspiring **Longmen Caves** ⑮ (Longmen Shiku; daily 7am–7pm; charge), a Unesco World Heritage Site, are situated 12km (8 miles) south of Luoyang along the banks of the Yi Jiang (Yi River). An elaborate ensemble of Buddhist statuary in stone, the remarkably varied carvings stretch for about 1km (²⁄₃ mile) on both sides of the Yi Jiang and encompass the artistic toil of three dynasties: the

The North

an eerie resting place for expired monks comprising more than 240 brick-and-stone stupas, each containing the ashes of an accomplished monk. The oldest stupas are from the 9th century AD.

Song Shan

The several dozen mountain peaks stretching west from Shaolin Si comprise the holy range of **Song Shan**, forming the central axis of Daoism's five sacred mountains (see pp.36–8). Nestled in the hills surrounding Dengfeng – a town in the heart of the mountains, about 13km (8 miles) east of Shaolin – are some fascinating historic sights. The Songyang Academy **Songyang Shuyuan** (daily 7.30am–6pm; charge), 3km (2 miles) north of Dengfeng, is one of China's four most influential ancient academies.

Zhengzhou

The lively city of Zhengzhou, about 80km (50 miles) east of Dengfeng,

is the capital of Henan province and an important railway junction straddling the crossroads of China's main east–west (Shanghai–Xi'an) and north–south (Beijing–Guangzhou) lines. There was a fortified settlement here as early as the Shang dynasty, some 3,500 years ago, but all that remains of that period are the high, packed-earth foundations of the Shang-era walls located in the southeast of the modern city.

The most intact ancient building in the downtown area is the **Chenghuang Miao** (City God Temple; daily 9am–5pm). Founded more than 600 years ago, during the Ming dynasty, its buildings have undergone a recent restoration, and the walls of the main hall are adorned with freshly painted murals depicting the city gods of China's biggest urban centres.

Kaifeng

An hour's bus ride east of Zhengzhou, **Kaifeng** ⑰ is one of China's most enduring ancient capitals, retaining enough historic sites to hint at

Martial arts training, Shaolin

A temple festival at Kaifeng

Bowuguan; 26 Yingbin Lu; daily 8.30–11.30am, 2.30–5.30pm; charge) on the south side of Baogong Lake.

Shandong

The final stretch of the Yellow River passes through Shandong, with its hilly peninsula extending into the Yellow Sea. Tai Shan, China's holiest Daoist mountain, along with Qufu, hometown of China's beloved Confucius, is a big draws for visitors. The former German colony of Qingdao is an ideal place to take in the coast.

Tai Shan

Considered to be China's most sacred Daoist mountain, **Tai Shan 18** lies 80km (50 miles) south of Jinan, close to the main Beijing–Shanghai railway line. Popular Chinese religion treats

its former glory, yet largely resisting indiscriminate modern development. It rose to prominence as a regional capital in 364 BC before reaching its pinnacle in the Northern Song period (AD960–1127), when it was believed to be one of the world's biggest cities.

In Kaifeng's far northeast corner, just inside the city wall, is one of its only Song-period relics: the **Iron Pagoda** (Tie Ta; daily 7.30am–6.30pm; charge), a 13-storey, 56m (184ft) brick structure soaring prominently in the middle of **a** park. The octagonal tower gets its name from the dark-brown glazed tiles that adorn its exterior, which from a distance look like cast iron.

For an overview of the city's past, including some relics from the former Jewish community (see right), visit the **Kaifeng Museum** (Kaifeng

Kaifeng's Jewish Community

Small enclaves of Jews are believed to have settled in northwest China as early as the Han dynasty (206BC–AD220), but those who migrated from Central Asia to Kaifeng during the Northern Song (960–1127) are considered the progenitors of China's longest-running Jewish identity. The city once had a notable Jewish presence – a synagogue stood near the town centre until the late 19th century, and three stelae inscribed with imperial versions of their history are displayed in the Kaifeng Museum. Yet by the 1870s assimilation and intermarriage had largely eradicated their presence. Today, around 800 local families can trace their lineage back to Jewish roots.

A Qingdao beach

mountains as living beings: as well as creating clouds and rain, their stabilising power perpetuates the cosmic order. Shamans and emperors have performed sacred rituals here for four millennia. *For more on Tai Shan, see p.36.*

Qufu

Qufu ⑲, the hometown of Confucius (551–479 BC), located 140km (90 miles) south of Tai Shan, has been transformed over the years into a monument to China's greatest philosopher and an ambitious tourist attraction. Confucian ideology was given imperial status in the Han dynasty by Emperor Wudi, and subsequent emperors granted the great sage's descendants lavish titles and property. Originally built in the 16th century during the Ming dynasty, the **Kong Family Mansion** (Kong Fu; daily 8am–5pm; charge), was home to the Kongs (Confucius' family name) until 1948, when, with the Communist victory imminent, the last of the line left for exile in Taiwan.

Qingdao

At the end of the 19th century, an ambitious Germany was looking for a place in China to plant its colonial aspirations. After two German Catholic priests were killed by Boxer rebels in 1897, German troops were sent in to establish a presence at **Qingdao** ⑳. In true imperial style, the Chinese were quickly forced into an agreement to lease the surrounding Bay of Jiaozhou to Germany. In a short period of time, a modern, German-style city was constructed, with villas, a deepwater port, a cathedral and a main street called Kaiser Wilhelmstrasse.

German expertise is to be thanked for the success of Tsingtao (the old Wade-Giles system of spelling Qingdao) Beer. The **Tsingtao Brewery** (daily 8.30am–4.30pm; charge) features a museum and visitor centre. Aside from beer, Qingdao is perhaps most famous for its beaches, although the city itself is also appealing with relics of the colonial past, including 19th-century German-style buildings.

ACCOMMODATION

Though finding budget accommodation in Dalian and Harbin can be tricky, most other northern cities offer a range of hotel options: Xi'an, in particular, has a plentiful range of accommodation. Qufu and Pingyao are increasingly adding courtyard-style hotels with traditional decorations and furnishings for a more discerning traveller. Many visitors to Inner Mongolia opt to stay in traditional yurts.

Accommodation Price Categories

Prices are for a standard double room in peak season

$ = under Rmb300
$$ = Rmb300–600
$$$ = Rmb600–1,000
$$$$ = Over Rmb1,000

Baotou

Baotou Hotel
33 Gangtie Dajie
Tel: (0472) 536 5199
www.baotouhotel.com.cn
This sizeable hotel is comfortable, affordable and convenient. It also houses the city's main CITS office. **$**

Dalian

Dalian Hotel
4 Zhongshan Square
Tel: (0411) 8263 3111
dl-hotel.com
Dalian's most impressive historical hotel, built in 1914 by Japanese occupiers. **$$**

Dengfeng

Shaolin International Hotel
20 Shaolin Lu
Tel: (0371) 6286 6188
www.shaolinhotel.com
Dengfeng's highest-calibre hotel – and the one used for most international package tours to the Shaolin area – this four-star abode has a vast lobby area and a wide range of rooms, as well as a handful of restaurants specialising in regional Chinese cuisines. **$$**

Harbin

Shangri-La Hotel
555 Youyi Lu
Tel: (0451) 8485 8888
www.shangri-la.com
First-class service and comfort, with views of the Songhua River and CBD. **$$$$**

Songhuajiang Gloria Inn Harbin
257 Zhongyang Avenue
Tel: (0451) 8463 8855
Decent three-star hotel with a great location near Zhaolin Park and the Songhua River. **$$**

Hohhot

Garden Hotel
Wulanchubu Xilu
Tel: (0471) 491 5499
Located in the east of town (2km /1½ miles southeast of the station), this is a good budget option. **$**

Holiday Inn Hohhot
33 Zhongshan Xilu
Tel: (0471) 635 1888
www.holidayinn.com/hihohhot
Located in the heart of Hohhot's shopping district. There's a well-equipped business centre and health suite, and the Jade Vine Restaurant serves tasty Cantonese,

The Dalian Hotel

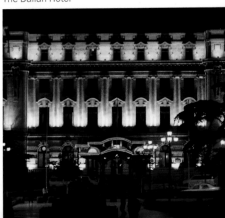

Sichuan and Hunan dishes. **$$–$$$**

Kaifeng
Dajintai Hotel
23 Gulou Jie
Tel: (0378) 6255 2888
Located in the heart of the Old Town, astride the night market, the Dajintai is the best value in Kaifeng, featuring large, comfortable doubles and an inclusive breakfast. **$**

Luoyang
Mingyuan Hotel
20 Jiefang Lu
Tel: (0379) 6390 1066
Comfortable large rooms and dorms and a convenient location south of the railway station make this a good choice. **$$**

Tianxiang Hotel
56 Jinguyuan Lu
Tel: (0379) 6393 5439
Convenient budget option for independent travellers, just a few minutes' walk south of the railway station and offering an array of economically priced rooms – many of them recently renovated. **$**

Qingdao
Oceanwide Elite Hotel
29 Taiping Lu
Tel: (0532) 8299 6699
There are unrivalled views across Qingdao Bay from this well-equipped hotel in the Old Town. **$$–$$$$**

Qingdao Old Observatory Hostel (YHA)
21 Guanxiang Er Lu
Tel: (0532) 8282 2626
This clean, well-managed hostel is located in a renovated observatory and offers great views of the city. Helpful English-speaking staff and fast internet access are on hand. **$**

Qufu
Queli Hotel
1 Queli Jie
Tel: (0537) 486 6818
Traditional courtyard building with modern facilities, close to most of Qufu's tourist sights. **$$**

Qufu International Youth Hostel
Gulou Beijie
Tel: (0537) 441 8939
Hostel close to all the main sights, with dormitories, twin and family rooms.

Shenyang
Haiyue City Plaza Hotel
83 Zhongshan Lu
Tel: (024) 6250 1888
Modern four-star hotel in the city centre offering very competitive rates for its spacious rooms. **$**

Xi'an
Bell Tower Hotel Xi'an
110 Nan Dajie (SW corner of Bell Tower)
Tel: (029) 8760 0000
www.belltowerhtl.com
Its location within easy walking distance of Xi'an's main tourist sites, friendly service and reasonably priced rooms have made this three-star hotel a perennial favourite. It also houses the city's most useful CITS office. **$$$**

Qixian Youth Hostel
1 Beixing Jie
Tel: (029) 6229 6977
A good budget option set in an old-style courtyard dwelling. Has a reasonable location southwest of the railway station. **$**

Sofitel Xi'an
319 Dong Xinjie
Tel: (029) 8792 8888
Xi'an top hotel, situated around 1km ($2/3$ mile) northeast of the Bell Tower, has a full range of facilities and unrivalled levels of comfort and refinement. **$$$$**

Xi'an Hotel
58 Chang'an Beilu
Tel: (029) 8766 6666
This ageing Chinese-standard four-star is reasonably priced and conveniently located for excursions to the sights in the south of the city. **$$**

RESTAURANTS

North Chinese cuisine tends to be heartier than in the south, and its noodles, potatoes and bread should be pleasant to the Western palate. Coastal towns Dalian and Qingdao offer plentiful seafood, usually extremely fresh. Shaanxi is known for a varied cuisine that reflects its long history as a trading crossroads. Packing the alleys north of the Great Mosque at Xi'an are rows of Muslim street vendors selling inexpensive mutton and beef dishes as well as desserts and sweet porridges. The Mongolian diet relies heavily on the grazing animals raised as part of the nomadic lifestyle – sheep, cattle and horses – either in the form of their meat or the dairy products that they yield. In Hohhot and Baotou, where the Chinese influence is strongly felt, the preferred mutton dish is thin slices of mutton in hotpot.

Restaurant Price Categories

Prices are for a full meal per person, with one drink

$ = below Rmb50 (below US$7.50)
$$ = Rmb50–100 (US$7.50–15)
$$$ = Rmb100–150 (US$15–22.50)
$$$$ = over Rmb150 over US$22.50)

Dalian

Wanbao Seafood Restaurant 万宝海鲜舫
108 Jiefang Lu
Elegant place specialising in lobster and sea urchin. **$$$$**

Xiandai Shishang 现代食尚
59 Changjiang Lu
Centrally-located at Zhongshan Square, this Dongbei restaurant strives for fashionable decoration and high-quality dishes. **$$**

Harbin

Huamei Xi Canting 华梅西餐厅
112 Zhongyang Dajie
Established in 1925 and claiming to be the mainland's oldest foreign restaurant, this famous Russian spot serves bortsch and other classics. **$$**

Xiangcun Dayuan 乡村大院
13 Dashun Jie
Dongbei cuisine and raucous nightly Red Army song performances. **$$**

Hohhot

Malaqin Fandian 马拉沁饭店
34 Xinhua Dajie
The most famous place for mutton hotpot, where large groups share animated evening feasts. **$$**

Kaifeng

Kaifeng's night market (开封夜市; Kaifeng Yeshi) is one of China's biggest, and a great place to eat. Hui Muslim vendors dole out kebabs and noodles.

Xinsheng Restaurant 新生饭庄
66 Gulou Jie
An affordable venue with big, comfortable booths and a helpful picture menu with a range of standard Chinese favourites. **$$**

Luoyang

Tianxiang Restaurant 天香饭店
56 Jingyuyuan Lu
This modest restaurant serves spicy Sichuan cuisine and gets packed out with Chinese tourists during lunch and dinner. **$**

Sweet and sour pork

Pork and choi sum

Qingdao

Yunxiao Lu and Minjiang Lu are two dedicated food streets with good local, Korean and Japanese food. There are dozens of seafood places in the streets around St Michael's Church on Zhonghsan Lu and near the beach on Nanhai Lu.

Haixian Chufang 海鲜厨房
55 Yunxiao Lu
Provides a menu wall of photos, tanks of live seafood and helpful staff. **$$**

Lao Zhuan Cun 老转村山东菜馆
112 Minjiang Lu
Popular restaurant serving local cuisine. **$$**

Xi'an

Lao Sun Jia 老孙家
364 Dong Dajie
One of Xi'an's most famous restaurants, where Chinese and foreign tourists alike come to sample *yangrou paomo*, a lamb stew filled with coin-sized chunks of flatbread. **$**

Wuyi Fandian 五一饭店
351 Dong Dajie
Located on the ground floor of the May First Hotel, this cafeteria-style canteen serves northern Chinese food such as noodles, dumplings and steamed buns. **$**

Xi'an Roast Duck Restaurant 西安烤鸭店
369 Dong Dajie
This no-frills, two-floor restaurant serves up generous portions of roast duck along with plum sauce and thin crêpes in which to wrap it all. It fills up quickly at lunchtime. **$$**

SPORTS AND ACTIVITIES

Frozen Harbin and the surrounding area offer many winter sports and an international-standard skiing resort at Yabuli. The beaches of Qingdao are perhaps China's most popular destination for water sports, while ancient Shaolin attracts kung fu enthusiasts from around the world.

Skiing
Harbin
Yabuli Ski Resort
Shangzhi City
Tel: (0451) 534 5888
www.yabuliski.com
China's premier skiing resort, offering nine intermediate pistes and a beginner slope. Season runs from November to March.

Sailing
Qingdao
Qingdao International Sailing Club
No. 1 Bathing Beach

Tel: (0532) 8286- 4645
One of the best places in Qingdao – venue for Olympic sailing events in 2008 – to rent a small boat, with or without lessons.

Kung fu
Shaolin Tagou Kung Fu School
Within Shaolin Temple Scenic Spot
Tel: (0371) 6274 9627
www.shaolintagou.com
Reputed to be the largest kung fu school in China, the Tagou school provides classes for students in many styles of martial arts, either by day or as part of a longer programme.

TOURS

Much of northern China is easily accessible to the independent traveller. You might consider relying on a tour guide to experience Changbai Shan Nature Reserve or to explore the grasslands of Inner Mongolia.

Changbai Shan Nature Reserve

CITS
14 Xinmin Street, Changchun, Jilin
Tel: (0431) 564 2401
Organises tours to Changbai Shan Nature Reserve. Note: tours are usually not available in winter.

Grassland

Anda Guesthouse
Qiaokao Xijie, Saihan District, Hohhot
Tel: (0471) 691 8039

www.andaguesthouse.com
This guesthouse arranges reliable horse-trekking, camel-riding and camping tours of the grasslands, as well as visits to a remote section of the Great Wall.

Educational

Smithsonian Journeys
www.smithsonianjourneys.org
Small group tours led by university professors. Destinations include Xi'an and the Great Wall.

FESTIVALS AND EVENTS

In north China you can experience a range of events, from Qingdao's hugely popular beer festival to the astonishing ice sculptures of Harbin.

January

Harbin Ice Lantern Festival
Centred on Zhaolin Park, this month-long event features extraordinary ice sculptures including animals, plants, mythical figures and famous buildings lit up from inside by coloured lights. The detail and sheer size of the sculptures defy belief. 🛝

August

Qingdao International Beer Festival
Usually held in August, the Qingdao Beer Festival is a hugely popular event, celebrating the city's brewing history with parades, performances and well-stocked beer halls.

September

Tai Shan Mountain Climbing Festival
Early September
'Mountain Climbing' in fact refers to hundreds of runners ascending the holy mountain en masse. Mountaineering competitions also take place, as well as folk performances.

Qufu Confucian Cultural Festival
September 28
Celebrations and performances accompanied by ancient music and dance take place at the Temple of Confucius and the Cemetery of Confucius in Qufu to mark the birthday of the great sage.

Harbin Ice Lantern Festival

Back in 1927, at the height of the Peasant Revolution in rural Hunan, Mao Zedong memorably declaimed that 'Revolution is not a dinner party'. He wasn't wrong: for the next half-century of civil war, foreign invasion, starvation and general mayhem prevailed across China. But Mao died in 1976, and in the intervening three-and-a-half decades, China has undergone a sea-change. Today, revolution is indeed a dinner party – if you want it to be so.

How can this be? It seems contradictory, but in many ways today's 'Communist China' is the epitome of state capitalism, a predominantly young society where emphasis is placed not on class warfare, but on getting ahead and, above all, getting rich. Relatively few of China's burgeoning middle class are old enough to remember the disasters of the **Great Leap Forward** (1958–61) and the **Cultural Revolution** (1966–76), let alone the **Civil War** that ended with Communist victory in 1949. Instead, they learnt about revolution from their parents and grandparents, without fully experiencing its travails.

As China has prospered, curiosity about the revolutionary past has grown, while adulation has diminished. No longer a quasi-deity or a figure of fear, Mao has become a cultural icon, with Mao watches, coffee cups and knock-off revolutionary posters for sale on high streets from Beijing

Mao Zedong still looms large in Yan'an

Market stall souvenirs

to Guangdong. Today both Chinese and overseas visitors are free to discover this past through visits to once-venerated revolutionary sites and even through unexpected culinary experiences – by sampling, for example, a millet and tapioca dinner in a converted Beijing bomb shelter at the market in Xicheng District.

Of course, the revolution remains at the core of the PRC's identity, and there's nowhere better to gain a sense of this than in the heart of Beijing, at **Tiananmen Square**. Apart from the intrinsic drama of the vast square flanked by Soviet-style behemoths, evocative revolutionary experiences can be savoured at the daily **flag-raising ceremony** (at the northern end of the square) and visits to the **Chairman Mao Mausoleum** and **Great Hall of the People**. The Socialist Realist **Monument to the People's Heroes** standing nearby exemplifies revolutionary times past. Elsewhere in China there are similar monuments at either end of the great **Nanjing Bridge** across the Yangzi River, built in 1968 as a symbol of national self-sufficiency at the height of the Sino-Soviet split.

Shanghai offers the hallowed **Site of the First National Congress of the Chinese Communist Party**, the teacups and chairs still arranged as though Mao Zedong and Zhou Enlai might return at any minute. Visit Mao's birthplace at **Shaoshan** in Hunan province for a chance to see both **Mao Zedong's Childhood Home** and the nearby **Museum of Comrade Mao** – this is the best place to witness the quasi-religious

The Mao Mausoleum, Tiananmen Square

fervour that the Great Helmsman still commands from some Chinese. Then there is **Jinggang Shan** in Jiangxi province, the 'Cradle of the Revolution', where Mao Zedong and General Zhude launched the Long March in 1927; the **Zunyi Conference Site** and **Long March Museum** at Zunyi in Guizhou; and the yellow loess caves of **Yan'an** in rural Shaanxi, final destination of the marchers and Mao's base from 1936–47.

Revisiting the Revolution

Shanghai and the Lower Yangzi

Shanghai is the most famous city in China and one of the brightest urban stars on the planet. Beyond are the flatlands of the lower Yangzi and the ancient cities of Hangzhou and Suzhou around the historic Grand Canal. Further west lies Nanjing, a former Imperial capital city

Shanghai

 Population: 19 million (urban area)

 Local dialling code: 021

 Local tourist office: Shanghai Tourist Information Centre, 303 Moling Lu (South Exit of Shanghai Railway Station); tel: 6353 9920

 Local newspapers/listings magazines: Shanghai: free listings magazines include *City Weekend* (**www.cityweekend.com.cn**) and *That's Shanghai* (**www.thatssh. com**). *Time Out* magazine is another good source of information, although the website is currently Chinese only. The *Shanghai Daily* (**www. shanghaidaily.com**) newspaper also has listings and occasional reviews, while the website **www.meet-in-shanghai.net/** is another resource.

 Main post office: 395 Suzhou North Road; tel: 6393 6666; daily 7am–7pm

Broad, flat and supersaturated with people, the Yangzi Delta region fully captures the essence of China. In addition to the amazing city of Shanghai, this history-rich area is home to the Grand Canal that once linked Nanjing to Suzhou and Hangzhou, and all three of those cities are former capitals that can lay claim to a historic array of cultural attributes, from tea-growing and silk production to famous sights like the West Lake in Hangzhou. The area is dotted with water towns that once sent rice, tea, ceramics and other goods up and down the Grand Canal, and now, fully restored, provide a close-up look at a vanished way of life.

But the Yangzi Delta is far more interested in the present, and the future. At the forefront of China's rapid modernisation, the region – with Shanghai at the helm – has benefitted from a rash of shiny new train stations, airport terminals, ports, highways, high-speed railways, bridges and other public works, with many more on the way. The Delta has also reclaimed its 1,000-year-old crown as the country's epicentre of trade and production, leaping into modernity in just two decades, and now a key contributor to the economy of China and the wider world.

Shanghai

The economic powerhouse of the east coast, **Shanghai ❶** attracts the lion's share of China's inbound investment, having catapulted itself onto the world stage at a speed that has no historical precedent. Rich in history, throbbing with street life and filled with colourful local street-level details as well as dramatic modern attractions, this is a must-see city for all visitors to China. Shanghai richly illustrates the contrasts and contradictions that make the country so fascinating: rich and poor, modern and ancient, global and local, urban and provincial, all exist side by side in a fast-changing, super-crowded,

Pudong, high-rise business district

money-mad urban experiment that is like nothing else on earth.

The Bund

The **Bund ❹** (Waitan) became Shanghai's centre of trade and commerce in the mid-1800s, and today the imposing classical buildings lined up along the Huangpu River are the city's signature landmark. In April 2010, the famous strip emerged from a year-long renovation that added further lustre to this great urban vista. A new tunnel now carries most of the car and truck traffic beneath the boulevard, reducing street traffic and adding to the appeal.

Stroll along the **riverside promenade** (🛗) along the Bund and gaze across the Huangpu, with its barges, ferries, pleasure boats and freight ships, to the fast-changing, ultra-modern skyline of Pudong.

There are now broad sidewalks in front of the historic buildings on the other side of the street, making it easier to view these architectural beauties from up close. Among the favourites are the **old Hongkong & Shanghai Bank Building** (12 Zhong Shan East No.1 Road), with its signature domed

Shanghai and the Lower Yangzi

The Bund Sightseeing Tunnel

roof and its wonderful interior atrium filled with murals of old bank outposts, while next door is the **Customs House** (13 Zhong Shan East No.1 Road), with the iconic clock tower that chimes every quarter of an hour. The old Hongkong Bank Building (now the Pudong Development Bank) is another of more than 20 period-piece buildings that line the iconic curved street.

The Bund is also home to some of the classiest nightclubs and restaurants in town, many of them nestled inside the colonial-era buildings with splendid views across to the Pudong skyline – the futuristic buildings lit up with a spectacular array of attention-grabbing light displays every evening. **Three on the Bund** and **Bund 18** – the numbers refer to their addresses on Zhongshan East No.1 Road – are the most successful makeovers. Bund 18, home to Bar Rouge nightclub, Mr and Mrs Bund restaurant and a handful of boutiques

and coffee shops, is an authentic renovation that retains many original features. Three on the Bund, home to Laris, Jean-Georges and New Heights restaurants, a giant Armani shop, an art gallery and other attractions, is a total revamp that replaced the original interiors with a spacious modern design.

The most famous building on the Bund is the **Fairmont Peace Hotel** (20 Nanjing Road East), an Art Deco masterpiece that opened in 1929 as the Cathay Hotel, featuring graceful vertical lines and a central symmetry that climaxes in a green apex at the top of the building. In 2010 it emerged from a two-year renovation that restored its former glory and re-established it as one of the classiest hotels in Asia.

Nanjing East Road and People's Park

At the base of the Fairmont is **Nanjing East Road**, a 2km (1¼-mile)

The view along the famous Bund

thoroughfare that connects the Bund waterfront to People's Park. This packed pedestrian street is a mecca for tourists from China and the world, and a walk along its length provides an essential slice of Shanghai. There is plenty of local shopping to be done on Nanjing East, but people-watching is the primary pastime, preferably from one of the many sidewalk cafés.

People's Park (Renmin Gongyuan) is a welcome patch of greenery filled with fountains, ponds and shady pathways that is circled by tall buildings and embraced by the non-stop throb of the city. Four of the finest museums in Shanghai can be found here. The **Shanghai**

Shanghai and the Lower Yangzi

Shanghai Transport

 Airports: Shanghai Pudong International Airport is 30km (18 miles) east of the city. A new freeway connects the city to the airport, and taxis are the easiest way to make the trip: to/from People's Square should cost around Rmb180.

The Maglev (magnetic levitation) train whisks passengers between Pudong Airport and Longyang Station, which connects to metro line 2. It can reach 430kmh (270mph), and journey time is just 8 minutes – although Longyang is still 30 minutes or more from the city centre. Service is from 6.45am–9.40pm, and tickets are Rmb50 one-way (Rmb40 if you show your boarding pass).

Shuttle buses depart at 15- to 25-minute intervals on various routes into the city. Fares (Rmb18–30) are collected on board.

Hongqiao Airport, the main domestic hub, is on the west side of

Shanghai, about 20 minutes (if roads are clear) from downtown by taxi (around Rmb50). Hongqiao is also connected to metro line 2, and there are shuttle buses.

 Metro: With 11 lines and 266 stations, Shanghai has a comprehensive subway system. Fares start at Rmb3, and trains run 5am–11.30pm.

Buses: Cheap, plentiful taxis and a good subway system mean that only a small minority of visitors will need to use Shanghai's crowded bus network.

 Taxis: One of Shanghai's great deals – taxis (all are metered) can be hailed anywhere off the street, cost only Rmb11 at flagfall, and average around Rmb15–30 for a city-centre journey.

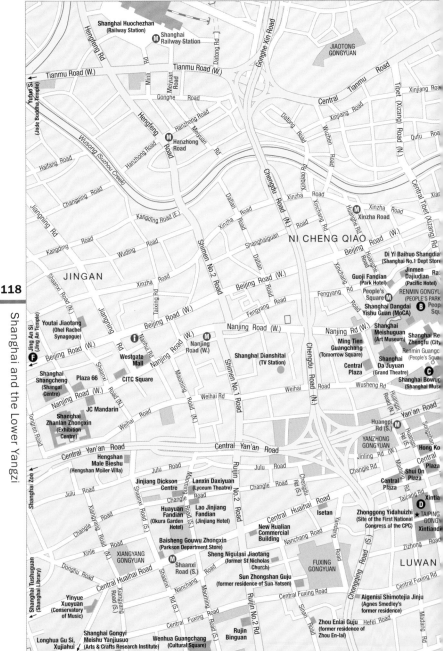

Shanghai

0 _____ 500 m
0 _____ 500 yds

Duolun Xiandai Meishuguan (Duolun Museum of Modern Art)
Hongkou Gongyuan

Tanggu Road
Tanggu Road
Minhang Road
Wuchang Road
Changzhi Rd

Shanghai Dasha (Broadway Mansions)
Pujiang Fandian (Astor House Hotel)
Daming Road
Nanxun Rd

Haining Road
Anqing Road
Sichuan Road (N.)
Wuchang Road
Zhapu Road
Wusong Road

Haining Road
Henan Road (N.)
Fujian Road (N.)

Tiantong Road

Tiantong Road

Central Sichuan Rd

Huangpu

Waibaidu Qiao

Changzhi Road

Renmin Yingxiong Jinianbei (Monument to the People's Heroes)
Waitan Lishi Bowuguan (Bund History Museum)

Nos 33-53 (former British Consulate)
No.27 (former Jardine & Matheson Co.)
No.24 (former Yokohama Specie Bank)
No.23 Zhongguo Yinhang (Bank of China)
No.20 Heping Fandian (Fairmont Peace Hotel, former Cathay Hotel)

HUANGPU GONGYUAN

Zhongshan

Waitan Canguang Sui Dao (Bund Sightseeing Tunnel)

Dongfang Mingzhu Guangbo Dianshi Ta (Pearl Oriental TV Tower)
Shanghai Guoji Huiyi Zhongxin (SICC) (International Convention Centre)

Beijing Rd (E.)

Chen Yi

No.19 Heping Huizhong Fandian (Swatch Art Peace Hotel, former Palace Hotel)

Central Ningbo Rd

Shandong Road
Central Fujian Rd

Beijing Road
Ningbo Road
Tianjin Road
Nanjing Rd (E.)

Jiujiang Road
Nanjing Rd (E.) Ⓜ

PUDONG

Zhen Da Guangchang (Super Brand Mall)

Lujiazui Rd

Ningbo Road
Shanxi Road
Central Henan Rd

Ningbo Road

Jiujiang Road

Hankou Road
Central Henan Rd

Bund 18 (former Chartered Bank Building)

No.13 Laohaiguan (Customs House)

No.12 Pudong Fazhan Yinhang (former Hongkong & Shanghai Bank)
No.5 Huaxia Bank/ M on the Bund
No.3 Three on the Bund

BINJIANG GONGYUAN (RIVERSIDE PARK)

Hualian Dept Store

Nanjing Road (E.)
Jiujiang Road

Hong Miao (Holy Trinity, Red Temple)

HUANGPU

Fuzhou Road

Hankou Road
Zhejiang Road
Central Fujian Rd
Shandong Road

Guangdong Rd

Fuzhou Road

Yan'an Road (E.)

...urch)
...ang Road
...Road

No.2 (former Shanghai Club)
Bund Centre
Shanghai Ziran Bowuguan (Museum of Natural History)

Benliang Dadao

Science & Technology Museum

Waitan Tianwentai (Meteorological Signal Tower)

Jinling Dong Lu Ma Tou (Jinling Pier)

Yan'an Road (E.) Tunnel

Ⓐ

Huangpu

Zhongshan No.1 Road (E.)

Jinling Road (E.)
Yan'an Road (E.)

Fujian Rd (S.)
Shandong Rd (S.)
Henan Road (S.)

Jinling Road (S.)

Yong An Lu Shichang

Ruose Tang (St Joseph's)

Renmin Road

Chengshi Guihua Zhenshiguan (Urban Planning & Exhibition Centre)
Da Shijie (Great World)
...anghai ...yue Ting ...ncert Hall)

Fuyou Lugu Wanshi Chang (Fuyou Road Sunday Antique Market)

Fuyou Road (S.)

Chenxlangge (Nunnery)

Fuyou Road

...ing Rd

Zhejiang Rd (S.)
Jinling Rd (S.)
Yunnan Rd (S.)

Fuyou Lu Qingzhensi (Fuyou Rd Mosque)

Yuyuan Shangchang (Yu Garden Bazaar)
Ⓔ YU YUAN
Huxinting Chashe (Teahouse)

Renmin Road
Zhongshan No.1 Road (E.)

Dongmen Rd

Road

Huaihai Rd (E.)

Dajing Lu Shichang (Market)

Cang Bao Lou (Cang Bao Bldg)
Shanghai Old Street

Chenghuang Miao (City Temple of Shanghai)

Dongmen Rd

Zhonghua Road

...ling Rd

Tibet (Xizang) Road (S.)
Renmin Road

Dajingge (Tower)

Dajing Road

Baiyun Guan (Taoist Temple)

Central Fangbang Rd

Xilinhou Rd

Dongtai Lu Shichang (Antiques Market)

Fuxing Road (E.)

Xiaotaoyuan Qingzhensi (Peach Orchard Mosque)

Fuxing Road (E.)

NANSHI

Guangqi Road (S.)

Fuxing Road (E.)

...zhong

Tibet (Xizang) Road (S.)
Renmin Road

...ntral Fuxing
...Road

Zhaozhou Road

Zhonghua Road

Henan Road (S.)

Wen Miao (Confucius Temple)

Zhonghua Road

Zhonghua Road

Zhonghua Road

Dongjiadu Rd

LAO XI MEN

...ei Road

Road (E.)
Daji Road

Hunan Stadium

Yingxun Rd

Daxing Street

Lujiabang Road

Pu'an Road

Nancangjiang Rd

Museum **C** (daily 9am–5pm; free) boasts a superb collection of Chinese art housed in a comfortable building and accompanied by explanations in several languages. The **Shanghai Art Museum** (daily 9am–5pm; charge) hosts global exhibitions, and has an excellent collection of modern Asian art, while the **Shanghai Urban Planning and Exhibition Centre** (Tue–Thur 9am–5pm, Fri–Sun 9am–6pm; charge), with its much-admired enormous diorama of the Shanghai cityscape, also attracts sizeable crowds. These three are joined by the pocket-sized **Museum of Contemporary Art** (daily 10am–6pm, Wed until 10pm; charge), a former greenhouse that specialises in carefully curated displays of contemporary Asian art.

Xintiandi

The city's top dine-and-drink area is **Xintiandi D**, an old lane-house district 1.5km (1 mile) south of the park that was converted into an open-air mall in 2002 and filled with high-end restaurants, coffee shops, nightclubs and boutiques. Xintiandi is not an authentic renovation, as many of the original *shikumen* (stone gate) homes were moved or rebuilt to make the area more retail-friendly, but it does give a sense of the old style.

Between People's Park and Xintiandi is the east–west thoroughfare **Huaihai Road**, a stretch of retail outlets anchored by Times Square Mall, which features the popular Zara, famous for its budget-friendly fashions, and Chaterhouse Booktrader, which has a large selection of books about China.

Old Town

Shanghai's **Old Town** (Nanshi), south of the Bund near the river, remains the most authentic Chinese

Morning exercises at People's Park

Crowds at the Mid-Lake Teahouse

vendors selling Mao trinkets and mahjong sets and T-shirts and 'antique' posters from the 1930s, plus myriad other knick-knacks. The cosy confines of Yu Garden itself offer a more serene experience. The Ming-era garden is rendered in classic Yangzi style, with moon bridges, jagged 'West Lake' rockery, four-season garden layouts with flowers and plants that bloom or leaf throughout the year, and graceful balconies that overlook trickling ponds and streams.

Former French Concession

The beloved old **French Concession**, with its classic architecture, intimate lane-house neighbourhoods and low-rise buildings, is a quintessential slice of Shanghai. Few of the city's must-see sights are here, however; instead, its enduring appeal lies in its quiet charm, subtle delights and rich, compact density, while the shady canopies and patchwork bark of the ever-present Eurasian plane trees are a defining feature. The area is book-ended by a pair of large open spaces, Zhongshan Park in the east and Xujiahui Park in the west.

neighbourhood in the city. Its narrow winding lanes and local homes are alive with sights and sounds, and its atmosphere harks back to an older, more traditional China. Its cultural opposite is the nearby Cool Docks, a new restaurant and nightlife complex on the Old Town riverfront, that has emerged as one of the hottest dine-and-drink complexes in the city.

The top attraction in this neighbourhood is **Yuyuan Bazaar** and Garden, a warren of lanes and buildings wrapped around the Ming-era **Yu Garden** ❸ (Yu Yuan; daily 8.30am–5.30pm; charge 🏠) and punctuated by the celebrated **Mid-Lake Teahouse** (257 Yuyuan Road; daily 5.30am–10pm). The bazaar is packed with

> ### Take a Breather
>
> New Heights restaurant (新视角餐厅酒廊; 3 Zhong Shan Road East No.1; tel: 6321 0909) sits atop Three on the Bund, and its wrap-around outdoor balcony provides by far the finest views of the Bund and Pudong. The food is merely acceptable, but its trump card is a comfortable bar perfect for those who want to soak up the sights.

121

Shanghai and the Lower Yangzi

Nanjing Road West is lined with upmarket shops

Nanjing West Road

With its high-end malls, luxury outlets and soaring office towers, Nanjing West is the modern face of Shanghai. Walking its streets are the most stylish shoppers and best-dressed office workers in town, who are joined by bag-toting tourists in search of the latest fashions. But the luxury veneer is thin, and near Nanjing Road are lane-house neighbourhoods bursting with local life, and tree-lined streets filled with mixed – though still upscale – residential districts sprinkled with cafés, nightclubs, boutique hotels and other attractions.

The neighbourhood oasis is Jing'an Park and Temple, a leafy retreat filled with goldfish ponds, jagged rockery, a children's play area and towering plane trees, while nearby **Jing An Si** ❶ (7.30am–5pm; charge) is a Buddhist shrine that features a Ming-era copper bell and some stone Buddhas, among other antiquities. Like most temples in China, it is more popular as a tourist attraction than as a place of worship.

Xujiahui

On the southern fringes of the French Concession, and free from its low-rise building constraints, the city explodes into a high-rise hub of shopping malls, warehouse stores, and apartment and hotel and office blocks, all of them humming with humanity. Xujiahui has historical sights, notably **Xujiahui Catholic Church** and **Longhua Temple** (7am–4.30pm; charge), but much of it is new, including Grand Gateway Mall, Shanghai Stadium and Shanghai Indoor Stadium. Xujiahui offers genuine bargains, and its low prices and central location make it popular with tourists and residents alike.

Further west, in Gubei and Hongqiao, Shanghai becomes a suburban swirl of residential compounds, local shopping streets, school campuses, office buildings and the like, all connected by vast clusters of highway. In their midst are a few tourist attractions, including **Shanghai Zoo** (daily 7am–6pm,; charge; ), and **Shanghai Botanical Gardens** (daily 9am–4pm; charge).

Hongkou and Suzhou Creek

Further to the north, **Hongkou** is a diverse patchwork of neighbourhoods where luxury hotel towers and beautiful old buildings sit side by side with traditional residential quarters that seldom see tourists. **Suzhou Creek**'s most famous attraction is **50 Moganshan Road**, a collection of lanes filled

Jing'an Temple

with art galleries of all sizes, from small boutiques to warehouse-sized spaces with giant sculptures and wall-to-ceiling paintings. M50 comes alive at night, when buyers and browsers and artists prowl the galleries in search of bargains, inspiration and entertainment.

Also popular is **Duolun Street**, a 1 km (⅔ mile) semi-pedestrian strip in Hongkou dotted with bronze statues of the Chinese writers and filmmakers who lived in Shanghai 100 years ago. The most famous is Lu Xun, and he is joined in bronze by many others, including Charlie Chaplin, who visited the city in 1931.

The Suzhou Creek area is also home to the **ERA Intersection of Time Circus** (Shanghai Circus World, 2266 Gonghexin Road; www.erashanghai.com; daily 7.30pm; charge),

Shanghai and the Lower Yangzi

⚐ SHANGHAI TOUR

Enormous though it is, Shanghai is a great city to explore on foot, because its central core is surprisingly small. In just a single day, therefore, a determined walker can enjoy many of the city's top sights.

Start at People's Park, a leafy oasis filled with shaded walkways, lotus ponds and Yangzi garden sculpture. The park also features four fine museums, including the free-of-charge Shanghai Museum and the popular Shanghai Urban Planning and Exhibition Centre.

Walk east from the park along pedestrian-only Nanjing East Road, the most famous street in the country and a mecca for tourists from all over China. The street is lined with open-air coffee shops, ice-cream parlours and restaurants, as well as prestigious shops.

Follow Nanjing East Road until you reach the Huangpu River – around 1.2km (¾ mile) from People's Park – and stroll onto the Bund, which emerged from a year-long renovation in April 2010. The sidewalk that fronts the colonial buildings is now much broader, with improved sightlines of the architecture that lines this classic boulevard. The riverside promenade is also roomier, and a tunnel beneath the Bund has relieved much of the area's car and truck traffic.

This is one of the world's top urban vistas: to the east, the Pudong side boasts countless one-of-a-kind modern skyscrapers, while the Shanghai side features the imposing old buildings of the Bund. Among the favourites are Customs House with its clock tower, and Hongkong & Shanghai Bank Building, with its signature dome, but those are just two of the 15 or 20 masterpieces along this historic street. The most famous is the Fairmont Peace Hotel, an elegant Art Deco tower topped by a pyramidal green peak.

Many of the old buildings are filled with modern restaurants, coffee shops, cafés and nightclubs. Bund 18 boasts two good restaurants, some high-end fashion boutiques and Bar Rouge,

The Customs House on the Bund

Tips

- Distance: 5km (3 miles)
- Time: a full day
- START: People's Park
- END: the Bund
- Points to note: to start the tour, take the subway to the People's Park station.

a lively late-night lounge that would not be amiss in the opium-saturated Shanghai of old. And at Three on the Bund, New Heights offers superb views from its wrap-around top-floor balcony.

From anywhere along the Bund, visitors can enjoy the Pudong skyline. Dominating the eastern horizon is the 492m (1,614ft) Shanghai World Financial Centre (SWFC), which features the world's highest hotel – the Park Hyatt – plus two observation decks. Next to the SWFC is the beautifully textured Jin Mao Tower, with its blue-and-grey glass facets that sparkle in the sun. The Jin Mao is one of China's best-loved buildings, and no trip to Shanghai is complete without a visit to Cloud Nine Bar on the 87th floor.

Next up is a real treat: crossing the Huangpu River by ferry boat. Shanghai does have its bargains, and the Rmb2 boat ride across the Huangpu is one of them. The little ferry leaves the dock at the south end of the Bund every 12 minutes, negotiates the barge- and boat-laden river, and docks in Pudong a few minutes later.

Bars along the Bund have great views

A half-hour stroll from the Pudong-side dock through Riverside Park brings you to the Pearl Oriental TV Tower. Take an elevator into one of the hot-pink balls, and view the work-in-progress that is Pudong. From here the entire metro area is on display, filled with high-rise towers and apartment blocks and construction sites and spaghetti-strand highways that seem to stretch for ever.

From the base of the Pearl Tower, the Bund Sightseeing Tunnel is just a block away. This five-minute ride is an only-in-Shanghai experience: visitors enter a plexiglass pod and ride the rails, as lasers flash and tunnels sparkle, accompanied by otherworldly sound effects. This psychedelic train ride is a perfect goodbye to Pudong, and an easy way to return to the Bund.

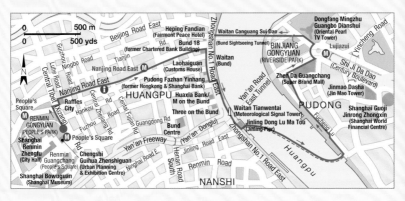

a fast-paced and professional show featuring performers from the best acrobatics schools in China. The slickly produced show involves dozens of breathtaking acts of balance, magic and acrobatics, all to the accompaniment of live music.

Pudong

Old Shanghai is admired for its charming concession neighbourhoods and historic buildings, but **Pudong ⑥** is something else entirely. The 522-sq km (202-sq mile) Pudong New Area was conceived in the late 1980s, and building began in earnest in the early 1990s, when the Pearl Oriental Tower was begun. Today, the New Area is a busy beehive of building sites, construction cranes and roadwork, as it packs a century's worth of city-building into two decades.

The heart of Pudong is Lujiazui, the waterfront area dominated by the blazing pink balls of the **Pearl Oriental TV Tower** (8am–9.30pm), the twinkling pagoda-like exterior of the **Jin Mao Tower** (10am–10pm) and the 492m (1,614ft) **Shanghai World Financial Centre** (8am–10pm), which rises from the flat soil like a giant curved sail. All three towers feature eagle-eye views of the sprawling city of Shanghai, and all three will soon be joined by the even loftier Shanghai Tower.

The Lujiazui waterfront is home to a cluster of tourist attractions such as **Super Brand Mall**, the **Shanghai Aquarium** (9am–9pm; charge), **Riverside Promenade Park**, the **Bund Sightseeing Tunnel** (see

p.125; Mon–Thur 8am–10.30pm, Fri–Sun 8am–11pm; charge), and the **Shanghai History Museum** (daily 8.30am–9.30pm; charge), along with a selection of cafés and restaurants.

Further east are **Century Park**, the city's largest, plus its newest museum, and top concert hall: the **Science and Technology Museum** (Tue–Sun, 9am–5.15pm; charge), and the **Oriental Arts Centre** (425 Dingxiang Road). Still further east are the

Jin Mao Tower and acrobats

Maglev train, the international airport and the expat enclave of Jinqiao, until Pudong finally fades into the vast, featureless expanse of farms, factories, and residential blocks that typifies rural China.

The Grand Canal and the Water Towns

To the north and west of Shanghai are a series of towns and cities strung along the length of the ancient **Grand Canal**, perfect for a day trip from the city. With its landmark completion 1,400 years ago, this venerable waterway connected Beijing to Hangzhou, and in the process it helped forge an empire. Although the northern section is long gone, the southern half remains a commercial corridor, and still connects Hangzhou to the Yangzi.

Suzhou

Suzhou ❷ is an essential city for anyone who wishes to gain a deeper appreciation of China. On the one hand, it is a charming historic town filled with lovely gardens, pagodas, silk works, waterways and ancient moats, while the Grand Canal itself slices through the centre of town. It is built around a lattice-work of 24 canals, home to small, intimate gardens tucked away behind houses and hidden between narrow streets.

On the other hand, it is also a sprawling, chaotic, traffic-filled boom-town surrounded by a pair of high-powered industrial zones: Suzhou has benefited from the nation's new wealth as much as any Chinese provincial city. The main shopping street, **Guanqian Jie**, is lined with clothing

Century Park, Shanghai's largest park

and shoe shops and fast-food restaurants, and there are several pedestrian-friendly strips filled with upscale bars and restaurants. There is also the shiny new Rmb170 million (US$25 million) **Suzhou Science and Cultural Arts Centre** (www.sscac.com.cn), which features theatres, a cinema, café and cultural centre.

Suzhou's gardens

Away from the commercial hustle, the city's **classical gardens** are its most famous attraction. The principles of

Shopping tips

Shanghai Cybermart, a cluster of electronics vendors offering rock-bottom prices on every computer-related item imaginable, sits at the corner of Huaihai and Xizang roads. Not far from there is Dongtai Road Antique Market; ignore the Mao heads and name chops and stone lions and other gimcracks, and instead browse the nearby shops that restore and sell genuine Art Deco-era antique lamps and furniture.

Chinese garden construction – creating an illusion of the universe in a small space, and achieving a year-round seasonal balance of plants – are apparent throughout the old part of the city. **Wangshi Yuan** (Master of the Nets Garden; 7.30am–5.30pm; charge) is a delightful and compact garden that dates from the Southern Song period. Famous for its peony blooms in spring, the focus of the garden is a central pool circled by pavilions and walkways. Nearby is **Canglang Ting** (Blue Wave Pavilion; 7.30am–5.30pm; charge), a beautifully arranged oasis laid out next to a canal. Unlike the manicured gardens elsewhere in Suzhou, Blue Wave features a profusion of untamed vegetation.

The queen of Suzhou gardens, and one of the finest in all of China, is **Zhuozheng Yuan** (Humble Administrator's Garden; 7.30am–5.30pm; charge 🏛), a meticulously balanced blend of vegetation, water and rocks that covers an area of 4 hectares (10 acres). Each element of the garden has a layer of meaning, such as the seasonal pagodas, where lotus, osmanthus, plum and bamboo bloom or

leaf in different seasons, to provide year-round visual pleasure.

Close by is the **Suzhou Museum** (Tue–Sun 9am–5pm; free). Designed by famous Chinese-American architect I.M. Pei, whose family is from Suzhou, the building displays many of his signature design features, such as squares, rectangles and pyramids, plus abundant use of natural light. The exhibits are less interesting than the building, however.

At the **Suzhou Di Yi Si Chouchang** (Suzhou No. 1 Silk Mill; 9am–5.30pm; free), tourists can see how Suzhou's most sought-after luxury is made. This is a real factory, and from mulberry leaves to worms, to cocoons, to thread, and on to the gift shop, it guides visitors through the history of silk production in China.

Tiger Hill Pagoda (Huqui Ta; 7.30am–5.30pm; charge), in the northwest part of town, is another noteworthy attraction. And yes, it is leaning: at the top, the pagoda is 2.34 m (7ft 8in) off-centre, and it has twice been stabilised, once during the Ming dynasty, and a second time in 1961. The Ming effort was remarkable – it is the uppermost layer that straddles the top of the pagoda and sits off-centre, in an effort to rebalance the 48m (157ft) structure. The pagoda dates back to the 10th century, and is made entirely of brick – a relative rarity in Chinese construction.

Wuxi and Tai Hu

Wuxi ❸, easily reached by train from either Suzhou (30 minutes) or Nanjing (90 minutes), or by boat from

---

Suzhou Boat Trips

The area around the Suzhou Museum is a good place to arrange boat trips on the city's picturesque waterways. These depart from several areas on the rectangular main canal, the broad waterway that embraces the Old Town like a moat. None of the boats are a bargain, but the bigger vessels are less expensive, if you don't mind waiting for them to fill up with tourists.

Suzhou's Wangshi Yuan garden

third-largest freshwater lake, covers 2,420 sq km (934 sq miles) and is peppered with 48 islands. The romantic landscape of green and blue, veiled with fine mist, has made this lake the subject of many poems. Tour groups tend to muster at two main sites on Tai Hu: spring is the peak season at **Mei Yuan** (Plum Garden; 6am–6pm) overlooking the lake, while Yuantou Zhu, or Turtle Head Islet, is a peninsula that is popular for its walks, pavilions and amusement parks.

Hangzhou on the Grand Canal in about 13 hours, has a history that goes back 2,000 years. The city's importance grew with the completion of the Grand Canal, which still flows through the centre of town, beneath elegant arched bridges.

Just south of Wuxi, **Tai Hu**, China's

Yangzhou

Further northwest on the Grand Canal, two hours by bus from Nanjing, the attractive town of **Yangzhou ❹** dates back to the 5th century BC. **Daming Temple** (7.15am–6pm) in the northwest of town dates to the 5th century, although

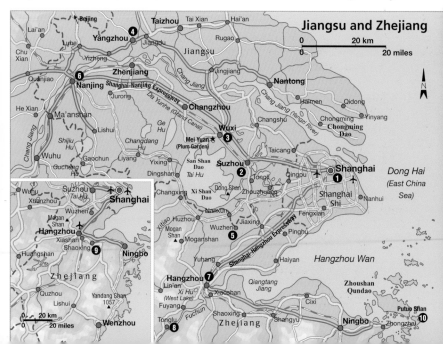

Jiangsu and Zhejiang

it was razed by the Taiping Rebellion and later rebuilt. The temple is notable for Jian Zhen Hall, dedicated to a monk who failed five times to reach Japan to promote Buddhism, before succeeding on his sixth trip.

The Water Towns

The border between Jiangsu and Zhejiang provinces (the area immediately south of Suzhou) is sprinkled with water towns – small villages connected to the Grand Canal that thrived on the silk, tea, ceramic and rice trades – and six of them, Luzhi, Nanxun, Tongli, Wuzhen, Xitang and Zhouzhuang, are Unesco World Heritage sites. These watery towns thrived during the Ming and Qing dynasties, and each of them, with their cobbled paths, graceful arched bridges, labyrinthine canal networks and exquisite tiled roofs, provides a tantalising glimpse of Old China.

Zhouzhuang, an hour and a half by car from Shanghai, packs a lot of history into just a few blocks. Among the highlights are Zhang's House, a sprawling mansion with six courtyards, 70 rooms filled with antiques, and a canal running through the courtyards.

Tongli is 20 minutes from Zhouzhuang by car, and two hours by boat. It is larger than Zhouzhuang, with wider canals, broader sidewalks and more trees. Highlights include **Tui Si Yuan** (Garden of Seclusion and Meditation; 7.30am–5.30pm), and the canal-side tables at its local teahouses.

Wuzhen , formerly the richest of the water towns, is two hours from Tongli. A branch of the Grand Canal serves as the town's main street, and the houses have back doors that open straight onto the water. Wuzhen is famous for traditional crafts; some shops make wooden barrels and some spin cotton into cloth, while others produce silk fans, rice wine, cotton slippers and brass buckles.

Nanjing

Nanjing is the most authentic and original large city in eastern China,

Nanjing	
Population: 6 million	**Buses:** There are several bus stations, but the largest – with express services to Shanghai, Suzhou and other delta destinations – is on Zhongyang Lu, about 5km (3 miles) straight north from Xinjiekou roundabout.
Local dialling code: 025	
Airport: Lukou Airport is 40km (26 miles) southeast of the city.	
Trains: The main railway station lies just north of Xuanwu Lake, some 3km (2 miles) from the centre of town. Some trains stop at the West Station, on the banks of the Yangzi. Ultra-fast new trains cover the 350km (220 miles) to Shanghai in around 1 hour 15 minutes.	**Key areas:** The 1912 District, similar to Xintiandi in Shanghai, is filled with restaurants, bars, nightclubs and upmarket boutiques. For a more local dining experience, the area around Confucius Temple (Fuzi Miao) has good local restaurants, plus plenty of souvenir and clothing shops.

Zhonghuamen Gate, is a Ming-style garden residence housing the **Taiping Tianguo Lishi Bowuguan** (Taiping Museum; 8am–6pm; charge). The turbulent rise and fall of the quasi-Christian 'Kingdom of Heaven', popularly known as the Taiping Rebellion, is well documented here in both Mandarin and English.

North and east of Xinjiekou

Xu Yuan, 15 minutes' walk northeast of Xinjiekou on Changjiang Lu, is a pleasant recreated Ming-dynasty garden, home to the freshly renovated **Tianchao Tian Gong** (Palace of the Heavenly Kingdom; 8am–5pm; charge) once occupied by Taiping leader Hong Xiuquan.

Further northwest stand two reminders of the Ming dynasty, **Gulou**, the Drum Tower, and **Zhonglou**, the Bell Tower (daily 8am–5pm; charge). Drum and bell towers were

and is refreshingly different from other urban areas on the Yangzi Delta. This former capital isn't a rapid-fire commercial city like many of its neighbours, and due to its relative lack of investment, Nanjing is calmer, quieter and better preserved than its Yangzi neighbours.

The **Xinjiekou roundabout** marks Nanjing's epicentre, and is packed with people, shops, vehicles of all descriptions, offices, banks and hotels. Here the 25-year-old Jinling Hotel stands out like a beacon, towering above the traffic; take the elevator to the top for a bird's-eye view of the city.

South of Xinjiekou

In the southern part of the city, near

131

Shanghai and the Lower Yangzi

> **The Taiping Rebellion**
>
> Led by Hong Xiuquan, the Taiping Rebellion ignited in Guangdong province and carved a devastating swath of destruction throughout southern and central China. The rebels captured Nanjing in 1853, making it the capital of their 'domain', before Qing troops finally defeated the rebels in the mid-1860s. In the official history, Hong's unique take on Christianity – he believed he was the younger brother of Jesus Christ – has been erased, and he has been reinvented as a reformist patriot trying to overthrow the decaying (and foreign) Qing dynasty.

The Sun Yatsen Mausoleum, Nanjing

common in all imperial cities. The Drum Tower – whose purpose was to warn the city of attack – was completed in 1382, just 14 years into the reign of the first Ming emperor, while the Bell Tower was completed six years later.

In the eastern part of the city, next to Zhongshanmen Gate, is the **Nanjing Museum** (Nanjing Bowuguan; 9am–4.30pm; free), which has an extensive collection of ceramics, jade, lacquerware, textiles, bronzes, porcelain and stone figures.

Sun Yat-sen Mausoleum, Zijin Shan and the Ming Tombs

For many Chinese, the **Sun Yat-sen Mausoleum** (Zhongshan Ling; daily 6.30am–6pm; charge) is Nanjing's best-known attraction, built in honour of the man who helped found the Chinese Republic in 1911. The size of the monument is staggering, covering 8 hectares (20 acres), and at

the end of the tree-lined avenue is a climb of 392 granite steps leading up to the blue-tiled memorial hall.

Sun Yat-sen's choice of the **Zijin Shan** (Purple Mountains) as the site for his tomb was not without historical precedent: over 500 years earlier, the Ming emperors – having made Nanjing their southern capital – were also interred in these hills. The first Ming emperor, Hong Wu (1327–98), built his tomb, known as Mingxiao Ling, here. A 'sacred path' known as the Shixiang Lu (Stone Statue Road) survives, and is lined with elegant stone carvings – soldiers on one side and animals, both real and mythical, on the other.

To the east of the tomb in **Linggu** (Valley of the Souls) is **Linggu Si** (daily 8am–5.30pm; charge combined with Sun Yat-sen Mausoleum), a temple built at the end of the 14th century and restored many times since. Nearby is the 60m (200ft) Linggu Ta, a pagoda built in 1929. On

The Great Yangzi Bridge

The Great Yangzi Bridge at Nanjing opened in 1968 and has been a symbol of Chinese national pride ever since. When relations between the former Soviet Union and China soured in 1960, the Chinese built the bridge – which had been a Soviet-funded project until then – with their own design and resources. A stroll through **Great Bridge Park** (daily 7am–6.30pm) affords excellent views.

the same mountain stands an observatory, accessed by a chair-lift which provides a splendid panorama of the city.

Hangzhou

Celebrated for its famous West Lake and cherished for its tea, temples and mist-shrouded hills, **Hangzhou** ❼ is among the prettiest cities in China. Once the capital of the sophisticated Southern Song dynasty, it marks the

southern end of the Yangzi Delta, where the canals, rivers and flat, fertile land give way to the hilly interiors and rugged coastline of Zhejiang province.

West Lake (Xi Hu)

Although there are some 30 West Lakes in China, the one in Hangzhou is by far the most famous. The eastern shore of **West Lake Ⓐ** (🏛) is close to the town, while forested mountains, often shrouded in mist, surround the other shores, lending the landscape a romantic allure. Add in a series of pagodas, pavilions, causeways and elegant little bridges, and the overall effect is the quintessential classical Chinese scene – albeit one compromised by the presence of large tour groups for much of the time.

The best way to take it all in is to stroll or cycle along the Bai Causeway to Gu Shan Island at the northern end of the lake, before heading south on

Hangzhou's West Lake

the longer Su Causeway.

On the northern shores of West Lake, the pagoda at **Baochu** Ⓑ (open access) stands tall against the sky, a symbol of the city. It was built in 968, then destroyed and rebuilt several times. On the northwestern shore, the **Mausoleum and Temple of Yue Fei** Ⓒ (Yuefen He Yuemiao; 7.30am–5.30pm; charge) commemorates the Southern Song general who resisted the northern invaders, but, in time-honoured Chinese fashion, was falsely charged, executed and later exonerated.

To the west of the lake, at the end of Lingyin Lu and easily reached by bus, is **Lingyin Si** Ⓓ (Monastery of Hidden Souls; daily 7am–6pm; charge), founded in AD326. Since the second half of the 10th century, the rock walls of the mountain have been carved with about 300 Buddhist sculptures and inscriptions.

Beyond these figures is the monastery, one of the most famous Buddhist sites in China. Inside the temple is **Tianwang Dian** (Hall of Heavenly Kings), where a statue of the Maitreya Buddha can be seen, guarded by the two Heavenly Kings standing at its side. The gilded statue of the Sakyamuni Buddha, more than 20m (66ft) high and made of camphor wood, is in Daxiongbao Dian (Precious Hall of the Great Heroes).

On the east shore of the lake, close to the urban attractions of Xihu Tiandi and Qinghefang Gujie *(see below)* is the **West Lake Museum** Ⓔ (Xi Hu Bowuguan; daily, 9am–5pm, closed Monday mornings; charge), showcasing rare cultural relics and documenting the

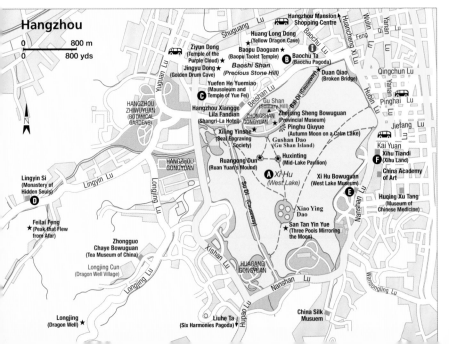

historical significance of the lake and its environs.

Modern Hangzhou

Xihu Tiandi , created by the developers that created Xintiandi in Shanghai, has a design based on West Lake landscaping and surrounding historic architecture, but it is mostly indoors, in brick-and-tile structures that are linked to each other by stone paths. The area is home to a large collection of upscale bars and restaurants, both Chinese and international. Touristy **Qinghefang Gujie** (Qinghefang Old Street) features numerous curio stalls and traditional medicine shops.

More contemporary hotspots in this part of town include **Hangzhou Mansion**, a shopping area filled with luxury shops selling global brands, and **Nanshan Road**, a lively strip that is home to beer gardens, nightclubs, live music and the like.

Outside Hangzhou

Heading west from town, Hangzhou Bay becomes the Qiantang River, which is called the Fuchun further upstream. The river is famous for its tidal bore, a surging wave of foamy water that roars up the river each day; the tide flows with extra vigour during the full moons of autumn.

Further upriver is **Tonglu** ❽, home to the remarkable **Jiangnan Suspended Temple** (8am–5pm; charge) built into a cliff face and supported by a series of pillars, which also support pathways and houses, all clinging to the side of the cliff for dear life.

Shaoxing ❾, 60km (38 miles) southeast of Hangzhou, is famous throughout China for its culinary rice wine, and the picturesque canal town is also notable as the birthplace of Lu Xun, the great early 20th-century writer. His **Former Residence** (Lu Xun Guju; daily, 8.30am–5pm; free), and the **Lu Xun Memorial Hall** (Lu Xun Jinianguan) stand on Lu Xun Street in the south of the city. The best way to appreciate Shaoxing's charms is to amble alongside the town's canals.

The island of **Putuo Shan** ❿, the easternmost of China's four sacred Buddhist mountains (see p.39), can be accessed by regular ferries from Shanghai, Ningbo and Hangzhou.

Shanghai and the Lower Yangzi

ACCOMMODATION

Shanghai has an extensive range of accommodation, from old classic buildings and compounds, some of them newly renovated, to modern glass-and-steel towers managed by the world's top hotel companies, to stylish boutiques carved from unique niche venues and decorated in wild modern eclectia. Hangzhou, Suzhou, Nanjing and the rest of the Yangzi Delta do not have the same range of options as Shanghai, but they offer a variety of accommodation and plenty of choice. Nor is everything super-expensive; if you look hard enough, excellent bargains will appear, many of them privately managed and all of them delivering perfectly acceptable overnights at wallet-friendly prices.

The newly-renovated Peace Hotel

The Bund

Captain Hostel
37 Fuzhou Road
Tel: (021) 6323- 5053
www.captainhostel.com.cn
This long-time low-budget favourite has a fine Bund location, just a few minutes from Nanjing Road East and close to the river-front. **$**

Fairmont Peace Hotel
20 Nanjing Road East, the Bund
Tel: (021) 6138 6950
www.fairmont.com
A famous old Art Deco gem that is one of the best-known buildings in China, the Fairmont emerged from a sensitive renovation in mid-2010. Now one of the classiest hotels in Asia. **$$$$**

Peninsula Shanghai
32 Zhongshan Road East, the Bund
Tel: (021) 2327 2888
www.peninsula.com
The Peninsula opened in late 2009 on a prime piece of property on the Bund, becoming the first all-new luxury hotel to open on the fabled waterfront in almost 80 years. **$$$$**

Waldorf Astoria
51 Guangdong Road
Tel: (021) 6323 8288
www.waldorfastoria.com
The beautiful new Waldorf opened in late 2010, with a new tower joined to a 1911 heritage building. Both buildings deliver old-world style, with plush ballrooms and Bund views. **$$$$**

Old Town

YMCA Hotel
123 Xi Zang Road South
Tel: (021) 6326 1040
www.ymcahotel.com/english/index.htm
The well-known Jinjiang YMCA is set in a classical-style 1929 building with a Chinese pagoda roof, and it features a range of options, from hostel-style dorm rooms (US$15 per night), all the way up to suites ($100 per night). **$–$$$**

People's Park

Langham Yangtze The Boutique
740 Hankou Road
Tel: (021) 6080 0800
yangtzeboutique.langhamhotels.com.cn
The pocket-sized Langham reopened in

2009 in a 1934 Art Deco-hybrid building, with gorgeous Deco-inspired interiors, plush and padded rooms, and superior service. Some of the rooms have balconies. **$$$$**

Hongkou and Suzhou Creek
Motel 168
300 Huoshan Road
Tel: (021) 5117 1111
www.motel168.com
Delivers everything the budget traveller could want: clean rooms, free broadband and a business centre, along with a smattering of spoken English. It is one of about 70 Motel 168s in Shanghai. **$**

Pujiang Hotel, or Astor House
15 Huangpu Road
Tel: (021) 6324 6388
www.pujianghotel.com
The atmospheric old Astor opened in 1906 and is ripe for a revamp, but stay there before that happens, because for now, the venerable Pujiang is the most authentic old building in the city. **$$$**

Nanjing West Road
Motel 268, or Xiang Yang Hotel
1 Xiangyang Road North
Tel: (021) 5403 7658
en.motel168.com
This new property on Xiangyang Road, not far from busy Huaihai Road, draws rave reviews from budget travellers. The ubiquitous 268 brand is more upscale than the 168, but delivers similar amenities. **$**

PuLi Hotel and Spa
1 Changde Road
Tel: (021) 3203- 9999
www.thepuli.com
An oasis of Southeast Asian spa culture in the heart of town. An urban resort filled with spa treatments, and park views. **$$$$**

Ruitai Jing'an Hotel
178 Taixing Road
Tel: (021) 6272 2222
www.ruitaijahotel.com
This small but perfectly adequate hotel is

proof that it doesn't take a fortune to spend a comfortable night in Shanghai. Just a few steps from Nanjing Road West. **$$**

Hangzhou
Fuchun Resort
Fuyang Section, Hangfu Yanjiang Road
Tel: (0571) 6346 1111
www.fuchunresort.com
A beautifully designed, super-upscale resort with a serene ambience, excellent cuisine, a challenging 18-hole golf course and one of the most memorable swimming pools in Asia. **$$$$**

Lakeview Hotel
Huancheng Road West
Tel: (0571) 8707 8888
A Chinese-managed hotel with a downtown location two blocks from West Lake, and standard three-star amenities including a swimming pool. **$$**

Nanjing
Crowne Plaza Nanjing Hotel and Suites
89 Han Zhong Road
Tel: (025) 8471 8888
A city-centre location in the heart of Nanjing, with modern amenities and a superior location atop a 60-storey building that provides superb views of the ancient capital. **$$**

Jinling Star Metropole Hotel
168 Longpan Road, Xuan Wu District
Tel: (025) 8689 1888
This very reasonable option enjoys a pretty

Astor House Hotel, aka the Pujiang Hotel

setting near Purple Mountain, and is conveniently close to the train station. Its two restaurants dish up light and lively Cantonese and Huiyang specialities. **$$**

Mandarin Garden Hotel
9 Zhuangyuan Road, Nanjing
Tel: (025) 5220 2555
This big four-star fairly bristles with old-world imperial decor, while behind the red-and-yellow trim lies a range of amenities and room sizes. **$$**

Suzhou
Garden Hotel Suzhou
99 Dai Cheng Qiao Road
Tel: (0512) 6778 6778
www.gardenhotelsz.com

The modern four-star Garden is set in a delightful, history-rich compound where the rich and powerful once lived. The courtyard is like a museum, with plaques and photos of former residents like Chiang Wei-guo (son of Chiang Kai-shek), and Lin Biao, who plotted his famous failed overthrow of Mao Zedong from this very spot. **$$$**

Hotel One
379 Chang Jiang Road, New District, Suzhou
Tel: (0512) 6878 1111
www.hotelone.com.cn
A business-friendly boutique hotel that opened in 2007 with postmodern decor, free mobile telephone service, English-speaking staff, along with swimming pool, spa and other five-star features. **$$$**

RESTAURANTS

Shanghai is irresistible to superstar designers, chefs and restaurateurs from around the world. Mix this together with a broad spectrum of venues and a variety of cuisines, and add a frantic populace that eats out nightly, and you have one of the world's great dining cities.

Restaurant Price Categories
Prices are for a full meal per person, with one drink
$ = below Rmb50 (below US$7.50)
$$ = Rmb50–100 (US$7.50–15)
$$$ = Rmb100–150 (US$15–22.50)
$$$$ = over Rmb150 (over US$22.50)

The Bund and Old Town
Kebabs on the Grill
505 Zhongshan South Road, near Fuxing East, inside Cool Docks
Tel: (021) 6152 6567
Fat roasted lamb and marbled beef kebabs, combined with the occasional all-you-can-eat specials, plus a riverside location in the trendy new Cool Docks development. **$$$**

Lost Heaven on the Bund 花马天堂
17 Yan An East Road (near Sichuan South Road)
Tel: (021) 6330 0967
www.lostheaven.com.cn
Featuring a mélange of Thai, Burmese and Yunnanese influences, with dazzling displays of flavour and texture which will stimulate

the most jaded palates. **$$**

Sun with Aqua 水族館
2/F, 6 Zhongshan East No. 1 Road
Tel: (021) 6339 2779
The Bund's first Japanese restaurant is an eye-catching venue with cutting-edge decor and an open kitchen. **$$$$**

Nanjing Road West
Cantina Agave 西拓餐厅
291 Fumin Road and Changle Road
Tel: (021) 6170 1310
www.cantinaagave.com
Generously spiked margaritas, indoor-outdoor seating and excellent Mexican food have made it an instant hit. Reservations are recommended. **$$$**

Chambar
139 Xing An Road
Tel: (021) 5306 2551
www.cham-bar.com
A classy new Belgian-style bistro that offers 18 beers – all from Belgium – plus a well-stocked wine cellar, and a menu that features exquisite French cuisine. There's also a lounge, pool table and terrace. **$$$$**

Chun Kitchen 春餐厅
124 Jinxian Road, near the corner of Maoming Road South
Tel: (021) 6256 0301
Chun has four tiny tables and two nightly seatings (6pm and 8pm), and guests eat what owner Ms Qu has bought fresh in the local market that day. The fish, snails, eels, pork ribs and other offerings are sweet, stewed, oily and very Shanghainese. Reservations are required. **$–$$**

La Creperie 永瑞餐厅
1 Taojiang Road, near Fenyang Road
Tel: (021) 5465 9055
lacreperieshanghai.spaces.live.com
A fine café that specialises in sweet and savoury crêpes: think sweet crêpe with stewed apple with butter and caramel, or savoury buckwheat crêpe with camembert cheese and smoked ham. It also serves the perfect accompaniment – dry Breton cider. **$$**

Former French Concession Bistro Burger
291 Fumin Road, in Mansion Complex
Tel: (021) 6170 1315
Beautifully cooked burgers, rich milkshakes and a surprisingly large selection of french fries, backed by sinful desserts and fine American microbrews, draw the crowds. **$$**

Hengshan Café 衡山小馆
308 Hengshan Road, by Gao'an Road
Tel: (021) 6471 7127
This very popular and inexpensive café features pan-Chinese dishes like steamed fish, barbecue pork, roast duck, stewed ribs and crispy stir-fried vegetables, all of them beautifully done and very reasonable. Make reservations. **$$**

Jesse Restaurant 吉士酒家
41 Tian Ping Road, near Huaihai Middle Road
Tel: (021) 6282 9260
This charming little cafe serves the tastiest Shanghainese food in town – red-cooked pork ribs, lion's head meatballs, steamed and fried fish – as evidenced by the clusters of hungry people waiting outside. **$$**

Kappo Yu 割烹雄
33 Wu Xing Road, near Huaihai Road
Tel: (021) 6466 7855
Serves *kaiseki*, the imperial Japanese cuisine typified by freshness, light flavours, clever presentation and a myriad of small elegant dishes. Open for dinner only. **$$$$**

Lost Heaven Yunnan 花马天堂
38 Gao You Road, near Fuxing West Road
Tel: (021) 6433 5126
www.lostheaven.com.cn
The menu features exotic mushrooms, vegetables, spices and other signature preparations from Yunnan province, and the design is subtle but dazzling: don't miss the two-storey wall made from blocks of *pu-er* tea. **$$$**

Mr Willis
3/F, 195 Anfu Lu
Tel: (021) 5404 0200
Mr Willis hews tightly to the time-honoured bistro formula: first-rate ingredients simply cooked and carefully dressed up in hints of herb and citrus and spice. The menu is dominated by classics like lamb shank, roast chicken and rib-eye, and the mains are reinforced by a solid wine list and superb side dishes. Reservations recommended. **$$$**

Qimin Organic Hot Pot 齐民有机中国火锅
407 Shanxi North Road by Beijing West Road
Tel: (021) 6258 8777
Using carefully selected organic ingredients and no MSG. **$$**

Restaurant Martin 马丁餐厅
811 Hengshan Lu (inside Xujiahui Park)
Tel: (021) 6431 9811
Basque staples like cod, squid, lamb and

lobster, served in a classic red-brick mansion in the middle of Xujiahui Park. Each dish is beautifully crafted. **$$$$**

Sichuan Citizen
30 Donghu Lu
Tel: (021) 5404 1235
At Citizen, the *gong bao* chicken is fatter and juicier, the dry-stewed fish is firmer and fresher, and the garlic and chilli oil and *ma la* spice are used tactically, rather than carpet-bombed on top of everything, as they are in cheaper Sichuan joints. **$$**

Western Shanghai
XinJiang Style Restaurant 新疆风味饭馆 维吾尔餐厅
280 Yi Shan Road, near Nan Dan Road
Tel: (021) 6468 9198
From the Muslim far west of China comes Xinjiang food, featuring hearty lamb and chicken and potato dishes, along with the famous home-made flatbread. This big, boisterous restaurant, complete with dancers in ethnic uniforms, is by far the best in this part of town. **$$$**

Hangzhou
Elm Garden
Si Yan Jing, Man Jue Long Road (near Hu Pao Road)
Tel: (0571) 8715- 3033
Located in a tourist spot famous for its sweet-scented laurel trees, Elm Garden is a country-style restaurant that serves simple but tasty dishes of local chicken, fish and seafood,

Dishes at the Hengshan Café

each of them alive with the characteristic mild freshness of Hangzhou cuisine. **$**

Kui Yuan Guan 奎元馆 (解放路总店)
154 Jie Fang Road, near Zhongshan Middle Road
Tel: (0571) 8702 8626/8706 5921
A traditional Hangzhou noodle restaurant, with many varieties of noodles from soup to cold to stir-fried. Very popular with visitors and locals alike. **$**

Tsing-Teng Teahouse 青藤茶馆
Floor 2, Yuan Hua Plaza, 278, Nanshan Road
Tel: (0571) 8702 2777/8702- 0084
This teahouse is a popular gathering place for locals. It offers a variety of tea, snacks, dim sum, and other small dishes in a traditional Chinese setting, along with many special types of Hangzhou tea. **$$**

Wei Zhuang 味庄, (aka Zhi Wei Guan) (知味观杨公堤店)
10–12 Yang Gong Di (Yang Gong Causeway)
Tel: (0571) 8797 0568/1913
A Chinese-style pavilion built on the West Lake, with a dream-like environment that duplicates an ancient royal palace. The food here is superb. **$$$**

Nanjing
Bai Wei Zhai Teahouse (Hundred Taste Teahouse) 鸡鸣寺百味斋社
1 Ji Min Temple Road
Tel: (025) 5771 3690
This little classic is located in the famous Ji Min Temple near Xuan Wu Lake. Every dish has an auspicious name and is served with a 'lucky instrument'. A fine selection of tea and superb vegetarian noodle dishes. **$**

Islamic Green Willow Restaurant 清真绿柳居
248, Tai Ping South Road
Tel: (025) 8664 3644
A rare combination of Islamic cuisine – lots of mutton, but no pork – and vegetarian selections, in a classic old venue in the center of Nanjing . Also does traditional dim sum. **$$**

Revolving Palace & Mei Yuan Restaurant 金陵饭店璇宫与梅苑餐厅
36/F & 2/F, Jin Ling Hotel, Han Zhong Road
Tel: (025) 8471 1888
A pair of fine restaurants in one of the most famous hotels in Nanjing, Mei Yuan offers fine Huai Yang cuisine, one of the mildest and most refined of China's eight major cuisines. The Revolving Palace has a superb 360-degree view across Nanjing. **$$-$$$$**

Suzhou
Song Helou 松鹤楼
141 Guangqian Street
Tel: (0512) 6770- 0068
Old-school Chinese charm, along with classic delta cuisine. Try the fried mandarin fish in sweet-sour sauce, the *wuxi* spare ribs and the light and silky tofu with crab egg. **$$$**

Yakiniku Suzhou
3, Li Song Road, Ligongdi Lakeside
Tel: (0512) 6265 6776
Peaceful lake views and a range of Japanese food from sushi to barbecue, accompanied by long sake list, are the specialities of the house. The Japanese barbecue set meals are especially good, featuring melt-in-your-mouth marbled beef and fresh seafood. **$$$**

Zapata's Waterfront Bar and Restaurant
158 Xinggang Street, on Rainbow Walk
Tel: (0512) 6767 2780
This perennial hotspot lures the crowds with its *feng shui*-friendly lake views, generous cocktails, sizzling spicy fajitas and bountiful burgers, while occasional DJs and live bands adding further midnight flair to this bright and lively venue. **$$–$$$**

NIGHTLIFE AND ENTERTAINMENT

The Yangzi Delta in general is typified by rapid change and quick turnover, and this is especially true of Shanghai's nightlife scene. From friendly pubs with tree-lined courtyards, to lounge bars lined with peach-and-purple lights and acres of plush cushion, to DJ-fuelled dance clubs and live music venues that don't rev up until midnight, this part of China has it all.

The Bund
Glamour Bar
6/F, 20 Guangdong Road
Tel: (021) 6350 9988
www.m-theglamourbar.com
The Glamour Bar evokes the rarefied ambience of the 1930s, although with modern spotlighting, updated fancy drinks and fine service. Its views of Pudong are superb.

Hongkou and Suzhou Creek
Vue Bar 非常时髦酒吧
Hyatt on the Bund, 32/F, 199 Huang Pu Road
Tel: (021) 6393 1234 ext 6348
shanghai.bund.hyatt.com/hyatt/hotels/entertainment/lounges
Everyone ignores the outdoor hot tub that sits in the middle of Vue Bar, probably because they are distracted by the eye-popping alfresco views of Pudong and the Bund.

Former French Concession
Boxing Cat Brewery 拳击猫
82 Fuxing Road West, by Yongfu Road
Tel: (021) 6431 2091
www.boxingcatbrewery.com
Nicely located in a renovated villa on a classy, tree-lined concession street. American-style craft beers, with lots of malty flavour and plenty of hops, with burgers, fries, sliders and a selection of breads and dips.

The Camel
1 Yueyang Road, near Dongping Road
Tel: (021) 6437 9446
www.camelsportsbar.com
Big, bright and bristling with TV screens, The Camel opened in 2010 to serve a key demographic: British expats who crave football, cricket, rugby and other Commonwealth sports.

Cotton's

132 Anting Road, corner of Jianguo Road West
Tel: (021) 6433 7995
www.cottons-shanghai.com
It's one of the best post-prandial options in town: a couple of Chairman Mao cocktails on the patio of this classy Concession-era mansion, under the sweeping boughs of the ever-present plane trees.

Paulaner Brauhaus 宝莱纳餐厅

150 Fen Yang Road
Tel: (021) 6474 5700
www.paulaner-brauhaus.com/shanghai/welcome
With its vast, park-like grounds, cavernous interiors, and vast outdoor patio that beckons on balmy evenings, Paulaner is easily the most famous dine-and-drink venue in Shanghai.

Nightclubs

Lan Club 兰会所

102 Guangdong Road
Tel: (021) 6323 8029
www.lan-global.com
Lan established itself as a firm favourite soon after its 2008 opening. The classy Bund venue is a four-floor party palace with friendly service and plenty of dance space, plus lounge, restaurant, rooftop garden, private rooms and eclectic Old China decor.

M1NT 铭特酒吧

318 Fuzhou Road
Tel: (021) 6391 2811
www.M1NT.com.cn
A lavish nightclub perched atop a 24-storey building five blocks from the Huangpu River, M1NT presents seasoned DJs, a spacious dance floor, restaurant, rooftop party area and a super-sized shark tank.

Sin Lounge 欣酒吧

23/F, Want Want Plaza, 211 Shimen 1 Road, next to Four Seasons Hotel
Tel: (021) 6267 7779
www.sinshanghai.com
A juicy red apple at the door, a snake-like entry hall, massive floor space, Garden of Eden jungle decor and high-flying city views await visitors, along with generous cocktails and deep, soulful house and tech-house music.

Live Music

Chinatown 中国城

471 Zhapu Road, near Wujin Road, Hongkou
Tel: (021) 6258 2078
www.chinatownshanghai.com
Wed-–Sat, show 8pm–2am
Chinatown is a lush three-storey club dressed in 'olde Shanghai' decor, while the revue presents light-hearted skits, silly jokes, and song-and-dance numbers that combine cabaret, burlesque, comedy and vaudeville.

House of Blues and Jazz 布鲁斯和爵士酒吧

60 Fuzhou Lu, near Sichuan Middle Road
Tel: (021) 6323 2779
This gem of a club opened in 2008 in a renovated mansion on a quiet Bund backstreet, and has a firm following that is attracted to its unpretentious but upscale atmosphere, and excellent bands that play soul-infused blues and jazz.

JZ Club JZ俱乐部

46 Fuxing Road West
Tel: (021) 6431 0269
www.jzclub.cn
While most jazz venues in Shanghai play blues and pop music and even show tunes, JZ remains the real thing, with an ongoing selection of fine jazz musicians from China and overseas, plus an excellent house band.

The Glamour Bar on the Bund

SPORTS, ACTIVITIES AND TOURS

People in Shanghai don't spend much time with sports, either as players or as spectators. One exception is golf, a bourgeois badge of honour. Beyond that, the Shanghai Shenhua football team performs in front of sparse crowds, while Formula One, ultra-popular when it first opened in 2004, has dwindled in popularity.

Golf

Yintao Golf
In Qingpu, 20km (14 miles) from downtown.
Tel: (021) 6976 2222
This 18-hole course is open to non-members.
Rmb690 weekdays, 990 weekends.

Football

Hongkou Stadium
30 minutes from downtown.
Tel: (021) 5666- 8969
The season begins in March and ends in November, with weekly games.

Formula One

Anting, 90 minutes north of downtown
www.formula1.com
Shanghai's US$320 million circuit is the most sophisticated F1 venue in the world. In 2009, the main event was moved from October to April, but that move may be temporary.

Bicycle Tours

China Cycle Tours

Tel: (1376) 111 5050
www.chinacycletours.com
For Rmb80, China Cycle will deliver your bike, with lock, helmet, map and lots of good advice, and pick it up 24 hours later. Guided bike tours Wednesday evening, for Rmb50.

Guided Architecture Tours

Luxury Concierge
Tel: (135) 0166 2908
luxuryconciergechina.com
Spencer Dodington, a US architect, shares his knowledge of Shanghai's historic buildings.

Walk Shanghai
www.walkshanghai.com
Excellent, knowledgeable tours.

Gang of One
Tel: (139) 0160 8284
www.gangofone.com.cn
Photographer Wang Gang Feng's tours open doors to people's homes, providing a perspective rarely seen by outsiders.

FESTIVALS AND EVENTS

With the loud and blazing exception of Chinese New Year, traditional Chinese festivals are little observed in Shanghai. Arts festivals, however, are steadily growing in popularity and importance.

January/February

Chinese New Year and Lantern Festival
There are fireworks at midnight on the first and fourth nights, then on the 14th and final night the area around Yu Yuan Garden comes alive with glowing lanterns.

March

Shanghai Literary Festival
Glamour Bar, 6/F, 20 Guangdong Rd

Tel: (021) 6253 7115
Author presentations, held in front of large, enthusiastic audiences.

June

Shanghai International Film Festival
Shanghai Film Art Center, 160 Xinhua Rd
Tel: (021) 6253 7115
An Asia-centric affair that introduces films both eccentric and popular.

Yangzi River Region

Rich in history and filled with inspiring scenery, the fabled Yangzi River slices through central China for 6,300km (3,900 miles) – the world's third-longest river – forcing its way through the Three Gorges to the plains beyond. The populous provinces that flank the river teem with human activity but also feature mountains and wilderness, and are emblematic of China in every way.

Chongqing

 Population: 33 million (municipality); c.5 million in urban area

 Local dialling code: 023

 Airport: Jiangbei Airport is 25km (14 miles) north of downtown.

 Trains: There are two main railway stations: most long-distance trains use Chongqing Bei Zhan (North Station) in Jiangbei District, 5km (3 miles) north of the centre, but Caiyuanba Station, 2km (1¼ miles) southwest of downtown, is also used.

 Buses: Long-distance buses use Caiyuanba Bus Station, next to the rail station of the same name.

 Key areas: In the heart of downtown, Minsheng Lu and Wuyi Lu are replete with small restaurants, street stalls and nightlife offerings, as is the area several blocks southwest of Chaotianmen Dock. Restaurants and bars can also be found on Nanan Binjiang Lu, on the south bank of the Yangzi and up the hill on nearby Nanbin Lu – many featuring fine night-time views of the city.

The central provinces of China are the country's industrial heartland, its gargantuan cities and sprawling factory towns linked by the mighty Yangzi, which the Chinese call, appropriately enough, the Chang Jiang (Long River). It is, indeed, the longest river in China, extending for 6,300km (3,900 miles) from its source on the Tibetan Plateau to the delta near Shanghai. The river traditionally divides China into north and south.

From Chongqing, the waters flow east through the Three Gorges and the Three Gorges Dam, the classic route for cruises. Downriver from Yichang the Yangzi becomes slower and wider, and its silt-laden light-brown water rolls through densely populated flatlands, passing the great cities of Wuhan and Nanjing. It is navigable by ocean-going vessels as far as Wuhan, nearly 1,000km (620 miles) upstream from its mouth on the East China Sea.

Chongqing

The teeming city of **Chongqing** ❶ is the starting point for cruises along the Yangzi, sitting at the point where the Jialing joins the main river, a strategic location that has long guaranteed its role as a trading centre. Its location on a rocky promontory is rare among Chinese cities, and the Old Town is a collection of winding alleys connected by steep flights of stairs. Yet Chongqing is also one of China's fastest-growing boom-towns, complete with futuristic skyscrapers, traffic jams, neon lights and a huge influx of people from rural areas swelling the population.

During World War II the National-ist government of Chiang Kai-shek retreated from Nanjing to Chongqing and made it their capital, because its foggy weather made it harder for Japanese bombers to find. Provincial status resumed after the war, and the city quickly grew into the industrial powerhouse that it is today.

The area around **Jiefang Bei** (Libera-tion Square) is the heart of the city, and there are many narrow, winding back-streets to explore. Steep steps lead from the tip of the peninsula down to the riverbanks and **Chaotianmen Dock**, where cruise ships await. Nearby is the **Huguang Guild** (Huguang Huiguan; 9am–6pm; charge), an extended clan dwelling and temple complex that gives an interesting account of the city's history.

Back uphill, not far from Chaotian-men and hidden in a narrow side street, is a small Buddhist temple, **Luohan Si**, noted for 500 painted terracotta sculp-tures. The **Three Gorges Museum** (Sanxia Bowuguan; Tue–Sun 9.30am–5pm; free) by Renmin Square has well-presented exhibits with some English captioning. To the south, visit **Pipa Mountain Park** (Pipa Shan Gongyuan; 6am–10pm; free) for tremendous views across the city; the night-time display of neon-lit buldings is impressive.

The new face of Chongqing

Along the Yangzi: Chongqing to Yichang

The serene 650km (405-mile) down-river cruise from Chongqing to Yichang is not just about admiring the spectacular gorge scenery. It also provides a fascinating look at modern China. Postcard-perfect hilltop pagodas, ancient half-moon bridges, Qing-era towpaths and secluded forest temples share the surrounding hills with enormous new concrete bridges, ambitious roadworks, vast cement embankments and other unsightly aspects of China's booming economy. There are also the smoke-belching

Chongqing Maidens

Chongqing is said to have the prettiest girls in China: they are slim from climbing up and down its steep hills, they acquire spicy attitudes from its fiery cuisine, and their soft fair skin is a result of the city's near-perpetual fog and moisture.

The Three Gorges Dam. Cruise ships take around four hours to pass through the locks

rising up 30m (100ft) from the river's edge. During high water, the reservoir behind the Three Gorges Dam reaches the bottom of the pavilion, where a wall has been built to protect it.

Sanxia (Three Gorges)

Sanxia ❷, the famed **Three Gorges**, are what most tourists have come to see. The first of the gorges is **Qutang** (Qutang Xia), the steep-walled canyon famously depicted on the Rmb10 note, and the first of the three famous gorges. Qutang Gorge is the shortest,

Yangzi River Region

factories and crowded cities that have long been hallmarks of the area.

The first major stop downriver from Chongqing is **Fengdu**. Known as the 'Ghost Town' for its demon statues housed in temples, it was largely submerged by the Three Gorges Dam reservoir. Before the waters rose, the inhabitants were offered three choices: move to a government-supplied farm on higher ground, move elsewhere in China, or move to a relocation village and receive a one-time payment of between Rmb100,000 and 450,000, depending on their previous circumstances. More than 80 percent of the 100,000 displaced villagers chose the first option.

About 80km (50 miles) further downstream is **Shibaozhai** (Stone Treasure Fortress; daily 8am–5pm; charge), a regular stop on cruise-boat itineraries. During the reign of Emperor Qianlong (1736–97), a temple was erected on top of a rock

just 8km (5 miles) long, but it is the most spectacular, as near-perpendicular mountains pinch the gorge to a width of 100m (330ft) and make navigation through the narrow passage harrowing.

After Qutang Gorge and before the next gorge (Wu Xia) is the town of Wushan, where the Daning He joins the Yangzi. Upstream along this tributary are the beautiful **Xiao Sanxia** (Three Small Gorges). The journey involves transferring to smaller vessels which struggle against the Daning He's strong currents, but the effort is

worthwhile, as the exquisite scenery is one of the highlights of a Yangzi cruise. At one point wooden coffins can be seen tucked into a tiny ledge high up on a mountain. These coffins belong to the Tujia people, descendants of the Ba, a lost culture from the Bronze Age.

Back on the Yangzi, the 45km (28-mile) long **Wu Xia** (Witches' Gorge) is relatively calm. Surrounded by 12 tall peaks with poetic names, it is steeped in legend; in this case, troublesome dragons have been turned to stone by the goddess Yaoji. The

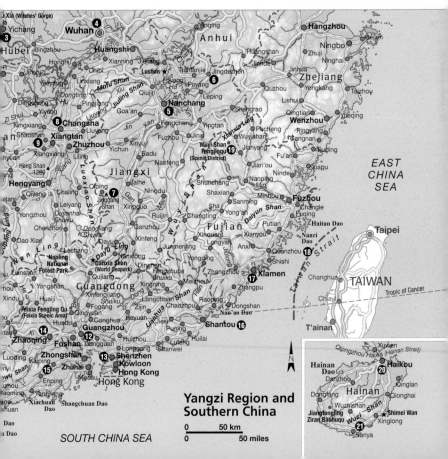

Yangzi Region and Southern China

0   50 km
0   50 miles

Witches' Gorge is so named because the sun never shines into its deepest and most shadowy recesses.

The last, longest and – before the dam slowed the current – most dangerous of the Three Gorges, **Xiling**, stretches for 66km (41 miles). Smack in the middle of Xiling Gorge is the **Three Gorges Dam** at Sandouping. Here, cruise boats descend through five monstrous locks, sharing the vast pools with container ships bearing gravel, sand, coal and other raw materials of industrial China. The descent through the five locks takes about four hours, and watching the giant gates open and close, and observing the boat's downward slide as the water is pumped out, is one of the highlights of the trip. Ascending boats go upriver through a parallel set of five locks.

Most boats stop below the Three Gorges Dam to allow tourists a look at its industrial immensity; a grassy park about 1km (⅔ mile) from the

dam affords fine views. Downriver from the dam is perhaps the most fascinating stretch of the Yangzi: the remainder of Xiling Gorge. Here, the river surges through the canyon unimpeded, offering the most authentic and original experience on the cruise. Of particular note is the village of Shibei, where the river makes a 110° turn. Here, a retreating Chiang Kai-shek fought a landmark battle against the Japanese, and his effort is marked by obelisks commemorating the occasion. The water on this flows fast and strong, and runs 50m (165ft) deep.

Most boats dock at **Yichang** ❸, an orange- and rice-growing village that has morphed into a large city, as many people who either worked on the Three Gorges Dam, or were displaced by it, have relocated here. A handful of passenger ferries continue downstream from Yichang to Wuhan and Shanghai, five days downriver – although the vastly improved road network is a far quicker option.

A new bridge spans the Yangzi upstream from Yichang

Yangzi River Region

Kite sellers at Yichang

preserved 2,000-year-old corpse of a Western Han-dynasty official can be seen. **Yueyang** in Hunan province is situated at the point where the Yangzi meets wildlife-rich Dongting Lake. Its best-known sight is **Yueyang Lou** (Yueyang Tower; daily 8am–6pm; charge), one of the region's most famous pavilion towers.

Wuhan

The industrial and commercial city of **Wuhan ❹**, halfway between Chong-qing and Shanghai at the confluence of the Chang and Han rivers, is a major hub for visits to central China. An enormous metropolis, it is actually a merger of three once-distinct settle-ments: Wuchang, Hankou and Han-yang, all now municipalities in their own right. Taking advantage of their privileged positions along the Yangzi as well as major rail and road networks, the cities comprise one of the country's most dynamic economic hubs.

Downstream from Yichang

The ancient town of **Jingzhou** has an impressive Ming-dynasty **city wall** and a **museum** (Tue–Sun 8am–4pm; charge) where the remarkably well-

---

The Great Dam of China

The US$60 billion Three Gorges Dam, fully 2.3km (1½ miles) across and 135m (442ft) high, has been in operation since 2003. As well as generating electricity, the dam has tamed the hitherto deadly floods, and has also made the Yangzi far deeper and thus safer for navigation.

Yet the mammoth project remains controversial. The creation of a vast reservoir forced the relocation of 1.5 million people, and buried countless artefacts for ever. The raised water level behind the dam has also made the celebrated Three Gorges somewhat less impressive.

But the biggest effect is environmental. A pool of polluted water has replaced the fast-flowing river and caused the extinction of numerous species of fish. Migratory species like the 4m (13ft) Chinese sturgeon can no longer reach their upstream spawning grounds.

The devastating Sichuan earthquake of 2008 damaged several dams further upriver, and caused many to question the wisdom of building the world's largest hydroelectric project in an earthquake zone.

Wuhan

 Population: 10 million

 Local dialling code: 027

 Airport: Tianhe Airport is 30km (21 miles) northwest of the centre.

 Trains: Wuchang Station is downtown on the south side of the river, while Hankou Station is in Jianghan District, a few minutes from downtown Hankou. Trains arriving from the north stop at Hankou, while those from the south usually call at Wuchang. A new station is under construction.

 Buses: Several bus stations serve Wuhan, none of them more than 30 minutes from the centre of town.

 Key areas: Hankou is the main focus for tourists. Inside Hankou, Jianshe Dadao District has a cluster of pubs and restaurants, while Jiefang Dadao and Zhongshan Dadao have dense concentrations of Western and local cafés and restaurants, with Zhongshan Dadao also offering hotels and guesthouses. Jianghan Lu and Jianshe Dadao are good areas for nightlife.

Of the three districts, **Hankou** – on the Yangzi's northwest bank and north of the Han River – has the most to offer in terms of accommodation and restaurants. Colonial European buildings near the waterfront serve as grandiose remnants of its role as a treaty port in the latter half of the 19th century.

Worshippers at Guiyuan Si in Wuhan

Wuchang, on the Chang Jiang's southeast side, is accessible via the Great Chang Jiang Bridge or regular public ferries from Hankou. The main sight is **Yellow Crane Tower** (Huanghe Lou; daily 7am–6.30pm; charge), looking down on the city from atop She Shan (Snake Hill). On Wuchang's eastern fringe is Dong Hu (East Lake), an expansive watery network situated within a huge park which makes for a pleasant retreat from Wuhan's suffocating summer heat. Nearby to the north is the **Hubei Provincial Museum** (Hubei Sheng Bowuguan; Tue–Sun 9am–5pm; free), dedicated primarily to antiquities excavated from the tomb of Marquis Yi, who died in 433BC. The exhibition is impressive and informative, with some captioning and displays in English.

Jiangxi

Together with neighbouring Hunan, Jiangxi province is best known in China for its revolutionary past and fiery cuisine. This corrner of China has

Beautiful scenery in northeastern Jiangxi

a dual identity: it has long been one of the country's most neglected areas, a forgotten backwater through much of history. Yet its isolation, combined with its mountainous landscapes and dozens of river networks, has attracted poets and philosophers for thousands of years, and generated countless works of art and literature. Economically, too, this landlocked but populous province has slowly been catching up with its rich coastal neighbours.

Nanchang

The provincial capital, **Nanchang ❺**, until recently known mostly for its role in the history of Chinese communism, is now at the forefront of another revolution: the rapid economic rise of China's 'second-tier' cities, many of them provincial capitals, which are benefiting dramatically from central government-led investment.

Nanchang's best-known historic site is the impressive nine-storey **Tengwang Pavilion** (Tengwang Ge; summer 7.30am–7pm, winter 8am–4.30pm; charge), which towers majestically over the Gan River. At night, an array of multicoloured lights brings its graceful flying eaves to life, and it is surrounded by a garden of elegant pavilions and weeping willows.

Around 2km (1¼ miles) to the east off Minde Lu, Nanchang's main commercial and nightlife thoroughfare, is **Zhu De's Former Residence** (daily 8am–5.30pm; charge). Together with Mao and Zhou Enlai, Zhu De led 30,000 Communist troops in the abortive 1 August 1927 Rebellion against the Nationalist forces. A pair of attractions, the **1 August Uprising Museum** (daily 8am–5.30pm; charge) and **1 August Square** (Bayi Guangchang), commemorate the date.

Elsewhere in Jiangxi

Tucked between the Yangzi's southern bank and the northern end of Poyang Lake is the rambling port of **Jiujiang**, entry point to **Poyang Lake**, where the large **Poyang Lake National Nature Reserve** attracts various species of crane each winter, along with other migrating waterfowl.

West of Poyang Lake in the north of Jiangxi, **Lushan** was a favoured retreat for missionary and expatriate families in the 19th century, and their European-style stone dwellings were later occupied by Nationalists and Communists alike. Some of the charming old buildings survive, and a few now operate as hotels.

Jingdezhen ⑥, in the northeast, is a historic kiln town and the manufacturing base of Jingdezhen porcelain, the most famous in ancient China. It still produces teapots, plates, cups and other ceramics in great abundance.

Celebrated as the cradle of the Chinese Revolution, the rugged mountains of **Jinggang Shan**, on Jiangxi's southwestern border, provided

shelter for the fledgling Chinese Red Army during fierce fighting with the Nationalists in the late 1920s and early 1930s. The village of **Ciping ⑦** served as a base for Mao Zedong and Zhu De after they united their divisions in 1927.

Hunan

The south-central province of Hunan has much in common with Jiangxi, encompassing as it does some sublime scenery and interesting old towns. Like its neighbour, it doesn't find its way onto many tourist itineraries, although associations with Mao ensure a steady stream of Chinese tour groups.

Changsha and Heng Shan

Located on the Guangzhou–Beijing rail line, the provincial capital **Changsha ⑧** is the largest city in Hunan, with a population of more than 10 million. It is not the most enticing city in China, yet neither is it devoid of attractions, foremost of which is the **Hunan Provincial Museum** (Hunansheng Bowuguan; daily 8am–6pm; charge). There are more than 110,000 artefacts within, most notably the 2,100-year-old Western Han tombs, corpses and coffins, as well as Shang- and Zhou-era bronzes.

Hunan's religious dimension is provided by the southernmost of the Daoist sacred mountains, **Heng Shan**, 120km (75 miles) south of Changsha. The mountain is reachable on foot from the town of **Nanyue** (see p.37).

Shaoshan

Mao's childhood home in **Shaoshan ⑨**, 90km (55 miles) southwest of Changsha, is a place of pilgrimage

Mao's 'little red book' was translated into over 30 languages in the 1960s and '70s

8am–5.30pm; charge), which traces the family ancestry back to a Ming patriot who fought the Mongols.

The far northwest

A one-hour bus ride from Zhangjiajie city (last bus at 6.30pm) lies Zhangjiajie village (Zhangjiajie Cun), the springboard for exploring **Wulingyuan Scenic Reserve** ⑩ (Wulingyuan Feng Jingqu; charge 🏵), encompassing some of China's most beautiful landscapes: the forests, crystal-clear lakes and dramatic sandstone crags were allegedly the inspiration for James Cameron's *Avatar*.

From the entrance there is a stunning 6km (4-mile) stroll along the valley floor, as well a handful of trails which climb the valley walls. Another climbing option is the one-of-a-kind Bailong Lift. Tacked onto a sheer cliff face, it whisks guests 326m (1,070ft) up the cliff in under two minutes.

Fenghuang

In the far west of Hunan is the ancient riverside town of **Fenghuang** ⑪ (🏵) home to Miao and Tujia minorities. The Tuo River runs through the old district, surrounded by the red-sandstone walls and grand old gateways, while Ming- and Qing-style architecture is lined up along the elegant stone-paved streets. The main focus for tourism is pedestrian **Dongzheng Jie**, which runs from the covered bridge of Hongqiao, past the 18th-century **Dongmenlou** (East Gate Tower) and into the thicket of low-rise buildings to the southwest of the river.

for many Chinese. Mao's image has suffered elsewhere, but in his hometown he remains a hero, and nothing can prepare visitors for the old-world propaganda laid on in this peaceful patch of Hunanese countryside. The mud-walled **Former Residence** (Mao Zedong Guju; daily 8am–5.30pm; charge) is surprisingly large, as Mao, who viciously persecuted 'rich peasants,' was himself a rich peasant. In the middle of the village is Bronze Square, where the **Museum of Comrade Mao** (Mao Zedong Jinianguan; daily 7.30am–5.30pm; charge), gives visitors a rundown of the life of the Great Helmsman, albeit glossing over key failures. Next to this is **Mao's Ancestral Temple** (Maoshi Zongci; daily

★ TRAIN TRAVEL IN CHINA

Train travel is central to the China experience, and no trip to the Middle Kingdom is genuinely complete without spending a night on a sleeper train. While much can be said for the gritty experience of riding in a six-berth 'hard sleeper' on a three-day trip through the vastness of central China, the country now offers a wealth of more comfortable options, from the luxury trains across the Tibetan Plateau to a fast-growing network of high-speed rail that is binding the country closer together.

Few visitors are likely to forget their first glimpse of a Chinese train station. The experience often begins with the act of buying a ticket, an activity that can be a ferocious battle in a chaotic scrum completely devoid of queues. Then there is the train station itself. Outside of any given station, clusters of waiting passengers share the broad concrete platforms with groups of migrant job-seekers coming and going from provincial towns, who eat noodles, play cards and smoke cigarettes as they await their trains. On a gentle summer evening, a unique atmosphere prevails, and the station fronts acquire an air of easy sociability. In any case, it is always nicer outside a Chinese train station than inside, as most are drab and featureless Communist-style affairs.

As for the trip itself, the romance of viewing China from a train window

The Beijing–Lhasa express makes its way across the Tibetan landscape

never fades. The vastness of the country slowly unfolds in a procession towns and factories and warehouses and fields, leavened by an occasional glimpse of wilderness. China is an epic country, and the train rides across it can be equally epic. The variety of landscapes is remarkable, from the rice paddies of the south to the fertile mountains of Yunnan, and from the yellow loess hills of the west to the barren semi-deserts of Tibet. The scenes within the train are equally compelling, if somewhat less romantic. In hard-seat class *(ying zuo)*, pyjamas are the dress of choice, and the time is whiled away in card games, mobile phones, tea-drinking and ceaseless chatter.

Yet, like everything else in modern China, rail travel is changing. One example is the way in which a train is now a ticket to the wide world beyond, as the railways connect to distant cities like Hanoi, Almaty and, most famous of all, Moscow. And they are moving upscale, as illustrated by the smart, modern express trains that whizz between Beijing and Shanghai, and the classy new carriages that roll across the Tibetan Plateau and over the 5,072m (16,640ft) Tanggula pass. A growing network of high-speed rails criss-crosses the country, bringing a whole new level of comfort to a time-honoured experience.

www.chinatravelguide.com is a useful resource for train times. Train tickets can be bought online through www. chinatraintickets.net and www.china-train-ticket.com.

Hard-sleeper *(yingwo)* is perfectly adequate, but the six-berth set-up can be a bit cramped

Most Chinese trains have individual compartments. Sliding doors open onto a corridor with pull-down seating

ACCOMMODATION

As elsewhere in China, accommodation in the Yangzi area is rapidly improving, and options are mushrooming, fuelled by growing tourism, most of it domestic, and by a surge in property investment, much of which has been ploughed into the building of residential property, including hotels. Accommodation tends to be inexpensive, even in the four- and five-star brackets, in the provincial cities.

Changsha

Huatian Hotel
300 Jiefang Donglu
Tel: (0731) 8444 2888
www.ehuatian.com/ehuatian/index.html
This venerable five-star has a long history, a city-centre location – and a good location – plus a restful interior courtyard and a fine Japanese restaurant. **$$$**

Xiaoxiang Huatian Hotel
593 Furong Zhong Lu
Tel: (0731) 8466 0888
www.xxht-hotel.com
A giant 600-room extravaganza of a property, the Xiaoxiang features cotton sheets and 24-hour butler service that complement its selection of suites, Hunan-Cantonese restaurant, teahouse and spacious lounge bar. **$$**

Chongqing

Harbour Plaza Hotel
Yu Zhong District, Wuyi Lu
Tel: (023) 6370 0888
www.harbour-plaza.com/en/
The first five-star hotel in Chongqing, the Harbour opened in 1998 in the commercial district, with unobtrusive but helpful service, and one of the best Cantonese restaurants in town. **$$**

Howard Johnson ITC Plaza
66 Qingnian Lu
Tel: (023) 6366 6666
www.itcmyway.com

Located in the prosperous central business district of downtown Chongqing, the Howard Johnson combines a good location with excellent English-speaking service, and 436 guest rooms with modern amenities. **$$$**

Sunrise Mingqing Hostel
23 Xiahongxue Lane, Yuzhong District
Tel: (023) 6393 1579
www.srising.com
The charming Sunrise offers 13 rooms in a 280-year-old former clan dwelling filled with old-world ambience and located in the brick-and-alley-filled old town section of Chongqing. The rooms, which overlook a leafy green courtyard, range from inexpensive dorms at Rmb60 per person, to a two-room suite for Rmb300. **$**

Nanchang

Galactic Peace International Hotel
10 Guangchang Nan Lu
Tel: (0791) 611 1118
www.glthp.com
The five-star Galactic is a local hotel that strives for international standards of service and accommodation. It features Chinese and Western restaurants, a swimming pool, abundant banquet space, and 390 rooms in a number of price ranges. **$$**

Jiangxi Hotel
368 Bayi Dadao
Tel: (0791) 620 6666
www.jxh.com.cn
The first five-star hotel in Nanchang, the Jiangxi combines comprehensive amenities – cosy tea bar, sauna, spa, and a spacious outdoor swimming pool set in park-like

surroundings – with a location in the heart of the city. Corner suites feature wrap-around balconies. **$$**

Wuhan

Howard Johnson Hotel
182 Yanjiang Dadao
Tel: (027) 8277 6666
plazapearlwuhan.hojochina.com/
plazapearl-wh-home.html
Located in the tourist-friendly Hankou District, the Howard Johnson features restful Yangzi River scenery and five-star amenities, including a revolving 41st-floor Thai restaurant that offers sweeping city views. **$$**

Jinjiang International Hotel
707 Jianshe Dadao
Tel: (027) 8578 6888
www.jinjianghotels.com
Operated by one of China's largest hotel chains, the 31-storey Jinjiang is a long-time favourite with in-the-know travellers, who appreciate its location and spacious rooms, many of which offer fine views of the rivers that surround the city. **$$**

Yichang

Guo Bin Garden Hotel
46 Chengdong Dadao
Tel: (0717) 633 1111
www.gbhy.com

Reception at the Huatian Hotel, Changsha

A garden-style hotel with leafy surroundings, a quiet ambience and restful views of the gentle Yichang countryside, along with all the amenities expected at this price range. **$$**

Yichang International Hotel
121 Yanjiang Dadao
Tel: (0717) 622 2888
no website
A well-run local hotel on the Yangzi River, the Yichang International offers river-view rooms, convenient links to the rest of the city and wallet-friendly room rates. **$**

RESTAURANTS

Spicy food is the norm upriver, and Chongqing especially is famous for its volcanic hotpots and incendiary stir-fries, fuelled by the liberal use of chilli peppers and Sichuan peppercorns, or *ma la*. There are clusters of restaurants around Nanbin Lu on the south bank of the Chang Jiang (take the cable car) and in the downtown area around the Liberation Monument (especially Bayi Lu and Minzu Lu). Downriver, the cuisine is mixed; the fiery fare of Hunan and Chongqing are plentiful, but so are the time-honoured techniques of braising and steaming, with fish and eels and other river life playing a large role in local diets. Wuhan's widest selection of restaurants is in the Hankou District, particularly along Zhongshan Dadao and its many side streets. The riverfront Yanjiang Dadao comes alive in the evenings with patio-seating hotpot establishments and an interesting sprinkling of Western-style bars and cafés. Wuchang also has plenty of dining options.

Changsha

Haoshishang 好食上
Hongfei Dasha, 245 Bayi Lu
Tel: (0731) 8446 3030
An atmospheric local restaurant that specialises in freshwater fish, shrimp, crabs and other signature Yangzi River delicacies. **$$**

Heshi Paigu 何氏排骨
313 Renmin Zhong Lu
Tel: (0731) 8412 1296
A 'hot and noisy' favourite where the wooden tables and chairs don't detract from its singular speciality: melt-in-your-mouth stewed pork ribs that are made according to a secret family recipe. **$$**

Huogongdian 火宫殿
93 Wuyi Dongl Lu
Tel: (0731) 8411 6803
A great place to sample a range of local specialities, with appetising Hunanese morsels served on dim sum-style trolleys. Make sure you try the cured chilli beef, and if you dare, have some smelly tofu, which Chairman Mao himself purportedly praised in 1959. **$**

Chongqing

De Zhuang Hot Pot (Qi Xing Gang) 德庄火锅（七星岗店）
148 Zhongshan Yi Lu
Tel: (023) 6352 1934
Said to be Chongqing's first ever hotpot restaurant, locals still consider it the title-holder over innumerable competitors around town, many of which are also extremely good, and equally spicy. **$**

Little Swan Hotpot 小天鹅
6/F, Chongqing Square, 22 Minzu Lu
Tel: (023) 6378 8811
Especially popular with Chongqing's foreign residents, Little Swan is more accommodating to non-Chinese-speakers than most other hotpot places, though no less spicy. **$$**

Tao Ran Ju 陶然居
15 Nanbin Lu, Nan'an District
Tel: (023) 8902 3118
Tao Ran Ju is one of the most popular

> **Restaurant Price Categories**
>
> Prices are for a full meal per person, with one drink
>
> **$** = below Rmb50 (below US$7.50)
> **$$** = Rmb50–100 (US$7.50–15)
> **$$$** = Rmb100–150 (US$15–22.50)
> **$$$$** = over Rmb150 (over US$22.50)

restaurants in Nanbin Lu's crowded Cuisine Street, which is well worth exploring for other local specialities. Offers upscale Sichuan cuisine in a traditional environment. **$$**

Waipo Qiao Fengwei Lou 外婆桥风喂楼
7/F, Metropolitan Plaza, 68 Zourong Lu
Tel: (023) 6383 5988
With its atmospheric Old China decor, this is an excellent place to sample a range of Chinese dishes, some with Sichuan influences. The most interesting menu items are imperial court dishes from the Qing dynasty. **$$–$$$**

Nanchang

Hongni Shaguo 红泥砂锅
Tengwang Pavilion, South Gate
Tel: (0791) 670 4888
Situated next to the Tengwang Pavilion, this is one of the best places to try the Jiangxi take on delicacies such as savoury *hongshao ruyu* (soy-braised mullet), crab-egg tofu and other local favourites. **$$**

Hunan Wang Caiguan 湖南王菜馆
99 Supu Lu
Tel: (0791) 623 8433
A popular restaurant that faces Bayi Park, and serves some of the city's most authentic Hunanese cuisine. **$**

Wuhan

Changchun Sucai Guan 长春素菜馆
145 Wuluo Lu, Wuchang
Tel: (027) 8885 4229
Part of the Changchun Guan Daoist temple complex, this delightful vegetarian restaurant exhibits a true mastery of the Chinese art of crafting delicious mock-meat dishes from soybean, wheat and other vegetable products. **$$**

Man Qi Lou z
136 Yanjiang Dadao, Hankou
Tel: (027) 8279 1563
This atmospheric riverfront avenue restaurant specialises in hotpot, with an emphasis on seafood. Outdoor patio seating is available when the weather cooperates. **$$**

Maojiawan 毛家湾
29 Shouyi Yuan, Wuchang
Tel: (027) 8832 6525
Cultural Revolution-era kitsch is the theme here, with youthful waitresses clad in sombre Red Guard attire serving peppery home-style Hunan dishes. It is tucked away on the north side of Shouyi Garden Snack Street, with no English sign. **$**

Yuan Ming Yuan 圆明圆
6 Jianghan Lu, Hankou
No Telephone
Dumplings of all shapes, sizes and substances are the main draw at this popular eatery, where locals order *baozi* by the dozen and chase them down with the tea of their choice. **$**

Yichang
The main concentration of restaurants is near the waterfront promenade, close to the intersection of Erma and Fusui roads.

Fuji Caiguan 福记菜馆
48 Fusui Lu
Tel: (0717) 622 2589
If you want genuine Hunanese food in all its peppery, garlicky, tongue-torching glory, Fuji is the place. Friendly staff. **$**

Wu Yue Wu Caifang 五月五菜坊
5 Erma Lu
Tel: (0717) 622 8777
A home-style diner with a selection of not-too-spicy Chinese standards, featuring high-quality pork, chicken and vegetable stir-fries to go with the rice and noodle staples. **$**

TOURS AND FESTIVALS
Cruising the Yangzi river is the focus for many visiting central China, but there are also specialist tours and colourful festivals to experience.

Yangzi Cruising
Websites such as www.discoveryangtze.com offer a useful overview of the options and costs, plus booking. *See also pp.23–24.*

President Lines
Tel: (023) 6365 4621
President offers less expensive local-quality cruises on a choice of Yangzi itineraries.

Victoria Lines
Tel: (023) 6163 7688
www.victoriacruises.com
The American-managed Victoria line offers a fleet of seven cruise liners, and a range of price tags and itineraries.

Yangzi Explorer
Tel: (852) 2824 9022/3179 5900

www.yangziexplorer.org
The most luxurious boat on the river, the *Yangzi Explorer* sails between Chongqing and Yichang.

Birdwatching
Poyang Lake National Nature Reserve in the north of Jiangxi province protects an important area of wetland, home to some spectacular birdlife, including Siberian cranes. Tours can be arranged in Nanchang.

Festivals
Yueyang Dragon Boat Festival
May/June
Miluo River, Yueyang, Hunan
One of China's largest dragon-boat competitions. The legend of Qu Yuan, the basis of the festival, originates from this area.

Southern China

China's subtropical southern coastal provinces (Guangdong, Fujian and Hainan Island) are vibrant and dynamic, offering everything from historical attractions through fine and varied cuisine to the country's best beaches. The interior of Guangxi, by contrast, offers a more relaxed pace of life and mesmerising rural scenery of an unparalleled beauty.

Guangzhou

Population: 10 million

Local dialling code: 020

Airport: Baiyun Airport is 30km (21 miles) north of downtown.

Trains: There are two main railway stations: most long-distance trains use Guangzhou East Station in Tianhe, 5km (3 miles) east of the centre. Guangzhou's main station, 2km (1¼ miles) north of downtown, also serves long-distance destinations and all local routes.

Buses: Long-distance buses use the Provincial Bus Station just to the west of the main train station. Opposite is the Provincial Bus Station, for most local and provincial buses.

Key areas: Dishifu Lu and Xiajiu Lu in Xiguan District (north of Shamian island) are good for restaurants. Restaurants and bars can also be found along the Yanjiang Lu riverfront. Haizhu Square, near the eponymous bridge, and nearby pedestrianised Beijing Lu are shopping hotspots.

Guangdong, Hainan and Fujian are among the richest and most developed provinces in China. This is especially true of the coastal regions, which have for centuries been associated with sea-faring, trade and overseas settlement. Most 'Overseas Chinese' trace their origins to these areas, and many have retained strong links with their ancestral towns and villages.

These subtropical southern lands differ from the ancient heartlands north of the Yangzi in many respects. Most obviously, the land is different, dominated by verdant green rice fields, with longer summers and milder winters. In terms of language, Cantonese and Fujianese are quite distinct from the northern dialect, Mandarin. Southern Chinese food – long familiar to the rest of the world as 'Cantonese' cuisine – is fresher and more subtle than that of the north.

Guangxi is different. Poorer, less developed and with minority nationalities making up almost 40 percent of the population, it is overshadowed economically by the other coastal provinces. It is, however, a favourite tourist destination, home to some of the most beautiful natural scenery anywhere in the world.

Guangdong

Foreigners have been visiting Guangdong for at least 2,000 years, as the provincial capital, Guangzhou, was China's first major seaport. It was the first Chinese town to receive Europeans (who called it Canton), when a Portuguese fleet arrived in 1514. Ever since, the province has maintained its gateway role; even during the years of political upheaval in the 1960s and 70s, Guangzhou kept open the nation's ties with foreign countries and with overseas Chinese, millions of whom have their roots here.

Guangzhou

With a population of more than 10 million, **Guangzhou ⑫** is one of China's richest and most progressive cities. It lies astride the Zhu Jiang or Pearl River, the country's fifth-longest river, which links the metropolis to

The Pearl River in the heart of Guangzhou

the South China Sea. The city is famed for its cuisine: dim sum, also known as *yum cha*, is at its very best here.

The most attractive part of Guangzhou is unquestionably **Shamian Island Ⓐ**, which evokes the atmosphere of 19th-century colonial Canton. This small residential enclave, shaded by banyan trees, was once home to a foreign colony in the era of the Western concessions. The stately European-style buildings, including old banks, factories and churches, have been spruced up, and Shamian's wide, shaded streets are free from the incessant traffic that plagues the rest of the city. A pleasant **riverside park** (🏛) affords a panorama across the busy stretch of water, with an endlessly changing procession of varied ferryboats, freighters, junks, low-lying sampans – and even the odd tanker and gunboat.

To the north of Zhongshan Lu, the main east–west thoroughfare through the heart of Guangzhou, a narrow street leads to **Liurong Si Ⓑ** (Temple of the Six Banyan Trees; daily 8.30am–5pm; charge), the city's principal Buddhist monument. Within its grounds

A residential lane in central Guangzhou

stands **Hua Ta** (Flower Pagoda), built in 1097 and a symbol of the city. The pagoda appears to be nine storeys high, each level with doorways and encircling balconies, but in fact contains 17 levels. There is a good view from the top. A few minutes' walk to the northwest is **Guangxiao Si ☉** (Temple of Bright Filial Piety; daily 6am–5pm; charge), a Buddhist temple preserved during the Cultural Revolution on the orders of Premier Zhou Enlai.

Further northeast, **Yuexiu Park ☉** (daily 6am–9pm) covers a 93-hectare (230-acre) site. In addition to its pretty gardens, lakes, pavilions and sports facilities, the park also contains the city's oldest building, **Zhenhailou**. Built in 1380, it now houses the **Guangzhou Museum** (Guangzhou Bowuguan; daily 9am–5.30pm 📷).

Dr Sun Yat-sen (1866–1925), who began his political career in the city, is honoured in Yuexiu Park by an obelisk 30m (100ft) tall. South of the park is an even more impressive monument, the **Sun Yat-sen Memorial Hall ☉**, built in 1931. This vast, modern version of a traditional Chinese building, with its sweeping blue-tile roofs, contains an auditorium big enough to seat nearly 5,000 people.

In early times Guangzhou had a significant Muslim population as a result of trade with the Middle East. The city is home to the oldest mosque in China, the **Huaisheng Mosque ☉** (daily 6am–5pm; charge to non-Muslims), supposedly dating from the 7th century.

Shenzhen

Shenzhen ⑬ is a busy Special Economic Zone on the border with

The Window of the World theme park near Shenzhen

Hong Kong, an economic miracle and magnet for overseas investors. For the typical overseas tourist venturing into mainland China for a day or two from Hong Kong, it provides a fascinating glimpse of changing China. It may lack cultural sophistication, but it makes up for this with bargain shopping, wild nightlife and various US-style theme parks.

The most popular of the theme parks is **Window of the World** (Shijie Zhichuang; daily 9am–10pm; charge ), a global Lilliput which showcases scale models of everything from Thai palaces to Japanese teahouses – to say nothing of the Eiffel Tower, one of the area's most prominent landmarks. Nearby **Splendid China** (Jinxiu Zhonghua; daily 9am–6pm; charge), does a similar job on Chinese landmarks. The adjacent **China Folk Culture Village** (Minzu Wenhua Cun; daily 9am–9-.30pm; charge) recreates the homes and lifestyles of the country's ethnic minorities.

Around the Pearl River Delta

The delta region is more famous for its

The Opium Wars

During the early 19th century, opium was imported by merchants from British India into China in defiance of Chinese prohibition. China's seizure and destruction of opium stocks caused war with Britain in 1839. Further disputes over the treatment of British merchants in Chinese ports resulted in a Second Opium War. Victorious, Britain forced the Chinese government into opening additional ports to unrestricted foreign trade, and for the cession of Hong Kong to Britain.

factories than tourist sights, but there are, nonetheless, a few places of interest. At **Humen** the First Opium War *(see box, p.163)* is commemorated at the **Opium War Museum** (Yapan Zhan-zheng Bowuguan; daily 8am–5.30pm; charge). On the coast 5km (3 miles) south of Humen town, related **Shajio Fortress** (Shajiao Potai; 8am–5pm; charge) is also worth visiting. Some 25km (16 miles) southwest of central Guangzhou, **Foshan** (Buddha Mountain) is famous for its venerable **Zu Miao** (Ancestral Temple; daily 8.30am–7pm; charge). Dating back to the 11th century, the Zu Miao's main effigy is a 3-tonne statue of a Daoist deity in charge of the waters whom the locals venerate in this flood-prone region.

Heading south towards Zhuhai and Macau, the countryside is less developed. The village of **Cuiheng**, where Dr Sun Yat-sen, the Father of Modern China, was born in 1866, lies to the southeast of Zhongshan. His house has been reconstructed and turned into the **Dr Sun Yat-sen Residence Memorial Museum** (Sun Zhongshan Guju; daily 9am–5pm; charge).

Elsewhere in Guangdong

One of Guangdong's most agreeable cities, **Zhaoqing** ⑭ sits on the Xi River, 110km (68 miles) west of Guangzhou. The main attraction is the **Seven Star Crags** (Qixing Yan), a range of limestone peaks that rise from a man-made lake in the north of town.

South from Zhaoqing, the area around **Kaiping** ⑮ is famous for its *diaolou* towers, multi-storeyed defensive village houses built from the early 17th century to the 1930s. Many display an ornate fusion of Chinese and Western architectural styles. The surviving diaolou – more than 1,800 in all – are scattered over a wide area, some hidden beside duck ponds in the backstreets of Kaiping, but most in the villages around the city, rising in surreal fashion from the emerald-green rice fields.

Two to three hours northeast of Guangzhou by bus is the town of **Conghua**, home to **Conghua Hot Springs**, a well-known destination famous for lychees and popular for its clean air and serene setting. **Chaozhou**, 40km (25 miles) north of Shantou, is a historic trading town, its attractive centre full of narrow lanes and a section of Ming-dynasty Wall bordering the Han River.

Near the border with Fujian, **Shantou** ⑯ is a port city that was opened to foreign trade after the Second Opium War. **Shipaotai** (Stone Fort Park; daily 7.30am–6pm; charge) preserves moated fortifications built in 1879 for coastal defence. The fort

Conghua is famous for its lychees

Diaolou towers stand tall amid the rice fields of western Guangdong

is squat and solid, its 5m (16ft) thick outer wall pierced by arched tunnels.

Fujian

Fujian enjoys close cultural and increasingly financial ties to the nearby island of Taiwan, with which it shares a common language and many cultural traditions. Though relatively unvisited by foreign tourists, this southeastern province certainly offers enough history, attractive scenery, folk traditions and other attractions to rank alongside some of the country's better-known destinations. Fujian has a long tradition of overseas migration, particularly to Southeast Asia; the diasporic communities have retained links to their homeland, and the money they send has made this corner of China one of the most prosperous regions in the country – enhanced, at least in coastal regions, by a vibrant economy.

Xiamen

One of China's more engaging cities, the port of **Xiamen** ⑰ has an attractive old centre and a beguiling off-shore haven, the island of Gulangyu (Xiamen itself is an island, linked to the mainland by a 5km/3-mile) causeway). Formerly known in the west as Amoy, it became wealthy during the expansive maritime trading years of the Ming dynasty. The port was opened to foreign trade after the Opium Wars, when Gulangyu became a foreign enclave, complete with elegant colonial buildings.

The **Old Town** is centred on lower Zhongshan Lu, and is a pleasant place to explore. On Siming Nanlu, about 2km (1¼ miles) south, is the **Overseas Chinese Museum** (Huaqiao Bowuguan; Tue–Sun 9.30am–4pm; charge), with an outstanding collection of pottery and bronzes gathered with the help of donations from the extensive overseas Fujianese community. There is also an informative section on the diaspora itself.

Gulangyu Island

Occupied by colonial powers until World War II, the island of **Gulangyu** is the main attraction, a laid-back museum piece of colonial architecture accessed via a five-minute ferry ride. Peace and quiet is a big part of the appeal – there are no vehicles (or even bicycles) allowed, although electric trains trundle slowly along the leafy lanes. The island is also known for its musical heritage; it can claim the world's highest per-capita piano ownership, and there is a Piano Museum *(see p.180)* and festival *(see p.181)*.

Close to the pier is **Xiamen Undersea World** (Haidi Shijie; daily 9.30am–4.30pm; charge), a modern

aquarium. Turn left from the pier to see the huge statue of **Koxinga**, a Chinese patriot who liberated Taiwan from the Dutch in the mid-17th century; the statue stands near the eastern shore of the island. Continue walking along the coast to reach the picturesque **Shuzhuang Garden** (Shuzhuang Huayuan; daily 6.30am–8pm; charge), beyond which a pleasant sandy beach extends along much of the island's southern coast.

Ascend **Sunlight Rock** (Riguangyan), the highest point on Gulangyu, for views across the red-tiled villas and verdant gardens to downtown Xiamen.

Quanzhou and the Southwest

A thousand years ago **Quanzhou** ⑱ was a significant port, with a lucrative position at the centre of the maritime silk trade. It prospered enormously during the Song and Yuan dynasties, when it was visited by Marco Polo and played host to Arab and Persian merchants. The port fell into decline following the restrictions on maritime trade imposed by the Ming emperors in the early 15th century. Still, it has retained its heritage remarkably well by Chinese standards, and all new buildings must follow height and design standards to keep them in harmony with the past.

The **Ashab Mosque** (Qingzhen Si; daily 8am–6pm; charge for non-Muslims) on Tumen Jie dates from 1009. It is said to be the only mosque in eastern China built along traditional Islamic, rather than Chinese, lines. English-language signs help to bring

Banyan trees and colonial architecture on Gulangyu Island

Traditional Hakka roundhouse, Yongding county

alive the past for the foreign visitor.

Islam was not the only foreign religion to reach Quanzhou, as is clear from the **Maritime Museum** (Haiwai Jiaotongshi Bowuguan; daily 8am–6pm; charge) on the northeast side of town. Nestorian crosses, carved fragments from Hindu temples, stones bearing the Star of David, Arabic inscriptions and even remnants of a 7th-century Manichaean shrine are on display. On the upper floor you will find an impressive survey of China's seafaring history and a sizeable display devoted to the expeditions of Admiral Zheng He (*see right*).

Kaiyuan Si (Kaiyuan Temple; daily 8am–5pm; charge) is Quanzhou's largest Buddhist temple, and one of China's most beautiful. The temple dates back to the late 7th century, but its two pagodas were later additions, constructed in the 13th century.

Yongding in southwest Fujian is unremarkable, but there is an unusual attraction northeast of town. A large earthen roundhouse built for defensive purposes by the local Hakka people and called **Zhenchenglou** is located near the village of Hukeng.

Admiral Zheng He

The Ming emperor Yongle was unique in the annals of Imperial China in that he pursued an active maritime policy – sending his favourite admiral, the Yunnanese Muslim eunuch Zheng He (1371–1433), to explore Southeast Asia and the Indian Ocean as far as the Red Sea and the coast of East Africa. Zheng developed Quanzhou into the main base for his 'treasure fleets', bringing wealth and development to the Fujian coast. Following Yongle's death in 1424, succeeding emperors abruptly turned their back on maritime trade: overseas voyages were outlawed in 1434; historians have pondered the economic consequences of this enforced isolation.

⭐ BLING BLING, IT'S THE NEW CHINA CALLING

The concept of universal austerity has never sat well with Chinese society. Chinese businessmen are legendary for their commercial acumen, and the dream of attaining wealth has always helped to sustain the poor. The Mao period comprehensively suppressed any entrepreneurial streak, but when Deng Xiaoping announced that 'to get rich is glorious', he struck a deep chord in the collective national psyche – and the Chinese have never looked back…

When Deng took over as paramount leader in 1978, China was still reeling from the excesses of the Cultural Revolution, the general population impoverished and malnourished, and the economy all but destroyed. Deng stated openly that 'Socialism is not the same as shared poverty', and set the nation on a course towards an autocratic free-market capitalist system.

But could even Deng have envisaged the changes that would transform China within just three decades? When Colin Thubron visited the country in 1985, he supposed that there were 'not more than a dozen privately owned cars in the whole country'. How times have changed… China is now the world's largest motor vehicle market, with sales of 13.6 million units in 2009.

Expensive jewellery on sale in Guangzhou

And it's not just cars. According to the 2010 *Hurun Wealth Report*, there are currently 875,000 US dollar millionaires in China, with figures rising by more than 6 percent annually. Beijing alone is home to more than 150,000 million-aires, with Guangdong and Shanghai close behind. Property prices in China's biggest cities have risen to rival London, Tokyo and New York – while Hainan, the preferred tropical playground of China's affluent *nouveaux riches*, has become so expensive that the local Hainanese can no longer afford to buy property on the island. Meanwhile, in the affluent suburbs surrounding Shanghai, themed estates based on Bavarian towns or English country villages are springing up, priced far beyond anything the ordi-nary person could ever possibly afford.

How are these emerging disparities affecting Chinese society? To be sure, the growing gap in wealth between the cities and the countryside, the coast and the interior troubles the ruling Communist Party and poses a threat to future stability. And yet an advertise-ment on Chinese TV shows two helicop-ters landing on the roof of a Shanghai skyscraper. A beautiful woman immacu-lately clad in white steps down from one, a similarly dressed man from the other. They ostentatiously display their gold Rolex watches as they climb into a white Rolls-Royce parked, inexplicably, on the penthouse roof. It's glitzy, it's bling – it's really rather offensive. But perhaps it brings hope to the millions who still echo Deng's vision: 'To get rich is glorious!' But then Deng also said: 'Some must get rich first'.

Upmarket shops and shopping malls are much in evidence in all major Chinese cities

The New China

Betting in Macau. The former Portuguese colony is cashing in on new levels of disposable income amongst the Chinese

There are other, similar roundhouses in the villages southeast of Yongding.

Wuyi Shan

In northwest Fujian, **Wuyi Shan** ⓳ is a Unesco-listed World Heritage Site with towering peaks and dense forest cradling a rich and unique ecosystem. Several trails head into the peaks; this is prime hiking territory, and is also known for its rafting. The various treks and tours will occupy a couple of half-days. The extraordinary 'hanging coffins', mostly made from whole trees, are concealed in caves high up on cliff faces. Carbon dating has revealed that they are more than 3,000 years old.

Hainan Island

Historically and geographically isolated and long thought of as a place of exile, Hainan Island has now come into its own as a tropical resort destination. It basks in year-round warmth, and there are plenty of palm-fringed beaches, particularly in the south

around Sanya, offering the best swimming and sunbathing in China.

Haikou

The island's capital, **Haikou** ⓴, is a pleasant city, with an unmistakably laid-back ambience. The Old Quarter in the north of the city centre is attractive, and features a promenade extending along Changdi Lu past clipped lawns and the banks of the Haidian River. Haikou attracts relatively few visitors, however, as most people prefer to head straight for Sanya and the south coast.

East Coast

These days most visitors fly straight to Sanya, but if you are travelling from Haikou along the east-coast highway, places of interest en route include some fine beaches around the village of **Qinglan** and Hainan's surfing centre at **Shimei Wan** (Shimei Bay). The nearby town of Xinglong is home to **Xinglong Tropical Botanical**

Uniquely for China, Sanya's beaches offer year-round sun, sand and sea

A typical resort development west of Sanya

Garden (Xinglong Redai Zhiwuyuan; daily 7.30am-6pm; charge).

Sanya and the South Coast

Sanya ㉑ was originally one of several fishing villages on the southern tip of Hainan, and fishing docks still occupy a focal point at the town's hub. The Sanya River divides the town from north to south, with the original settlement lying to the west. It's all pleasantly relaxed; shabbiness now rubs shoulders with a form of gentrification – numerous good restaurants have opened as well as upmarket teahouses. The rocky **Luhuitou Peninsula**, immediately south of Sanya, is dominated by a giant sculpture depicting the legend of a hunter and a deer. The statue is located in a hill park in the north of the peninsula, with superb views of Sanya City, Dadonghai Bay and other nearby beaches available from the highest point.

Five minutes southeast of the city centre by road, or a 45-minute walk, lies the sandy bay of **Dadonghai**. The whole of its beachfront has been developed, with mostly high-end hotels and resorts. Off the main road, side streets are wall-to-wall with seafood restaurants and beachwear and souvenir knick-knack shops. Palm-tree shade is a little scarce, although it's possible to rent chairs and tables under parasols. The water is clean, but deceptive currents mean that it's not suitable for children or weaker swimmers.

Yalong Wan (Yalong Bay), 20km (12 miles) to the east, is a gorgeous 7km (4½-mile) strip of pale, powdery sand; warm sunshine throughout the winter high season attracts the crowds, and activities include scuba-diving, deep-sea fishing and paragliding. Most tourists visiting Yalong Bay and Hainan's other beaches are either Chinese or Overseas Chinese, but increasing numbers of Westerners – especially Russians – are also being drawn to the area.

The Interior

Hainan's island culture is best typified by the livelihood of its minority Li and Miao peoples. Several Li and Miao villages can be reached around the town of **Wuzhishan** in the highlands north of Sanya, which has a fascinating **Minority Nationalities Museum** (Minzu Bowuguan; Tue–Sun 8am–5pm; charge) dedicated to the culture of the Li and the Miao. The **Jianfeng Ling Primeval Forest Reserve** (Jiangfengling Ziran Baohuqu), 110km (68 miles) northwest of Sanya, is a striking mountainous area that has been successfully reforested.

Guangxi

After Beijing, Shanghai and Xi'an, rural Guangxi is China's best-known tourist attraction, with the magical, almost mystical scenery around Guilin a perennial draw. Wind and rain has eroded the limestone hills into fantastic shapes, riddled with labyrinthine caves and grottoes.

With some peaks rounded and some sharply pointed, perpendicular cliffs and trees that sprout from the cracks to bend skyward, this is a dream-like landscape, familiar to anyone who has looked at a Chinese scroll painting.

Guilin

The provincial capital of **Guilin ㉒** has been a significant political and cultural centre since Tang-dynasty times (618–906), though at first glance there is little to see of this rich history – almost the entire city was razed by the Japanese army in 1944. Still, Guilin remains attractive. Parks and osmanthus trees lighten the urban landscape, and a few limestone peaks rise above the buildings. The Li River cuts through town, and many small restaurants offer river cuisine, such as fish, eel, frog, turtle, snail, shrimp and snake.

Guilin's 200m (650ft) **Elephant Trunk Hill** (Xiangbi Shan), topped by 500-year-old Puxian Pagoda, offers good views across the city. To the northwest, beside an 800-year-old banyan tree

The "End of the Earth" beach near Sanya, Hainan Island

Dragon-boat training, Guilin

The pre-eminent historical sight in Guilin is the **Palace of the Jinjiang Princes** (Jinjiang Wangfu; daily 8.30am–5pm; charge), a short stroll north of the city centre. This ancient city within a city has its very own karst mountain inside its walls (included in charge). **Solitary Beauty Peak** (Duxiu Feng; daily 7am–7pm; charge) rises up above the Ming buildings, and climbing the 300 or so steps to the pagoda at the top rewards you with the delightful view enjoyed by princes and poets over the centuries.

The Li River

The extraordinary beauty of the countryside south of Guilin is no secret, and a steady stream of riverboats (*see p.174*) make the scenic journey () along the Li River between Guilin and Yangshuo. The landscape in this region is dominated by the otherworldly limestone pinnacles rising sheer from the otherwise flat terrain of rice fields. Farmhands in conical hats work the

on the northern bank of the Rong Hu Lake, is an authentic remnant of the Old City. Further north the main hub of activity is the area around **Central Square** (Zhongxin Guangchang) and Zhongshan Lu. Between Central Square and the Li River, Zhengyang Lu pedestrian street is geared towards tourists, with a selection of restaurants, bars, galleries and souvenir stalls.

Guilin

 Population: 1.4 million

 Local dialling code: 0773

 Airport: Liangjiang Airport is 26km (16 miles) southwest of the city.

 Trains: The main railway station, Guilin Zhan, is centrally located on Zhongshan Lu. There are good rail links with China's major cities.

 Buses: The long-distance bus station is also on Zhongshan Lu approximately 200m/yds north of the railway station. Buses for Yangshuo leave from in front of the railway station as well as the long-distance bus station.

ℹ️ **Key areas:** There are restaurants and shopping malls all along Zhongshan Lu, and the area just north of Central Square has a number of good restaurants. Shazheng Yang Lu, slightly to the east of Central Square, is a pedestrian street with boutiques and some more upmarket restaurants.

Li River Boat Trips

Large, flat-bottomed tour boats usually leave early in the morning from the quay near the Liberation Bridge in central Guilin. (In the dry season, when the river is at its lowest, the first part of the journey is by coach.) With room for more than 100 passengers each, most of these vessels are quiet and serve a lunch cooked en route. The river traffic, meanwhile, keeps amateur photographers snapping in all directions at flat-bottomed tubs, hand-poled bamboo rafts, sampans and towboats.

rice terraces, while on the river villagers fish from bamboo rafts using trained cormorants.

The town of **Yangshuo** ㉓ lies amid spellbinding scenery on the west bank of the Li River, 60km (37 miles) downstream from Guilin. It has long enjoyed a prime position on the tourist trail, yet still exudes a riverside country-town feel, and for most visitors remains one of the most appealing of all destinations in China. Both town and surrounding countryside are easily explored by bike or on foot, while there's a good selection of reasonably priced accommodation in the town, and a wide choice of reasonably priced restaurants serving both Chinese and Western dishes.

Xi Jie (West Street) is the centre of the tourist scene, while **Chengzhong Lu** has a few pavement cafés and small guesthouses, and there are more hotels along **Binjiang Lu**, some with great river views. The atmosphere in town is surprisingly laid-back, and it's a great place to unwind or to come back to after a day biking through the

The amazing landscapes around Guilin continue below the surface

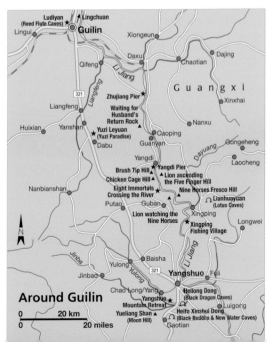

Around Guilin

Yangshuo is situated amid some of the most impressive karst scenery in the region

surrounding karst outcrops. If you are staying overnight in Yangshuo, don't miss the amazing Impressions of Liu Sanjie show. This beautifully choreographed musical extravaganza takes place in an open-air venue on the Li River, close to Yangshuo, with the karst peaks providing a perfect backdrop to the performance.

Around Yangshuo
A trip out to **Moon Hill** (Yueliang Shan), 10km (6 miles) southwest of town, is highly recommended; the view from the summit of the hill is simply magnificent. Yangshuo has become one of China's foremost adventure-sport capitals in recent years. Rock-climbing, boating, caving and ballooning trips can all be organised through operators in town. All three pursuits offer spectacular new perspectives on the karst landscapes. Rafting around **Yulong Qiao** (Jade Dragon Bridge) is a particular highlight. The **Yulong River** itself, a tributary of the Li, is accessible by bicycle and wonderfully scenic.

Elsewhere in Guangxi
The main road north from Guilin to Guizhou province gives access to yet more dramatic landscapes. Southeast of **Longsheng** ❷❹ town, the **Dragon's Backbone Terraces** (Longji Titian) are a series of steep hills layered with rice terraces. The effect is extraordinary, and highly photogenic. Basic accommodation can be found in **Ping'an**, a small Zhuang village positioned amid the terraces and within range of other minority villages.

The southern part of Guangxi is well off the tourist trail, but is not without interest. The port of **Beihai** ❷❺ on the south coast still sports 19th-century European buildings that recall its history as a treaty port (the best examples are near the waterfront); the town is also known for its beaches. Some 200km (125 miles) southwest of the provincial capital, Nanning, and en route to the Vietnamese border, the country town of **Ningming** is the jumping-off point for a boat trip along the scenic **Zuo River**.

ACCOMMODATION

Southern China, encompassing a number of the wealthiest regions of mainland China, offers some of its best hotels. Standards of service tend to be higher here than in other parts of the country. Prices in Guangzhou's hotels will rise around the time of the twice-yearly Canton Fair (second half of April and October). Hainan Island's tropical beach resorts become heavily booked during Chinese New Year, when prices skyrocket.

Accommodation Price Categories

Prices are for a standard double room in peak season

$ = under Rmb300
$$ = Rmb300–600
$$$ = Rmb600–1,000
$$$$ = Over Rmb1,000

Guangzhou

Garden Hotel
368 Huanshi Dong Lu
Tel: (020) 8527 4373
A Guangzhou institution, the Garden Hotel boasts a charming garden and waterfall as well as superbly decorated rooms. Facilities include tennis and squash courts. **$$$$**

Shamian Hotel
52 Shamian Nan Jie
Tel: (020) 8121 8288
Popular with foreign visitors, this is the best budget option on Shamian Island. **$–$$**

The Westin Guangzhou
6 Linhe Zhong Lu
Tel: (020) 2886 6868
www.starwoodhotels.com
Situated in the middle of the Tianhe District, Guangzhou's new shopping and business district, and close to Guangzhou East Station. **$$$$**

Garden Hotel, Guangzhou

White Swan Hotel
1 Shamian Nan Jie
Tel: (020) 8188 6968
www.whiteswanhotel.com
Situated on historic Shamian Island, this five-star hotel overlooks the Pearl River. The lobby area contains a number of boutiques and restaurants. **$$$**

Guilin

Guilin Fubo Hotel
27 Bin Jiang Lu
Tel: (0773) 256 9898
Large comfortable rooms, friendly service and a riverside location make up for the slightly frayed-at-the-edges feel. **$$**

Lijiang Waterfall Hotel
1 Shanhu Bei Lu
Tel: (0773) 282 2881
www.waterfallguilin.com
Centrally located, overlooking Shan Lake, the Lijiang Waterfall has large rooms and an array of first-class facilities, including an indoor pool, sauna and gym. **$$$**

HOMA Chateau
Dabu Town, Yanshan District
Tel: (0773) 386 7888
www.guilinhoma.com
Located beside the Yuzi Paradise sculpture park, 28km (18 miles) south of Guilin, the hotel is an integral part of the park. **$$$$**

Sheraton Guilin Hotel
15 Bin Jiang Lu, Guilin
Tel: (0773) 282 5588

www.sheraton.com/guilin
Close to all Guilin's beautiful sights, the Sheraton has a superb riverfront location. **$$$**

Quanzhou
Quanzhou Hotel
22 Zhuang Fu Xiang
Tel: (0595) 2228 9958
www.quanzhouhotel.com
Well situated for Quanzhou's major tourist sights, the hotel has a wide variety of rooms, varying from three-star to five-star quality. **$$$**

Sanya
Hilton Sanya Resort and Spa, Yalong Bay
Tel: (0898) 8858 8588
www.sanya.hilton.com
With its selection of swimming pools, chic sea-view rooms and good restaurants, this is a stylish resort hotel. **$$$$–$$$$$**

Landscape Beach Hotel
23 Haiyun Lu, Dadonghai Beach, Sanya
Tel: (0898) 8822 8866
Situated right next to the beach with bright, comfortable rooms, the Landscape is just a short distance from town. **$$**

Sheraton Sanya Resort
Yalong Bay National Resort District, Yalong Bay, Sanya
Tel: (0898) 8855 8855
www.sheraton.com/sanya
Beautiful tropical gardens, endless facilities and flawless service make this one of China's very best resorts. **$$$$$**

Shenzhen
Shangri-La Shenzhen
1002 Jianshe Lu, Shenzhen
Tel: (0755) 8233 0888
www.shangri-la.com
Well located for the railway station and close to the Hong Kong border, renowned for top-notch service and rooftop restaurant. **$$$**

Xiamen
Lujiang Harbourview Hotel
54 Lujiang Lu
Tel: (0592) 266 1383
www.lujiang-hotel.com
This historic, colonial-style hotel sits on Xiamen's busy waterfront and faces Gulangyu Island. Sea-view rooms are slightly more expensive. **$$–$$$**

Marine Garden Hotel
27 Tianwei Lu, Gulangyu Island
Tel: (0592) 206 2668
www.marinegardenhotel.com.cn
With 96 beautifully decorated rooms, indoor swimming pool and gym, this is Gulangyu Island's top hotel. **$$$**

Yeohwa Hotel
101 Yuehua Lu, Huli
Tel: (0592) 602 3333
www.xmmandarin.com
Formerly the Mandarin, this splendid hotel with its villa-style accommodation and beautiful gardens makes for a great five-star escape. **$$$$**

Yangshuo
Paradesa Yangshuo
116 Xi Jie
Tel: (0773) 882 2109
The Paradesa has a pretty landscaped garden and the best facilities to be found in Yangshuo town. **$$$**

Yangshuo Mountain Retreat
Wang Gong Shan Jiao, Feng Lou Cun Wei, Gao Tian
Tel: (0773) 877 7091
www.yangshuomountainretreat.com
A peaceful retreat in a glorious setting, the hotel's 22 rooms offer lovely views, either of the pretty Yulong River or the impressive karst outcrops surrounding the property. **$$**

Zhaoqing
Zhaoqing Phoenix Hotel
18 Hu Xilu, Gao Yao, Zhaoqing
Tel: (0758) 838 3888
www.zqphoenixhotel.com
This comfortable, 300-room hotel sits close to the famous Seven Star Crags. **$$$**

RESTAURANTS

Cantonese cuisine, one of the world's truly great culinary genres, finds its home in Guangzhou, a city overflowing with excellent eateries. Restaurants are spread out across the city, with a cluster in the streets north of Shamian Island. Fujian cooking features strong, salty flavours and, being a coastal province, lots of seafood. Hainan cuisine is usually lighter than other mainland cuisines and seafood predominates, although the island is probably most famous for its Hainanese chicken rice. Guangxi, not known for its own cuisine, has a strong Cantonese influence in the east and south. Yangshuo, with its numerous travellers' cafés, is one of the best places in China to find Western food.

Guangzhou

1920 1920西餐
183 Yanjiang Zhonglu, Guangzhou
Tel: (020) 8333 6156
With its German specialities and imported beers, this charming riverside café is just the place for lunch or dinner. **$$$**

Cow and Bridge 牛桥泰菜
2/F, Xianglong Huayuan, 175–181 Tianhe Beilu, Guangzhou
Tel: (020) 8525 0821
Good, authentic Thai food. All ingredients are imported from Thailand. **$$$**

Datong Restaurant 大同酒家
63 Yanjiang Lu, Guangzhou
Tel: (020) 8188 8988
Busy eight-floor Cantonese diner on the river with a huge menu. **$$**

Tao Tao Ju 陶陶居
20 Dishipu Lu, Guangzhou
Tel: (020) 8139 6111
This revered Cantonese restaurant has deservedly acquired a reputation across the Pearl River Delta. **$$$**

Guangzhou Restaurant 广州酒家
2 Wenchang Nanlu, near Xiajiu Lu, Guangzhou
Tel: (020) 8138 0388
Classic Cantonese dishes at this famous establishment with a fine dim sum buffet. **$$**

Guilin

Left Bank Café 滨江左岸
18 Binjiang Lu, Guilin
Tel: (0773) 288 2259
Next to the Li River and with good views of Seven Star Park, the Left Bank serves an ambitious range of dishes including steaks, burgers, pizzas and fried rice. **$$**

Lotus 洛特丝厅餐
HOMA Chateau, Dabu Town, Yanshan District, Guilin
Tel: (0773) 386 7888
www.guilinhoma.com
Beautifully presented Asian fusion food in this arty modern restaurant. **$$$**

Zhengyang Tang Cheng 正阳汤城
54 Zhengyang Lu, Guilin
Tel: (0773) 285 8553
A great place to sample Cantonese-style soups, with the restaurant producing over 30 different varieties daily. Apart from the soups try the Guilin noodles. **$**

Haikou

Jade 玉宫中餐厅
Sheraton Haikou Resort, 199 Binhai Lu, Haikou
Tel: (0898) 6870 8888
www.sheraton.com/haikou
Chaozhou specialities accompany traditional Cantonese favourites at this plush hotel eatery. **$$$$**

Lu Zhi Hai Xien Mai Tze Cheng 吕记海鲜美食城
38 Hai Xiu Donglu, Haikou
Tel: (0898) 6672 3925
A veritable 'seafood city' right in the heart of the town, this very popular establishment serves an array of fine Chinese-style seafood dishes. **$**

Quanzhou
Qing Yuan Chun 金洲大酒店
Quanzhou Hotel, 22 Zhuang Fu Xiang, Quanzhou
Tel: (0595) 2228 9958
www.quanzhouhotel.com
Elegant restaurant, featuring well-presented Cantonese favourites with an emphasis on seafood. **$$**

Sanya
The Big Kitchen 金茂三宫大酒店
Hilton Sanya Resort and Spa, Yalong Wan, Sanya
Tel: (0898) 8858 8588
www.sanya.hilton.com
Fusion cuisine at its finest; guests are encouraged to challenge the chefs with their own suggested ingredients. **$$$**

Spice Garden Pan Asian Restaurant 香料园亚洲餐厅
2F, Sheraton Sanya Resort, Yalong Wan, Sanya
Tel: (0898) 8855 8855
www.sheraton.com/sanya
In a casual atmosphere, cuisines to tempt the palate include Indian, Indonesian, Thai and Vietnamese. **$$$**

Wan Hao 万豪酒店
Sanya Marriott Resort and Spa
Tel: (0898) 8856 8888
www.marriott.com/syxmc
First-class Cantonese restaurant with some Hainanese specials also on the menu. **$$$**

Shenzhen
360 at the Shangri-La 360 度餐厅
Shangri-La Hotel, 1002 Jianshe Lu, Shezhen
Tel: (0755) 8396 1380

www.shangri-la.com
Superb views from the 31st floor coupled with first-class cuisine and a long wine list. **$$$$**

Phoenix House 凤凰楼
2/F, The Pavilion Hotel, 4002 Huaqiang Beilu, Futian, Shenzhen
Tel: (0755) 8207 8888
Renowned for its great Cantonese seafood dishes, and with its 30 VIP rooms the all-day *dim sum* can be savoured without the hustle of similar Hong Kong establishments. **$$**

Xiamen
Lujiang Restaurant 观海餐厅
Lujiang Hotel, 54 Lujiang Dao
Tel: (0592) 202 2922
This rooftop restaurant overlooking the harbour and Gulangyu serves a fine choice of dim sum along with some particularly toothsome Cantonese and Fujian specialities. **$$**

Nanputuo Si Vegetarian 南普陀寺餐厅
Nanputuo Temple, Siming Nanlu
Tel: (0592) 208 7281
This attractive temple restaurant serves up a selection of excellent Chinese vegetarian dishes. **$**

Tutto Bene 多乐意意大利餐厅
1-16 Jianye Lu (opposite Marco Polo Hotel)
Tel: (0592) 504 6026
The chef here prepares excellent pizzas and a wide variety of Italian-style pasta dishes. **$$$**

Sanya's Big Kitchen restaurant

Yangshuo

7th Heaven Café 桃源饭店
2 Cheng Zhong Lu, Yangshuo
Tel: (0773) 882 6101
This friendly café provides great breakfasts and good coffee along with a variety of Western favourites. An added bonus is the selection of medicinal Chinese soups. **$**

Café Too 自由人旅店餐厅
7 Cheng Zhong Lu, Yangshuo

Tel: (0773) 882 8342
Great value for breakfast and serves a fine choice of local dishes for lunch and dinner. **$**

Le Vôtre 乐得法式餐厅
79 Xi Jie, Yangshuo
Tel: (0773) 882 8040
This restored Ming-dynasty building with a large outside terrace is a rarity in China; it's an upmarket French restaurant, and they brew their own beer. **$$**

NIGHTLIFE AND ENTERTAINMENT

The larger cities of south China have seen numerous bars and clubs open in recent years, most of these becoming meeting places for China's ever more affluent youth. Guangzhou and Shenzhen both have a thriving nightlife scene, and the only way to get a handle on it is to pick up one of the numerous English-language free magazines aimed at expatriates, such as *That's PRD* (Pearl River Delta). Guangzhou, with its concert halls, museums and art galleries, is the cultural heart of Ssouthern China. Nightlife in Hainan is limited to a few bars and plenty of karaoke joints. Guilin and Yangshuo have a good range of visitor-friendly bars.

Guangzhou

Elephant and Castle Bar
363 Huanshi Dong Lu
Tel: (020) 8359 3309
A perennially popular expat favourite.

Hare and Moon
White Swan Hotel, 1 Shamian Nanjie
Tel: (020) 8188 6968
www.whiteswanhotel.com
For those staying in the Shamian Island area this relaxing hotel bar has a wonderful view of the Pearl River.

Xinghai Concert Hall
33 Qing Bo Lu, Ersha Dao, Guangzhou
Tel: (020) 8735 2222
Next door to the Guangzhou Museum of Art on Ersha Island, and home to the extremely accomplished Guangzhou Symphony Orchestra.

Shenzhen

LV8 (Level 8 Bar)
1F, Fa Zhan Xin Building, Renmin

Nan Lu, Luohu
Tel: (0755) 8222 5777
Amid the lively nightlife of Shenzhen, this place has quickly established itself as one of the most popular clubs.

Xiamen

Gulangyu Piano Museum
45 Huang Yan Lu, Gulangyu Island
Tel: (0592) 257 0331
Asia's largest piano museum is a monument to the extraordinary number of great pianists who have come from Gulangyu.

Soul Bar (Dusan Jiu Ba)
188 Hubindong Lu, Xiamen
Tel: (0592) 507 5078
This popular club and bar attracts some fairly big-name DJs from across the planet.

Yangshuo

Buffalo Bar
50 Xianqian Jie, Yangshuo
Tel: (0773) 881 3644
With regular quiz nights, pool competitions

and live music, this is a great place to chill out after a day spent cycling, trekking or rock-climbing in the area.

Impressions of Liu Sanjie
Tian Yuan Lu, Yangshuo

Tel: (0773) 881 1983
www.yxlsj.com
Over 600 actors and musicians in a spectacular nightly 70 minute dramatic show, all set against a magnificent natural backdrop. Starts at 8pm.

SPORTS, ACTIVITIES AND TOURS

Guangdong and the Pearl River Delta boast a number of first-class golf courses. For outdoor activities Guangxi's Yangshuo has become southern China's adventure-sport capital. Cycling, rafting, rock-climbing, trekking, boating and ballooning trips can all be arranged through tour operators in town.

Golf

Guangzhou Luhu Golf and Country Club
Luhu Congyuan, Lujing Lu, Guangzhou
Tel: (020) 8350 7777
www.luhugolf.com
Winding through the foothills of the Baiyun Mountains and around Luhu Lake, north of Guangzhou, this superb 18-hole course offers a real challenge.

Yalong Bay Golf Club
168 Qiong Dong Lu, Dongshan, Qiongshan, Hainan
Tel: (0898) 8856 5888
In the golfing community it's perceived to be the best course on the island.

Adventure Activities

China Climb
The Lizard Lounge, 45 Xianqian Jie, Yangshuo
Tel: (0773) 881 1033
www.chinaclimb.com
Exciting programmes for all skill levels in the karst outcrops surrounding Yangshuo.

Yangshuo Village Inn
Moon Hill, Yangshuo
Tel: (0773) 877 8169
www.yangshuoguesthouse.com
This eco-friendly operation offers various activities (caving, hiking, kayaking, etc) – and it's also a pleasant place to stay. 🍴

FESTIVALS

China's southernmost regions have their own unique festivals, reflecting local beliefs and culture.

Water Splashing Festival
Mid-April and late July
Hainan Island
Seen as a cool way to ward off bad luck and ill-health, this event is celebrated with great gusto. The island's Li and Miao minorities celebrate at the end of July. 🍴

Matsu (Mazu) Festival
April/May

South China coastal regions
This exuberant festival venerates Matsu, goddess of the sea and sailors (known as Tin Hau in Hong Kong, A-Ma in Macau). 🍴

Gulangyu Piano Festival
July/August (even-numbered years)
Gulangyu Island, Xiamen, Fujian
A bi-annual celebration of the island's unique musical heritage.

Hong Kong & Macau

China's two Special Economic Zones, Hong Kong and Macau, are unlike anywhere else in China. Heir to both Chinese and British traditions, Hong Kong is densely packed, rich, go-ahead and yet colourful, vibrant and visitor-friendly. Macau is rather different, a vision of colonial Portugal overlaid with a veneer of very glitzy Chinese consumerism.

Hong Kong & Macau

 Population: Hong Kong: 7 million; Macau: 540,000

 Local dialling codes: Hong Kong: 852; Macau: 853

 Local tourist offices: Hong Kong Tourism Board; Star Ferry Pier, Tsim Sha Tsui; tel: 2508 1234; **www.discoverhongkong.com** Macau Government Tourist Office;

Largo do Senado; tel: 2833 3000; **www.macautourism.gov.mo**

 Main police station: Hong Kong: tel: 2860 2000, Macau: tel: 2573 3333

 Main post office: Hong Kong: Connaught Place, Central; Macau: Avenida de Almeida Ribeiro

Han Chinese have been living in and around Guangdong for at least two millennia, but Hong Kong remained a backwater until it was ceded to Britain after the First Opium War in 1842. Famously dismissed by Lord Palmerston as 'a barren island with hardly a house on it', the new colony nevertheless developed into a vital trading link between Europe and China, and by 1997, when it returned to China, it had become one of the richest cities in the world, with a population of more than 7 million. Its opium merchant founders, though undeniably men of vision, could hardly have foreseen this spectacular development. Where once there stood an obscure fishing village, today Hong Kong Island, its skyscrapers set against a spectacular mountain backdrop, is dominated by grand financial institutions and enormous, impressively futuristic buildings. It is also home to some beautiful walks and, on the southern side, some good beaches.

Macau, by contrast, established by the Portuguese in 1557, has long been overshadowed by Hong Kong and remained an almost forgotten colonial backwater until its return to China in 1999. In the past decade, fuelled by the rapid rise in disposable income amongst middle-class Chinese, it has become the Las Vegas of the East, a gambling mecca studded with excessively ostentatious casinos and resorts. Yet the Old City – with its unique Sino-Mediterranean architecture,

Portuguese restaurants and ancient banyan trees – has happily survived the onslaught.

Hong Kong

Situated on China's south coast and surrounded by the Pearl River Delta and South China Sea, Hong Kong is renowned for its glittering skyline and magnificent natural harbour. As the entry point into China for many tourists, it makes for a memorable introduction to Chinese culture and an easy transition to mainland China. Bustling and crowded, it offers fabulous food, exciting nightlife and unparalleled shopping, all set amid a vivid visual and cultural backdrop.

The International Finance Centre Two

Hong Kong skyline, harbour and Star Ferry

Central District

Central is Hong Kong's business and financial hub, squeezed between the harbour and the steep slopes of Victoria Peak. Big money and futuristic architecture mingle with elements of earlier times, with wayside hawkers dangling novelties and pirated goods while incense sticks smoulder by tiny shrines.

Just to the west of the **Star Ferry Pier** is the gigantic **International Finance Centre Two ❶** (usually abbreviated to IFC). At 420m (1,378ft) it was, until recently, Hong Kong's tallest building. Walkways connect the Star Ferry Pier and IFC to the rest of Central via **Exchange Square ❷**, home to the **Hong Kong Stock Exchange** and featuring a collection of sculptures by Henry Moore and Ju Ming in the adjacent plaza.

This part of Central is the financial district, home to the headquarters of several major banks. Two of these are housed in iconic buildings: facing Statue Square is Norman Foster's US$1 billion **Hongkong & Shanghai Bank Building ❸**; further east rise the sharp

Hong Kong and Macau

angles of the gleaming 368m (1,209ft) **Bank of China Tower ❹**, designed by Chinese-American architect I.M. Pei. The former **Supreme Court Building**, now housing the Legislative Council, is a rare survivor of classical architecture.

Inland from the Star Ferry, **Des Voeux Road** is a blur of traffic and people. Here the **Landmark Shopping Mall ❺** is dedicated to designer goods. Five floors surround a vast atrium, around which walkways connect with neighbouring buildings such as **Chater House**, flaunting yet more upmarket shops. The next east–west road away from the harbour, **Queen's Road Central**, marked the waterfront before land reclamation began in the 1850s. Running between its shops and emporia and those of Des Voeux Road are two narrow lanes, **Li Yuen Street East** and **Li Yuen**

Street West, lined with stalls and outlets selling clothing, fabrics and counterfeit designer fashion accessories. Behind Queen's Road Central the terrain rises steeply. **D'Aguilar Street** leads up to **Lan Kwai Fong**, which together with neighbouring **SoHo** is a prime nightlife area.

Above Lan Kwai Fong on Upper Albert Road, the former **Government House** faces the lush and appealing **Zoological and Botanical Gardens ❻** (daily 6am–7pm; free 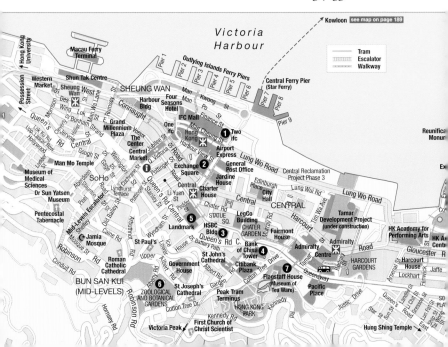), dating from 1864. In nearby **Hong Kong Park**, Flagstaff House is home to the **Museum of Tea Ware ❼** (Wed–Mon 10am–5pm; free), which is reputedly Hong Kong's oldest surviving colonial building. As Central's only large open space, the park is busy all day long, with t'ai chi practitioners first thing in the morning, joggers and office workers, and bridal parties posing against a backdrop of waterfalls and shrubs. The walk-through **aviary** (daily 9am–5pm; charge) is home to over 90 different species of birds from the rainforests of Southeast Asia.

Above Kennedy Road, the property prices rise as quickly as the altitude, culminating with the prestigious real estate around **Victoria Peak** (). Take the fantastically steep Peak Tram to the terminus at the **Peak Tower**, and admire the amazing views *(for more on the Peak, see pp.186–7)*.

Wan Chai and Causeway Bay

To the east of Central, **Wan Chai** and **Causeway Bay** are among the territory's most crowded and active districts, revealing the authentic flavour of modern Hong Kong. Despite its reputation, Wan Chai has lost much of its former risqué character, although there's still a lively bar and restaurant scene. Causeway Bay is one of Hong Kong's premier shopping districts.

On the Wan Chai harbour is the futuristic **Hong Kong Convention and Exhibition Centre** ❽, the venue for the Handover ceremony in 1997. Elevated walkways lead from here to **Lockhart Road**, a lively neighbourhood of bars and restaurants. To the south, **Queen's Road East** is home to the **Hung Shing Temple**, while the picturesque **Pak Tai Temple** is nearby on Stone Nullah Lane. Inland is **Happy Valley**, with its celebrated racecourse witness to Hong Kong's love for horse racing.

South Side

In contrast to the intensely built-up northern strip, the southern coast

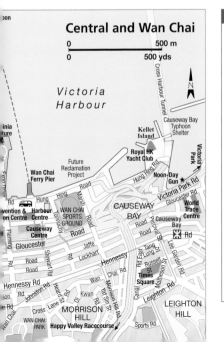

Central and Wan Chai

0 — 500 m
0 — 500 yds

Victoria Harbour

Cross Harbour Tunnel

N

Kellet Island

Causeway Bay Typhoon Shelter

Royal HK Yacht Club

Victoria Park

Wan Chai Ferry Pier

Future Reclamation Project

Noon-Day Gun ★

Hung Hing Road

Victoria Park Rd

Gloucester Rd

World Trade Centre

Convention & Exhibition Centre

Harbour Road

WAN CHAI SPORTS GROUND

CAUSEWAY BAY

Causeway Bay

MTR Rd

Causeway Centre

Gloucester Road

Jaffe Road

Hennessy Rd

Tang Lung St

Russell St

Times Square

Matheson St

Lee Garden Rd

Canal Rd

Leighton Rd

LEIGHTON HILL

Hennessy Rd

Lockhart Rd

Wan Chai Rd

Morrison Hill Rd

Cross Lane

Kwan

Yat Sin St

MORRISON HILL

WAN CHAI PARK

Happy Valley Racecourse

Sports Rd

One Country, Two Systems

Under the principle 'one country, two systems', Hong Kong is run on economic and political lines very different from those of the neighbouring mainland. A Special Economic Zone of Communist China, it is nevertheless one of the world's leading international financial centres, with a major capitalist service economy characterised by low taxation, free trade and minimal government intervention. The Hong Kong dollar is the ninth-most traded currency in the world, The Hong Kong Stock Exchange is the sixth-largest in the world, and as of 2010 Hong Kong's highly developed economy was ranked as the freest in the world by the Index of Economic Freedom for 15 consecutive years.

🚶 TOUR OF THE PEAK

Take the Peak Tram up to the dizzy heights above Central District. Gaze down on one of the world's most spectacular vistas before exploring the mountain on peaceful shady paths.

Victoria Peak

Hong Kong is so vibrant and intense that it is only natural to want to rise above it and get a clear view of the densely packed city and busy harbour. There is no better way to do this than to take the tram up Victoria Peak and revel in the clear air and unparalleled vista spread out below.

One of the world's steepest funicular railways, the Peak Tram has been in service since 1888. Its spectacular eight-minute ascent does not end at the summit of Victoria Peak (552m /1,811ft) but at the 1997-built Peak Tower (396m/1,300ft), from the top of which there are stunning 360-degree views of Hong Kong.

In the Tower

Indoor attractions include state-of-the-art virtual-reality rides and interactive games at the EA Experience, and Madame Tussaud's (charges for both), where you can pose with wax effigies of both Western and Asian celebrities. Throughout the Tower there are plenty of places to eat, snack and admire the view. Dining options range from refined Japanese or Cantonese cuisine and the elegant **Pearl on the Peak** to theme restaurants such as the Forrest Gump-inspired **Bubba Gump Shrimp Co**.

Across the road from the Tower is the Peak Galleria, less architecturally spectacular but with four floors of smart shops and restaurants, and a viewing platform. Also nearby is one of

The Peak Tram is one of the steepest funiculars in the world

Tips

- Distance: 4km (2½ miles)
- Time: Half a day
- START Peak Tram Lower Terminus, Garden Road, Central
- END Peak Tram Lower Terminus, Garden Road, Central
- Points to note: To reach the Peak Tram's lower terminus on Garden Road, walk up from Admiralty MTR through Hong Kong Park (this should take approximately 10 mins) or take bus 15C from the Central Ferry Piers via Connaught Road. Trams run approximately every 15 mins, 7am to midnight daily.

The view at night is mesmerising

the most relaxing places to take in the view, the Peak Lookout.

Around the Peak

Walk south from the Peak Tower to Lugard Road, the start of a gentle circular walk around Victoria Peak, which takes about an hour to complete. The tree-lined path winds past isolated colonial villas that rank among the most expensive and exclusive homes in the territory, a world apart from the high-rise metropolis below. On clear days (increasingly rare) you can see beyond the harbour and Kowloon to the Nine Dragon Ridge, which separates urban Hong Kong from the New Territories, and across to the hills stretching up to Shenzhen. Lugard Road merges with Harlech Road at a four-path junction and shaded picnic spot. The path winds east along the thickly wooded southern flank of the mountain back to the Peak Tower and the tram stop.

Up to the Top

Pause for refreshment at the Peak Lookout, then, if you're feeling sufficiently energetic, continue on up Mount Austin to the summit of Victoria Peak at 552m (1,811ft). On the way, make a detour into Victoria Peak Gardens for more elevated views and greenery. A path, the Governor's Walk, runs around the well-tended gardens, all that remains of the early governors' summer residence. Back by the tram station, enjoy a drink at **Café Deco** in the Galleria, watch the city light up as darkness settles, and have dinner

there before catching a tram back downhill.

Extending the Walk

If you feel like a longer hike, there are plenty more options from the Peak. From the crossing of Lugard Road and Harlech Road another path leads down into Pok Fulam Country Park, arriving after about 45 minutes' walk at Pok Fulam Reservoir, taking in the beautiful views en route. Continue on past ponies and retired racehorses at the Hong Kong Jockey Club Public Riding School to Pok Fulam Road, where you can catch a bus or taxi to Central or Aberdeen; or continue further along the Hong Kong Trail, which runs for 50km (30 miles) right cross Hong Kong Island. It is also possible to walk back to Central from the Peak Tower – just follow the marked paths downhill (allow around 45 minutes).

Tour of the Peak

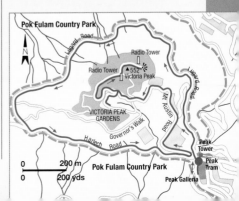

Neon lights and traffic jams in Tsim Sha Tsui

of Hong Kong Island is lined with beaches and countryside. **Aberdeen** has a character unlike any other town in Hong Kong, and is famous for its floating seafood restaurant. **Ocean Park** (daily 10am–6pm; charge ) offers a spectacular cable-car ride overlooking the South China Sea, the world's largest reef aquarium and numerous adventure rides. Further along the coast is bustling **Stanley Market** (daily 10am–7pm), a good place to shop for clothes, arts and crafts, and souvenirs. Also at Stanley is the **Maritime Museum** (Tue–Sun 10am– 6pm, Sat until 7pm; charge). The best beach is at **Repulse Bay**, but it gets very crowded on fine weekends.

Kowloon

Kowloon – the name means 'Nine Dragons' in Cantonese – starts at **Tsim Sha Tsui** (pronounced 'chim-sa-choi'). Although this is where the majority of tourists stay, Kowloon – particularly away from the main tourist areas around Nathan Road – is a little rougher round the edges than the glittering island across the harbour, and on the go later into the night.

From the **Star Ferry Pier** eastwards along the harbour, a waterfront promenade provides a great vantage point for viewing Hong Kong Island. At 8pm each night the promenade is the place to be for watching the Symphony of Lights, the world's largest sound-and-light show.

Next to the Clock Tower, the windowless **Hong Kong Cultural Centre** ❾ stages local and international

opera, classical music, theatre and dance. The complex abuts the **Hong Kong Space Museum** ❿ (Mon, Wed–Fri 1–9pm, Sat–Sun 10am–9pm; charge, but free on Wed), with IMAX movies on space travel and exhibitions of Chinese astronomical inventions. Opposite stands the venerable **Peninsula Hotel**.

At the bottom of **Nathan Road**, Kowloon's main north–south thoroughfare, hundreds of small tailors' shops, jewellers and electronics stores are crammed tightly together. Head north beyond shabby Chungking Mansions – home to curry houses and backpacker hostels – to reach the four minarets and large white marble dome of **Kowloon Mosque**. The pleasantly leafy expanse of **Kowloon Park** ⓫ lies beyond. Leading off to the east from the other side of Nathan Road, Carnarvon and Kimberly roads are lined with cheap clothing stores, while Knutsford Terrace – and further south, the areas around Peking and Mody roads – are the main nightlife zones.

Continue north on Nathan Road past Jordan MTR station, then turn left onto Kansu Street to reach the **Jade Market** (daily 9am–6pm), packed with stalls selling ornaments and jewellery. North from here is **Yau Ma Tei**. Shanghai Street leads north into an area once famous for its temples, but now renowned for the **Temple Street Night Market**. This area has numerous open-air restaurants, where oysters, prawns, clams, lobsters and fish are

Tsim Sha Tsui East Museums

Tsim Sha Tsui East is home to two of the best museums in Hong Kong. The **Hong Kong Science Museum** (Mon–Wed, Fri 1–9pm, Sat–Sun 10am–9pm; charge, but free on Wed) displays more than 500 scientific and technological interactive exhibits. Just opposite is the **Hong Kong Museum of History** (Mon, Wed–Sat 10am–6pm, Sun and public holidays 10am–7pm; charge, but free on Wed), charting the 6,000-year story of Hong Kong from Neolithic times right up to reunification.

laid out on beds of ice to tempt diners.

A sizeable area west of Yau Ma Tei has recently been reclaimed from the harbour. Here you will find Hong Kong's tallest building, the 118-storey, 484m (1,588ft) **International**

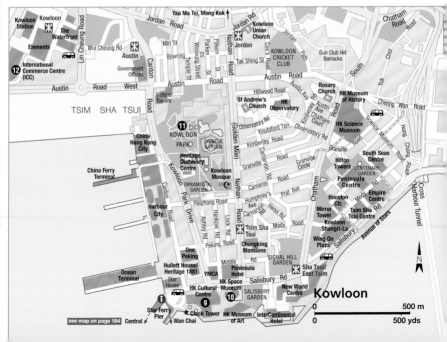

Commerce Centre ⑫ (ICC), located on top of the Kowloon MTR station (Airport Express line). Surrounded by luxury high-rise apartment towers, the viewing platform on the 100th floor is due to open at the end of 2010. The complex will also boast the world's highest hotel when the Ritz Carlton moves into the top 15 storeys in 2011.

Mong Kok is one of the most crowded, noisy and lively districts in the territory; long notorious for opium parlours and illegal gambling dens, it still has a certain reputation for sleaze. It is also known for several colourful street markets: the **Ladies Market** (noon–10.30pm), selling a mixture of clothes and souvenirs, the **Goldfish Market** (10am–6pm), the **Flower Market** (10am–6pm), and the **Yuen Po Street Bird Market** (7am–8pm), with hundreds of songbirds and beautiful birdcages for sale.

Further northeast, close to the old airport, is **Kowloon City Walled Park**. The infamous Walled City was a small area of the New Territories excluded from British control due to a legal loophole. The area deteriorated into a semi-lawless enclave which was left to its own governance. In 1987, with China's consent, 35,000 residents were resettled in housing estates, and the entire block was razed to the ground. The rather attractive park that replaced it, modelled on the Jiangnan garden style of the early Qing dynasty, has exhibits on the Walled City.

Due north, one of Kowloon's most colourful and popular places of worship, the **Wong Tai Sin Temple** (daily 7am–5.30pm; donation expected) on Lung Cheung Road, sits opposite an MTR station bearing the same name.

Hong Kong Transport

 Airport: Hong Kong International Airport is at Chep Lak Kok on the west coast of Lantau island. High-speed Airport Express Line trains (tel: 2881 8888; www.mtr.com.hk) travel to Hong Kong Station in Central in just 23 minutes, with stops at Tsing Yi and Kowloon. Trains depart every 10–12 minutes, from 6am–12.45am daily. One-way fare is HK$90–100. Taxis cost around HK$350 to Central, plus a HK$30 toll. There are also numerous shuttle buses going to locations across Kowloon and Hong Kong, and ferries to Macau and various points on the China coast.

 Metro: Hong Kong's MTR network is a model of efficiency and ease of use. Fares are low, but if you plan to use the network frequently, buy a multi-journey Octopus card (also valid on the Airport Express). Services operate between 6am and 1am.

 Trams and Buses: Hong Kong's clanking old trams are one of the sights of the city, and a great way to travel along Hong Kong Island's urban strip from Kennedy Town to Causeway Bay and beyond. Buses and minibuses operate everywhere and are fast and reliable. Buy tickets on board.

 Taxis: Hong Kong taxis are red in the city (Hong Kong Island and Kowloon), green in the New Territories and blue on Lantau. All are metered. It is possible to flag them down in the street, but at busy times you may have to go to a taxi rank. There are various surcharges for tunnels and harbour crossings.

The path leading up to the Ten Thousand Buddhas Monastery, Sha Tin

The temple hosts a row of fortune-tellers who can divine your future via the I Ching (Yijing) and other arcane Chinese oracles. East of Wong Tai Sin Temple and near Diamond Hill MTR station is the **Chi Lin Nunnery** (Thur–Tue 9am–4pm; donation expected), a reconstructed Buddhist temple complex.

New Territories and Islands

Hong Kong's New Territories are a contradiction. Some areas are as modern as anywhere else in Hong Kong, notably the New Towns such as Sha Tin and Yuen Long, but in other places time seems to have stood still. There is also scenic beauty aplenty, with fine beaches, lofty mountains and numerous beautiful islands.

New Territories

Sha Tin is one of Hong Kong's fastest-growing New Towns, with gargantuan housing projects occupying what was once an area of rice paddies. East of Sha Tin is the New Territories' most attractive area. In summer the beach at **Clear Water Bay** is packed with sunbathers, while nearby **Sai Kung Country Park** has wonderful scenery and a spectacular – if hard to access – stretch of sand at Tai Long Wan. **Sai Kung** itself is a seaside town known for its Chinese seafood restaurants; the most interesting part of the town is hidden behind **Tin Hau Temple**, where a maze of narrow alleyways leads past traditional herbalists and noodle shops interspersed with small family homes.

The western side of the Kowloon Peninsula has been reshaped by huge land-reclamation and construction projects that have redrawn the map, but still has points of interest. Surrounded by **Tsuen Wan** new town is **Sam Tung Uk Museum** (Wed–Mon

9am–5pm; free), a 200-year-old walled Hakka village complete with period furniture. In Tuen Mun, east of 583m (1,900ft) Castle Peak and adjacent to the Ching Chung light-rail station, is the huge **Ching Chung Koon Temple**, which serves as a repository for many Chinese art treasures, including 200 year-old lanterns and a jade seal over 1,000 years old.

Just outside **Yuen Long** are the walled villages of **Kam Tin**. The most popular for visitors is **Kat Hing Wai**. There are 400 people living here, all with the same surname, Tang. Built in the 1600s, it is a fortified village with walls 6m (20ft) thick, guardhouses on its four corners, slits for the arrows used in fighting off attackers, and a moat.

Lantau

Hong Kong's largest island, Lantau has changed somewhat since the construction of Chek Lap Kok Airport and the arrival of Disneyland, although much of the mountainous

The Big Buddha at Po Lin Monastery, Lantau

interior, southern and western coasts remain tranquil. Close to the airport, **Tung Chung** is an old fortress constructed in 1817. Its thick ramparts are still standing, as are six old cannons dating from the 19th century. Up on the hills above is the island's best-known attraction, the brightly painted **Po Lin Monastery** (daily 6am–6pm; free), with its giant Buddha. A cable car (🚠) links Tung Chung with the monastery, offering panoramic views. West of Po Lin is an excellent walking path that leads to **Yin Hing**, a monastery rich with traditional Buddhist paintings and statues. Lantau is also popular for its many long, smooth and often empty beaches.

The Dim Sum Tradition

In Hong Kong Chinese restaurants start serving dim sum as early as five in the morning. It has become a tradition for older people to gather to drink tea and eat dim sum after morning exercises, often while reading the newspapers. Consistent with this tradition, restaurants generally only serve dim sum until mid-afternoon. While dim sum ('touch the heart') was originally conceived as a snack, it has now become a staple of Chinese dining culture, especially in Hong Kong.

Cheung Chau

Cheung Chau is a fishing island, its curving harbour filled with boats of all sizes and shapes. Colourful **Pak Tai Temple** north of the pier is the island's most interesting shrine. The island is famous for its four-day Bun Festival, which usually takes place in May and is one of Hong Kong's most colourful events. Designed to placate the restless spirits of victims of pirates who once made their base here, giant bamboo towers covered with edible buns are erected in the courtyard of Pak Tai Temple.

Lamma

Lamma is rich in grassy hills and beautiful bays and renowned for its seafood restaurants. There are no high-rise buildings and no cars or proper roads – although the scene is spoilt somewhat by the presence of a huge power station on the western side of the island (albeit well hidden behind a large hill). The town of **Yung Shue Wan** at the north end of Lamma is home to many expat Westerners and has streets lined with small restaurants and bars. A concrete pathway runs much of the length of the island to the village of **Sok Kwu Wan**, which is famous for its seafood restaurants.

Macau

Since reunification with China, Macau has been developed into a leisure destination with elaborate and frankly rather vulgar resort and casino complexes designed to lure tourists from mainland China. A flavour of old Macau manages to survive in graceful old buildings redolent of Portugal, overlooking cobbled streets shaded by ancient banyan trees.

São Domingos church on Largo do Senado square, Macau

Macau City

Largo do Senado ❶ (Senate Square) is Macau's largest piazza; a handy tourist information centre is situated on the square (daily 9am–6pm). Nearby is the **Leal Senado ❷** (Loyal Senate; daily 9am–9pm) building, regarded by most as the best example of Portuguese architecture in Macau. At the northern end of the square is **São Domingos ❸** (St Dominic's), on the site of a chapel established here in 1597. The current church dates from the 17th century.

North from São Domingos stand the iconic ruins of **São Paulo ❹** (St Paul's; open access). Founded in 1557, it was destroyed by fire in 1835, and today only the classical facade remains. Overlooking São Paulo are the massive stone walls of the 17th-century **Fortaleza do Monte ❺** (Tue–Sun 7am–7pm; free ). The **Museum of Macau** (Tue–Sun 10am–6pm; charge) on the site of the fortress charts the history of the enclave.

South from Largo do Sendao are several Unesco historical sites including the Baroque-style **Santo Agostinho ❻** (St Augustine's). Further

The striking tower of the New Lisboa casino

Portuguese Outpost

In 1557 the Portuguese established the first European colony on Chinese soil in Macau, almost 300 years before the British claimed Hong Kong. It was the easternmost link in a string of Portuguese outposts that included Goa, Sri Lanka and East Timor. For much of its history it remained a quiet colonial backwater, overshadowed by the wealth and power of nearby Hong Kong. It was reunited with China in 1999.

south on Rua de São Lourenço is the elegant pale-yellow church of **São Lourenço ❼** (St Lawrence's), surrounded by a small garden.

Near to the foot of Barra Hill stands **A-Ma Temple ❽** (daily 7am–6pm), the oldest temple in the territory, dating back 600 years to the Ming dynasty. It is dedicated to Tin Hau, the patron goddess of fishermen. Close by is the **Maritime Museum ❾** (Wed–Mon 10am–5.30pm; charge, but free on Sun), tracing the maritime history of the South China Sea.

The 338m (1,110ft) **Macau Tower ❿** features an observation deck (daily 10am–9pm; charge) with 360-degree views of Macau; a look through its glass floors is not recommended for vertigo sufferers.

Further north, the **Colina da Guia**, the highest point in Macau, is crowned by the impressive **Guia Fortress and Lighthouse ⓫** (daily 9am–5pm; free). A cable car links the hilltop with a pleasant small park and aviary at **Flora Garden** below (daily 7am–6pm 🏛).

Cotai and Coloane

The two outlying islands of **Taipa** and **Coloane** are now linked by **Cotai**, a strip of reclaimed land that is home to the colossal **Venetian Casino Complex** and several other Vegas-style resort-casinos. In **Taipa village** some fragments of Old Macau survive. The **Taipa Houses Museum** (Tue–Sun 9.30am–5pm; charge) consists of five beautifully restored houses, while local history and developments are recorded in the **Museum of Taipa and Coloane History** (Tue–Sun 10am–6pm; charge).

For a taste of southern Europe, visit **Coloane village**. Its atractive Portuguese-style village square is crowded with restaurant tables at weekends and holidays.

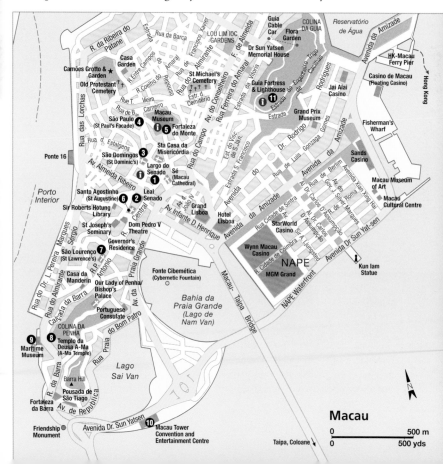

Macau

0   500 m
0   500 yds

ACCOMMODATION

Hong Kong's five-star hotels rank alongside the best in the world and there are plenty of them. Budget accommodation, on the other hand, is difficult to find especially on Hong Kong Island. Kowloon still has a few cheap options, the notorious Chungking Mansions being one. There's plenty of mid-range choice, but sometimes rooms can be cramped, although usually they are perfectly comfortable. Macau has a wide choice of accommodation, and prices are usually slightly lower than Hong Kong. If you are travelling from Hong Kong to get to Macau it's worth stepping into a travel agent before leaving, as they can often get substantial discounts on accommodation in Macau.

Hong Kong

Bishop Lei International House
4 Robinson Road, Mid-Levels,
Hong Kong Island
Tel: (852) 2868 0828
www.bishopleihtl.com
Run by Hong Kong's Catholic Diocese, this conveniently located property, only a few minutes' walk from both Admiralty and Central MTR stations, includes an exercise room and outdoor swimming pool. **$$**

Cosmic Guesthouse
12/F, Block A1, A2, F1 and F4,
Mirador Mansion, 54–64 Nathan Road,
Tsim Sha Tsui, Kowloon
Tel: (852) 2369 6669
www.cosmicguesthouse.com
A bargain right in the heart of busy Tsim Sha Tsui, the Cosmic boasts large, spotlessly clean rooms and a friendly atmosphere. All rooms have TV and en suite bathroom. **$**

The Excelsior
281 Gloucester Road, Causeway Bay,
Hong Kong Island
Tel: (852) 2894 8888
www.mandarinoriental.com/excelsior
Overlooking the Yacht Club and Victoria Harbour, this 864-room hotel with 22 immaculate suites provides a wide variety of excellent facilities and a pleasant environment. Great shopping opportunities nearby. **$$$$**

Four Seasons
8 Finance Street, Central, Hong Kong Island
Tel: (852) 3196 8899
www.fourseasons.com
Elegant and refined in the most postmodern manner, this sensational hotel uses harbour views to great effect and offers perfectly appointed rooms in either contemporary Chinese fashion or cultured Western style. **$$$$$**

InterContinental Hong Kong
18 Salisbury Road, Tsim Sha Tsui, Kowloon
Tel: (852) 2721 1211
www.interconti.com
Perfectly situated on the waterfront and close to the Star Ferry and Kowloon's prime entertainment district. The views across Victoria Harbour, especially at night, are spectacular. First-class facilities include a

The Peninsula and the Intercontinental

poolside spa, fitness centre and some of the best restaurants in Hong Kong. **$$$$$**

Island Shangri-La Pacific Place
Supreme Court Road, Central,
Hong Kong Island
Tel: (852) 2877 3838
www.shangri-la.com
Soaring 56 floors above Victoria Harbour, this glamorous retreat with its elegant decor, helpful staff, exceptional restaurants and beautiful, spacious rooms is the last word in state-of-the-art luxury. **$$$$$**

Kings de Nathan
473 Nathan Road, Yau Ma Tei, Kowloon
Tel: (852) 2780 1281
www.kingsdenathan.com
This comfortable budget hotel is just off Nathan Road and right next to the Temple Street Night Market. The Yau Ma Tei MTR station is very close, making access to anywhere in Hong Kong very straightforward. **$$**

Langham Place Hotel
555 Shanghai Street, Mong Kok, Kowloon
Tel: (852) 3552 3388
www.hongkong.langhamplacehotels.com
Not what you'd normally expect to find in the Mong Kok area, but the Langham is leading a revival of the district with its classy rooms all fitted out with state-of-the-art technology and stunning works of art. **$$$$**

Mandarin Oriental
5 Connaught Road, Central,
Hong Kong Island
Tel: (852) 2522 0111
www.mandarinoriental.com
Still going strong after more than four decades of impeccable service, the Mandarin Oriental has consistently ranked among the world's top hotels. Beautifully decorated throughout the property and very conveniently located in the heart of Central. **$$$$$**

The Peninsula
Salisbury Road, Tsim Sha Tsui, Kowloon
Tel: (852) 2920 2888
www.peninsula.com

Opulence at the Mandarin Oriental

This, the grand old dame of Hong Kong's hospitality business, has been a byword for impeccable service and colonial-style grandeur since 1928. Its eight restaurants and superb attention to detail make it one of the world's great hotels. **$$$$$**

Regal Airport
9 Cheong Tat Road, Chek Lap Kok, Lantau
Tel: (852) 2286 8888
www.regalhotel.com
If you've got an early flight then this is the best place to stay. It's directly connected to Hong Kong International Airport. Facilities include six restaurants and a splendid spa. **$$$**

Macau
Lisboa
2–4 Avenida de Lisboa
Tel: (853) 2888 3888
www.hotellisboa.com
This iconic hotel, famous for its casino, provides over 1,000 rooms each with ornate décor, an amazing number of very good restaurants and superb entertainment. **$$$$**

Pousada de Colôane
Estrada de Cheoc Van, Coloane
Tel: (853) 2888 2143
www.hotelpcoloane.com.mo

The Casino Lisboa

You might be forgiven for thinking you were somewhere in sunny Portugal at this quiet, family-run venture, overlooking Cheoc Van Beach. With its 30 double rooms decorated in typical Portuguese style, swimming pool and fine Portuguese restaurant, this makes for a relaxing break. **$$**

Pousada de São Tiago
Avenida da Republica
Tel: (853) 2837 8111
www.saotiago.com.mo
Part of the 17th-century Fortaleza de Barra, the Pousada de São Tiago is now one of Macau's most important historical buildings. This Portuguese-style inn features 23 rooms all embellished with dark wood, white linen, chandeliers and marble. **$$$$**

The Westin Resort
1918 Estrada de Hac Sá, Coloane
Tel: (853) 2887 1111
www.starwoodhotels.com
The perfect getaway from busy Macau and Hong Kong, this peaceful, secluded eight-storey resort hotel on Coloane Island provides spacious rooms with private outdoor terraces overlooking the beach. **$$$$$**

RESTAURANTS

Being one of the world's truly great cities, it's no surprise that as far as food is concerned everything is available in Hong Kong, although often at a price. On Hong Kong Island the main restaurant and street-food areas are around Lan Kwai Fong and SoHo

Restaurant Price Categories
Prices are for a full meal per person, with one drink
**$** = below HK$ 150
**$$** = HK$ 150–300
**$$$** = HK$ 300–500
**$$$$** = over HK$ 500

in Central and around Lockhart Road in Wan Chai. Kowloon is overflowing with places to eat, and in Tsim Sha Tsui most of the action is focused on the cluster of streets south of Kowloon Park, and also around Mody Road a little further to the east. Macau doesn't have the breadth of restaurant possibilities that Hong Kong has, but it does have some excellent local cuisine which features elements from the far-flung Portuguese colonies of old, combining with those from the European homeland.

Hong Kong
Bubba Gump Shrimp Co.
Level 3, The Peak Tower, 128 Peak Road, Hong Kong Island
Tel: (852) 2849 2867
www.bubbagump.com
As the name suggests, it's every conceivable shrimp creation known to man at this all-American theme restaurant. Portions

are large, and the selection of smoothies, quenchers and cocktails second to none. **$$**

Café Deco
Level 1–2, Peak Galleria, 118 Peak Road, Hong Kong Island
Tel: (852) 2849 5111
www.cafedecogroup.com
This, the largest restaurant atop The Peak,

serves a wide selection of international dishes with a strong emphasis on seafood, steaks and Thai favourites. There's some cool live jazz most evenings and stunning city and harbour views. **$$–$$$**

Gaddi's
The Peninsula, Salisbury Road,
Tsim Sha Tsui, Kowloon
Tel: (852) 2315 3171
On the go since 1953, Gaddi's has rightly built up an impeccable reputation within Hong Kong high society. French haute cuisine presented with flawless style and in splendid surroundings; unfortunately a jacket and tie are required at dinner. **$$$$**

Harlan's
Shop 2075, Podium Level Two, IFC Mall, 8 Finance Street, Central, Hong Kong Island
Tel: (852) 2805 0566
First-class International cooking featuring fine ingredients prepared with panache. Its long, delightfully exciting menu aims to attract Hong Kong's jet set and usually succeeds. **$$$$**

Hoi King Heen
Basement 2, InterContinental Grand Stanford Hotel, 70 Mody Road,
Tsim Sha Tsui, Kowloon
Tel: (852) 2731 2883
Believed by many to be the finest Cantonese cuisine in Hong Kong, quite a claim indeed, but the Hoi King Heen delivers time after time with its endlessly creative and novel adaptations of Cantonese classics. **$$$**

Hunan Garden
3/F, The Forum, Exchange Square, Central, Hong Kong Island
Tel: (852) 2868 2880
As the name implies, it's Hunan food that is on offer here. Hunanese cuisine is known for its sour and spicy flavours. Try the Fortune Hunan Ham or the braised bean curd with shredded meat and chilli. **$$**

Hutong
28/F, 1 Peking Road, Tsim Sha Tsui,

Kowloon
Tel: (852) 3428 8342
www.aqua.com.hk
An amazing location with stunning views of the Hong Kong skyline coupled with an intoxicating mix of antique and up-to-date Chinese decor. The menu offers classic northern Chinese cuisine with a contemporary twist. **$$$**

Luk Yu Teahouse
24–26 Stanley Street, Central,
Hong Kong Island
Tel: (852) 2523 5464
The city's most famous traditional Cantonese teahouse can be found in the heart of Central serving superlative dim sum. A hangout for HK's tycoons and criminal kingpins, it's a fun place to be. **$$**

Mak's Noodle
77 Wellington Street, Central,
Hong Kong Island
Tel: (852) 2854 3810
Mak's distinguished clients have included Chiang Kai-shek back in the 1960s, and the essential wonton recipe has remained the same ever since. If wonton noodle soup is what you are after, then this is the place to sample it. **$**

Peking Restaurant
1/F, 227 Nathan Road, Jordan, Kowloon
Tel: (852) 2730 1315
Authentic Beijing dishes, including the ever-popular Peking duck with pancakes, are

Mak's Noodles

served at this nostalgic blast from the past. The place is not much to look at inside, but the quality of the food makes up for this. **$$**

Le Tire-Bouchon
45A Graham Street, Central,
Hong Kong Island
Tel: (852) 2523 5499
www.letirebouchon.com.hk
This long-standing, traditional French restaurant serves a series of classic dishes including Tournedos Rossini and duck-liver salad, and some good wines from a comprehensive cellar. **$$$**

Yung Kee
32–40 Wellington Street, Central,
Hong Kong Island
Tel: (852) 2522 1624
www.yungkee.com.hk
With its rags-to-riches history spanning more than seven decades, the Yung Kee is truly a Hong Kong institution. Classic Cantonese dishes include its famed roasted goose with preserved trotter and a variety of abalone soups. **$$**

Macau
Fernando's
9 Praia Hac Sa, Coloane
Tel: (853) 2888 2264
A Macau institution, this beachfront eatery on Coloane Island serves wonderful Portuguese/Macanese specialities and a range of Portuguese wine. **$$**

A Lorcha
289 Rua Almirante Sérgio
Tel: (853) 2831 3193
This family-run place offers Portuguese classics like pork with clams, *feijoada* (pork-and-bean stew), Macanese seafood rice and *serradura* ("sawdust pudding"). **$$**

Tung Yee Heen
1/F, Grand Lapa Macau, 956–1110
Avenida da Amizade
Tel: (853) 8793 3821
With a fine mix of classic and contemporary Cantonese cuisine, a relaxed setting and attentive service, the Tung Yee Heen is one of Macau's best Chinese restaurants. Renowned for its all-day dim sum. **$$–$$$**

Le Tire-Bouchon

NIGHTLIFE

One of the liveliest cities in the world for nightlife, Hong Kong offers a limitless choice of venues, from seedy back alley bars to plush, state-of-the-art mega-clubs. There's also a thriving live music scene, one that's steadily grown over the last decade. The Lan Kwai Fong area in Central has every type of bar imaginable. Macau has recently been gaining a reputation for a lively bar, club and live-music scene, and the southern end of the NAPE (Novos Aterros do Porto Exterior or New Reclaimed Land of the Outer Harbour) is one of the best areas to go searching.

Hong Kong

Aqua Spirit
29–30/F, 1 Peking Road, Tsim Sha Tsui, Kowloon
Tel: (852) 3427 2288
A great place to watch the 8pm Hong Kong skyline light show.

Club 97
9 Lan Kwai Fong, Central, Hong Kong Island
Tel: (852) 2186 1897
It's been around for more than a quarter of a century, but still one of the hippest clubs in town.

Gecko Lounge
Lower Ground Floor, Ezra Lane, Lower Hollywood Road, Hong Kong Island
Tel: (852) 2537 4680
It's mostly live jazz on weekday evenings at this comfortable wine bar.

Joe Bananas
23 Luard Road, Wan Chai, Hong Kong Island
Tel: (852) 2529 1811
The clientele varies throughout the day, but this still remains one of the most popular bars in Hong Kong.

New Wally Matt Lounge
Ground Floor, 5A Humphrey's Avenue, Tsim Sha Tsui, Kowloon
Tel: (852) 2721 2568
One of the gay community's favourite hangouts, but everyone's welcome.

Rick's Café
Ground Floor, Luna Centre, 53–59 Kimberley Road, Tsim Sha Tsui, Kowloon
Tel: (852) 2311 2255

Aqua Spirit

This tried and trusted dance venue becomes an excited, heaving mass after midnight.

Macau

Moonwalker Bar
Ground Floor, Vista Magnifica Court Building, Avenida Doutor Sun Yat Sen
Tel: (853) 2875 1326
Excellent Filipino bands and singers will play any and all requests; they seem to know every popular rock song ever written.

Old Taipa Tavern
21 Rua de Negociantes, Taipa
Tel: (853) 2882 5221
This well-known watering hole in Old Taipa gets especially busy on Friday and Saturday nights, when the very good resident band gets going.

Oparium Café
'The Docks', Avenida Baia Nova
Tel: (853) 2883 8425
Plenty of loud, sweaty rock music played here, attracting a fairly young crowd.

Listings

ENTERTAINMENT

Bustling, cosmopolitan Hong Kong boasts an array of world-class entertainment and live-performance venues, attracting a pleasing mix of mainland Chinese and Western acts. Hong Kongers love to gamble, and with two busy horse-racing tracks – Happy Valley on Hong Kong Island and Sha Tin in the New Territories – they rarely miss an opportunity.

With Macau's status as gambling capital of Asia the territory has been able to raise its profile in other forms of entertainment. It can now rival Hong Kong's international pulling power and welcomes artists and performers from all over the world.

Hong Kong

AsiaWorld Arena
AsiaWorld-Expo, Hong Kong International Airport, Lantau
Tel: (852) 3606 8888
www.asiaworld-expo.com.hk
Hong Kong's largest indoor venue plays host to numerous international artists and sports events. Famous Western artists to have performed here include Elton John, Linkin Park and Kylie Minogue.

Happy Valley Race Course
Wong Nai Chung Road, Pau Ma Tei, Hong Kong Island
Tel: (852) 2966 8111
www.hkjc.com
Even if you've never been to a racecourse in your life, this place is worth a visit just to see the excitable local punters.

Hong Kong Cultural Centre
10 Salisbury Road, Tsim Sha Tsui, Kowloon
Tel: (852) 2414 5555
www.hkculturalcentre.gov.hk
Home to the Hong Kong Philharmonic Orchestra, the centre welcomes orchestras, ballet companies and dramatic productions from far and wide.

Hong Kong International Film Festival Society
21/F, Millennium City 3, 370 Kwun Tong Road, Kowloon
Tel: (852) 2970 3300
www.hkiff.org.hk
In April the society organises this well-respected film festival to showcase new

Witness the excitement at Happy Valley Race Course on Wednesday evenings

talent from all corners of the globe and screens movies at 11 theatres across Hong Kong. Other cinematic events are arranged throughout the year.

Macau

Macau Cultural Centre
Avenida Xian Xing Hai
Tel: (853) 2870 0699
www.ccm.gov.mo
Connected to the Macau Museum of Modern Art, the Centre is Macau's premier cultural events venue with regular theatre, concert and opera performances.

Sands Macao
Largo de Monte Carlo
Tel: (853) 2888 3388
www.sands.com.mo
Apart from being one of Macau's top casinos, the Sands Macao provides plenty of live entertainment every night.

SPORTS AND ACTIVITIES

Having never really been associated with sport of any kind, Hong Kong has recently forged a reputation for hosting some important world sporting events, including the annual Rugby World Cup Sevens, Hong Kong Marathon and the Hong Kong Open Golf Championship. Hong Kong has some excellent hiking trails, including the Dragon's Back on Hong Kong Island and the Maclehose Trail in the New Territories. For water sports, popular Repulse Bay on the southern side of Hong Kong Island is the place to head, with wakeboarding, windsurfing and scuba-diving much in evidence. Macau's Grand Prix is a major event.

Hong Kong

Hong Kong Sevens
Hong Kong Stadium
Tel: (852) 2504 8311
www.hksevens.com
For rugby enthusiasts this annual seven-a-side tournament held every March has become the world's leading event of its kind.

Macau

Macau Grand Prix
Central Macau
Tel: (853) 8796 2268
www.macau.grandprix.gov.mo
This annual event, taking place every November, attracts both car and motorcycle racers to its exciting street circuit.

FESTIVALS AND EVENTS

Hong Kong and Macau follow most of the usual traditional Chinese festivals, both religious and secular. In Hong Kong there is usually some event going on, whether it be of the sporting variety or an art happening. It's best to check the local listings magazines such as *HK Magazine* to find out what's happening and where.

Chinese New Year
January/February
Hong Kong's most lively and colourful festival, with fireworks exploding over the harbour and noisy street parades; look out for the vibrant flower markets. 👫

Cheung Chau Bun Festival
April/May
Praya, Cheung Chau Island, Hong Kong
www.cheungchau.org
Originally a religious festival held to drive away evil spirits, these days this week-long festival has become a riot of colourful parades and noisy musicians. 👫

Dragon Boat Festival
May/June
Hong Kong and Macau
Races are held at many different sites, but the most exciting can be seen at Stanley on Hong Kong Island's south coast.

Mid-Autum Festival (Moon Festival)
September/October
Hong Kong
Commemorating an uprising against the Mongols in the 14th century, locals consume 'moon cakes' and make their way to the city's parks to light paper lanterns; Victoria Park in Causeway Bay is especially renowned. 👫

Procession of the Passion of Christ
February/March
Central Macau
A uniquely Macau event, this Christian religious celebration involves the moving of a statue of Christ from St Augustine's Church to Macau Cathedral. After spending the night at the cathedral the image is borne through the streets to much fanfare.

Southwest China

No part of China is more culturally or scenically diverse, and more rewarding to explore, than the Southwest. Home to a colourful plethora of peoples and traditions, this largely mountainous area extends from the rice terraces of Guizhou to the tropical backwaters of Xishuangbanna, and from the urban charms of Chengdu to the isolated splendour of Yunnan's Himalayan wilderness.

Chengdu

 Population: 3.3 million in urban area; 10.2 million in greater Chengdu

 Local dialling code: 028

 Airport: Shuangliu Airport is 16km (10 miles) southwest of downtown.

 Trains: There are four main railway stations in Chengdu, but the two most useful stations for long-distance trains are the North Railway Station, 4km (2½ miles) north of the city centre, and the South Railway Station, 5km (3 miles) south of the centre.

 Buses: The three main bus stations are: Xinnanmen, not far south of the city centre; Chadianzi, northwest of the centre; and the North Bus Station, near the North Railway Station. All three serve destinations all over Sichuan and beyond. Xinnanmen serves Emeishan, Leshan and Jiuzhaigou.

 Key areas: Chunxi Lu, a little over 500m/yds to the east of Tianfu Square, is Chengdu's main shopping and restaurant street. Near Wuhou Temple, southwest of the city centre, Jinli Lu is a re-creation of an ancient commercial area and houses a number of good restaurants and fascinating shops.

Southwest China is enduringly popular with visitors because it offers a wide variety of cultures and cuisines unmatched elsewhere in this vast country. The dominant people remain Han Chinese, but closer to the southern and western frontiers a complex and dazzling ethnic tapestry unfolds, set amidst some of the most spectacular scenery imaginable. Far from the traditional Chinese heartlands north of the Yangzi River, much of the region is redolent of neighbouring Southeast Asia and Tibet, a world away from Beijing and Shanghai.

The great province of Sichuan is famous across China for its distinctively spicy cuisine and fertile rice fields, while in the west are wild mountains and forested valleys.

To the south and east, Guizhou is one of China's poorest and least developed provinces, but the relative difficulty of travel is amply rewarded by the colourful dress and distinctive architecture of the region's ethnic groups.

Finally, in the far southwest, Yunnan offers unparalleled opportunities for exploring minority cultures from the Dai to the Tibetan, as well as wonderful old cities like Dali and Lijiang. Set against a backdrop of snow-clad peaks, the province also offers some of the best trekking in China.

Sichuan

Sichuan is almost a country in its own right. With an area of 485,000 sq km (187,000 sq miles) it's as big as California, but the population of 85 million is about three times larger. It's also one of China's richest provinces. While Chengdu and the east is overwhelmingly Han Chinese, the mountainous west is home to 15 recognised ethnic minority groups, including a sizeable Tibetan population. Surrounded by mountains, the heart of Sichuan is the fertile Red Basin, a region capable of

Shops in Chengdu

producing three rice crops a year and supporting one of the most densely populated rural areas on earth.

Chengdu

Sichuan's pleasant capital, **Chengdu** ❶, is more than 2,000 years old, has a population of around 3.3 million in the city proper, and around 10.2 million in greater Chengdu, making it China's fifth-largest city. In contrast to some other Chinese urban centres, and despite rapid redevelopment, it has managed to preserve an atmosphere that evokes a sense of history. Balmy, often misty weather keeps the city green and full of flowers year-round.

Built on flat terrain, Chengdu can easily be explored on foot or by bicycle. It has something of a southern feel, with pleasantly colourful old streets lined by scores of small, traditional shops and restaurants, and pavements that remain crowded until late with traders, buyers and people out for an evening stroll. The commercial centre is located around Dongfeng Lu and Dong Dajie, southeast of the large Mao statue and the Exhibition Hall, and Tianfu Square subway station.

A large Mao statue dominates Chengdu's Tianfu Square

Chengdu has several attractive temple complexes. The **Temple of Marquis Wu** (Wuhousi; daily 7am–7pm; charge) is a complex of halls and gardens in the southern suburbs built to commemorate an honoured minister. Known in his lifetime (AD181–234) as Zhugeliang, he was posthumously ennobled for his role in unifying the region and developing its economy and culture.

Chinese literary pilgrims are drawn to another of the city's historic sites, the **Thatched Cottage of Dufu** (Dufucaotang; daily 7am–7pm; charge), a shrine, museum and park at the spot where the poet of the Tang dynasty lived in exile from the capital for several years. Dufu lived from 712 to 770 and wrote more than 1,400 poems, many of them regarded as the greatest in the Chinese literary canon.

The city's most popular Daoist temple, **Green Goat Temple** (Qingyanggong; daily 6am–8pm; charge) is a lively, garish complex where two bronze 'good luck' goats at the main altar have been rubbed smooth by worshippers seeking their fortunes. Close by is the centre of Zen (Chan) Buddhism in Sichuan, the 1,300-year-old **Wenshu Temple** (daily 8.30am–5.30pm; charge), which maintains its own company of woodcarvers, a vegetarian restaurant and outdoor teahouse.

It is worth visiting the **Tomb of Wang Jian** (Wangjian Mu; daily 9am–5.30pm; charge), in the northwest of the city. Wang Jian was a general during the last days of Tang emperor Lizhu's rule in the early 10th century. The building has three burial chambers. The centre chamber contains a sarcophagus between two rows of stone figures.

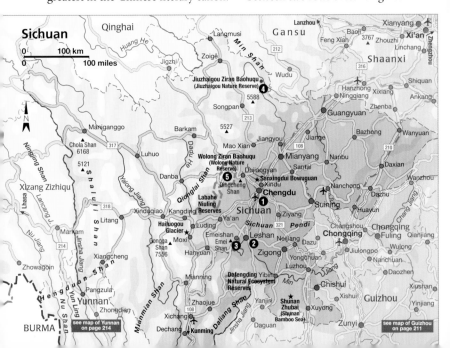

Green Goat Temple, Chengdu

Chengdu has a long tradition as China's pre-eminent city of teahouses. Many still operate along the north bank of the **Jin River**, serving covered cups of flower tea. Customers linger at courtyard tables, watching trinket vendors and pipe and tobacco salesmen ply their trade along the river promenade, or sometimes enjoying free performances of Sichuan opera or instrumental music.

Another restful spot is **Wangjianglou** (the River Viewing Pavilion Park; daily 6am–9pm; free ) along the south bank of the Jin River. More than 100 kinds of bamboo grow here. As in other traditional Chengdu parks, there are pavilions and towers, rock gardens, ponds and shady paths.

Around Chengdu

Sichuan is famous for its giant pandas. If you can't venture out to Wolong Reserve (see p.209) in the mountains of western Sichuan, the best place to see these gentle-looking beasts in something resembling the wilds is 11km (7 miles) northeast of central Chengdu, at the **Giant Panda Breeding Research Base** (daily 8am–6pm; charge), where more than 40 pandas have free run of some 30 hectares (80 acres) of bamboo groves. There's also a panda museum here. In closer confines, the **Chengdu Zoo** (daily 7.30am–6pm summer, 8am–5-.30pm winter; charge) has more resident pandas than any other zoo in the world.

Chengdu's largest and most renowned religious monument, located 28km (17 miles) north of the city, is the **Divine Light Monastery** (Baoguangsi; daily 8am–5pm; charge). The most photographed element of this sprawling establishment is the stupa, a slightly

Southwest China

Kuan Alley

Kuan Xiangzi (Kuan Alley), around five minutes' walk northwest of Renmin Park, has been restored to its Qing-dynasty glory, and while there is something contrived about its appearance, it is difficult not to appreciate this small pocket of Old Chengdu, which elsewhere is very much a 20th-century Chinese city. There are no notable attractions, but it makes for an interesting stroll, and there are restaurants and tea shops to linger in.

Leshan's Great Buddha

crooked 13-level pagoda. It was built of stone at the end of the Tang dynasty, replacing an ancient wooden pagoda on the same spot.

Qingcheng Shan, 64km (40 miles) west of Chengdu, is a Daoist peak and a great place for hiking amid a mountainous landscape of temples, caves and lakes. To the north is **Qingcheng Hou Shan**, a further expanse of rambling walks and trails. There is a steep but not too strenuous hike to the summit, where it's possible to shelter in temple tea gardens and take in the views.

Leshan

From the provincial capital of Chengdu, a three-hour drive on a modern expressway leads to the town of **Leshan ❷**, the base for visits to a monumental riverside Buddha, as well as to **Emei Shan**, one of the four sacred mountains of Chinese Buddhism.

Boats ferry visitors from Leshan to the site of the **Great Buddha** (Dafo; daily; charge 🅼). The giant figure overlooks the confluence of two rivers, the Dadu He and Min He, and is simply astonishing in scale. Carved from the cliff-side in the 8th century, its height is 71m (233ft), and the statue's feet are so large that 100 people are said to be able to sit on each one. The boats tie up some distance from the Buddha and passengers climb from the shore to **Dark Green Temple** (Wuyousi), with magnificent views of the surrounding rivers and nearby Mount Emei, the gate to Western Paradise.

Emei Shan

Dubbed 'the fairest mountain among the fair mountains of the world', **Emei Shan ❸** reaches an altitude of 3,099m (10,167ft). Daoists began erecting temples around the area in the 2nd century AD, but as Buddhism gained popularity from the 6th century onwards, the mountain became a sacred place of Buddhism. It has been a major pilgrimage centre for centuries, and although buses and cable cars now ascend the heights, the old-fashioned method of walking up is worth the effort for the fit.

At the foot of Mount Emei, foreshadowing the many temples ahead, are the **Crouching Tiger Temple** (Fuhusi) and the 16th-century **Loyalty to Country Temple** (Baoguosi). The latter is filled with plant life, housing small gardens and bonsai. It also contains the **Shengji Bell**, reputedly the second-largest in China (after

Emei Sunrise

Many visitors have time to spend only a night on the mountain in one of the basic inns before being driven to the summit before dawn to see the famous sunrise. At sunrise on **Golden Peak** (Jinding) pilgrims and tourists alike gather in the hope of seeing an optical phenomenon called 'Buddha's Halo'. Here you can see your shadow perfectly framed inside a bright halo formed when the morning sea of clouds is penetrated by the rising sun.

Beijing's Great Bell), and inscribed with Buddhist scriptures.

For more on Emei Shan, *see p.38.*

North and West Sichuan

In the northwest of Sichuan, close to the border with Gansu province and some 500km (300 miles) from Chengdu, **Jiuzhaigou Nature Reserve ❹** (Jiuzhaigou Ziran Baohuqu; charge) is a natural wonderland. The park was opened in 1978, and abounds with luxuriant montane forests, grassy steppes, brilliantly clear blue lakes, rivers and waterfalls, all set amid high mountains and peaks covered with eternal snow.

The **Wolong Nature Reserve ❺** (Wolong Ziran Baohuqu; charge), a 200,000-hectare (500,000-acre) sanctuary for the giant panda some 140km (85 miles) northwest of Chengdu, is three hours by bus from Dujiangyan, or four hours direct from Chengdu. It's by no means always easy to catch sight of the rather shy pandas in the wild, but a group of about 20 are on view in a smaller enclosure.

A macaque on Emei Shan. The monkeys can be aggressive

Cable cars asced to Hongfu Si above Guiyang

The setting is indeed lovely, and the wooded hills and hiking trails make the reserve a very worthwhile trip. The remote, pristine forests are a sanctuary for exotic wildlife such as snow leopards and golden monkeys, as well as pandas.

Guizhou

Guizhou is one of China's poorest provinces and remains a relatively unvisited backwater. Much of the landscape is mountainous and difficult to cultivate, and this has meant that Han Chinese settlement was both little and arrived relatively late. Much of the province is home to a fascinating ethnic patchwork of minorities. Guzhou is associated in Han Chinese minds with rural poverty and *maotai*, a potent and high-priced liquor fermented from sorghum, but it is also a welcoming and rewarding destination.

Guiyang

Guizhou's modest capital, **Guiyang** ❻, has little to entice visitors, but is strategically located in the centre of the province and makes a convenient base for setting out to explore surrounding areas. The **Provincial Museum** (Guizhousheng Bowuguan; Tue–Sun 9–11.30am, 1–4pm; charge) on Beijing Lu has displays relating to the province's ethnic tribes, and **Qianling Shan Park** to the west is a pleasant, wooded area of hills topped by the attractive Buddhist **Hongfu Si** (Hongfu Temple; charge), accessed by steps or cable car.

Minority Villages

Most visitors travel to Guizhou with the primary objective of visiting the ethnic minority areas. The far southeast of the province is home to the Dong minority, known for their construction of elaborate wooden towers and covered bridges, as well as for distinctive indigo-dyed clothing. The town of **Zhaoxing** ❼ is the main centre of the Dong people, and is a fascinating place with five impressive drum towers and five wind-and-rain bridges. Most other buildings in the town are of traditional wooden three-storey design.

The regional capital of **Kaili** ❽, connected to Guiyang by train and ringed by Miao minority villages, is a convenient base equipped with hotels, banks, restaurants and internet cafés. Ask at your hotel or at CITS in the Yingpanpo Binguan (Yingpanpo Hotel) for maps and details of the local festivals and markets in surrounding villages – it's best to try to coincide your exploration with festival dates if possible. The lovely Miao hamlets of **Matang**, **Chong'an** and **Shibing** to the north, as well as

Xijiang to the southeast, are among the many fascinating settlements spread across the hilly countryside around Kaili. *For more on ethnic minorities in the area see pp.47–9.*

Elsewhere in Guizhou

Zunyi ❾ is an undistinguished industrial town 165km (102 miles) north of Guiyang with significant revolutionary credentials. In 1935, roughly halfway through the epic Long March, the Communist army held a meeting here that paved the way for Mao Zedong to assume control of the Chinese Communist Party (CCP), and approved his strategy of promoting rural revolt among the peasantry. The event is memorialised at the **Zunyi Conference Site** (Zunyi Huiyizhi; daily 8.30am–5pm; charge) and the **Long March Museum** (Changzheng

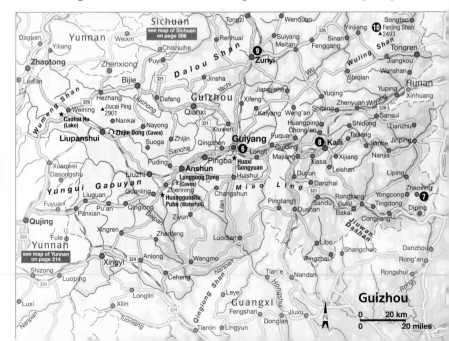

Bowuguan; daily 8.30am–5pm; charge).

In a karst region 100km (60 miles) southwest of Guiyang, the town of **Anshun** is primarily a place from which to reach the **Huangguoshu Waterfalls** and the **Longgong Caves**. Minibuses regularly depart Anshun for Huangguoshu, 45km (28 miles) to the southwest. If possible, time a trip to the 68m (223ft) falls during the summer rainy season, when the floodwaters are at their most forceful.

Tongren, near the border with Hunan to the east, is the access point to the mountain and forest reserve of **Fanjing Shan ⑩**, renowned for its diverse fauna and flora. Home to several rare species including the golden, or snub-nosed, monkey and the giant salamander, the reserve also sustains a remarkable diversity of trees and medicinal plants.

Further west in the mountainous **Wumeng Shan** region near Yunnan province, **Caohai Hu** (Caohai Lake) is a celebrated freshwater lake at the centre of a beautiful nature reserve.

Yunnan

China's southwestern province of Yunnan spans a huge region of forest and mountain linking Southeast Asia with the Tibetan Plateau. Consequently, there is an abundance of interest in the form of ancient cities, minorities and wonderful scenery.

Kunming

Yunnan's capital, **Kunming ⑪**, sits close to the northern shore of Dian Chi Lake at an altitude of 1,900m (6,200ft), an elevation that ensures pleasant temperatures throughout the year. The city has developed rapidly as

Downtown Kunming

a business centre for China's burgeoning economic links with Southeast Asia, and has unfortunately lost much of its former charm and atmosphere in the process. Nonetheless, there are some attractive neighbourhoods, and the climate remains wonderfully refreshing, with springlike temperatures for most of the year.

Kunming did not become an important centre until the Yuan dynasty (1271–1368), when the Mongols made it the provincial capital. Still, the city's most ancient landmarks, the two 13-tier pagodas **Xisi Ta** (West Pagoda) and **Dongsi Ta** (East Pagoda) in the southeast quarter (both 9am–8.30pm; charge) date back to the Tang dynasty. Nearby, the **Yunnan Provincial Museum** (Yunnansheng Bowuguan; daily 9am–5pm; charge) on Wuyi Lu has an extensive collection of ancient bronzes and informative exhibitions on Yunnan's minority cultures.

Yuantong Si (daily 8am–5pm; charge), in the northern part of town, has been Kunming's most important Buddhist temple for more than 1,000

Kunming's ancient Xisi Ta (West Pagoda)

years. A short walk west from here lies **Cui Hu** (Green Lake), with ornate boats on the water and bright pavilions on its shores. Slightly further afield, the city's most arresting historical attraction is **Tanhua Si** (daily 8am–5pm; charge), a lofty pagoda located approximately 3km (2 miles) east of the city centre down Renmin Lu. A climb to the seventh floor

Kunming

Population: 3.2 million (urban area)

Local dialling code: 0871

Airport: Wujiaba Airport is 9km (5½ miles) southeast of downtown.

Trains: Kunming is served by two railway stations. The main station is at the southern end of Beijing Lu, with routes to most major cities in China. Kunming North Railway Station at the north end of Beijing Lu services routes in southwest China and, when in operation, Vietnam.

Buses: The main long-distance bus station is located on Beijing Lu, a short walk north of the main railway station. Buses run to most destinations in Yunnan and adjacent provinces. The other main bus station is 2km (1¼ miles) to the east.

Key areas: For shopping and upmarket restaurants head for the area near the Flower and Bird Market on Zhengyi Lu. The University and Cui Hu (Green Lake) Park area northwest of downtown is filled with bars and cafés.

The Western Hills

The **Western Hills** (Xishan), which rise to 2,350m (7,700ft) immediately to the west of Kunming and Dianchi Lake, make an interesting day trip from the city, though the crowds can be overwhelming, particularly during Chinese holidays. The hike to the various temples provides some great viewing opportunities across Lake Dianchi. At 340 sq km (130 sq miles), this is one of the largest freshwater lakes in China, extending for 40km (25 miles) end to end.

provides splendid views across the city and nearby lake.

Around Kunming

With the beautiful **Western Hills** (Xi Shan; *see above*) and Dianchi Lake right on its doorstep, there

are numerous possibilities for day trips from Kunming. **Qiongzhu Si** (Bamboo Temple; daily 8am–6pm; charge) lies 13km (8 miles) north-west of the city. It is a hall of 500 idiosyncratic 19th-century statues of Buddhist saints and disciples, each uniquely sculpted to embody a Buddhist virtue. **Heilongtan** (Black Dragon Pool; daily 8am–6pm; charge), 11km (7 miles) north of the city, is more conventional. It is flanked by a Ming-era Daoist temple, and the nearby botanical garden has a collection of camellias, rhododendrons and azaleas.

At the summit of Phoenix Song mountain, 7km (4 miles) northeast of Kunming, stands **Jin Dian** (Golden Temple; daily 8am–5pm; charge), which is actually furnished with walls, columns, rafters and altars made of

Shilin, the Stone Forest

gilded bronze rather than gold. A cable car leads to the nearby **World Horticultural Garden** (Shiboguan; daily 8am–5pm; charge), with masses of colourful local blooms, rare trees and a tea plantation.

Some 126km (78 miles) southeast of Kunming and reached by frequent minibuses is the region's most famous tourist attraction, the **Stone Forest** ⑫ (Shilin; daily 8.30am–7pm; charge 🏠). This 'forest' of limestone rock formations is served by colourfully clad ethnic minority tour guides and is enduringly popular with Han Chinese tour groups.

Dali and Er Hai Lake

Dali ⑬ is an ancient walled city some 400km (250 miles) west of Kunming, and one of the most picturesque destinations in all of China. The surroundings could hardly be more spectacular,

with Er Hai Lake to the east and the steep Cangshan mountains to the west. Best of all are the local people, who are mostly members of the Bai ethnic minority, an outgoing people who treat travellers with generous hospitality.

The town, capital of the Bai Autonomous Region, is surrounded by a restored city wall with monumental gates at all four cardinal points. Within the walls are a number of tile-roofed shops and houses, many of which serve as souvenir shops, private travel agencies, hostels, and small cafés serving a truly international mix of generally inexpensive cuisines. Also within the Old City, it is possible to see some local historical treasures at the small **Dali Museum** (Dali Bowuguan; daily 8am–5.30pm; charge) on Cangping Lu.

Dali's most spectacular and famous attraction is the **San Ta Si** (Three Pagodas; daily 8am–7pm; charge), which are around 1km (⅔ mile) north of town. Well over 1,000 years old, the central tower is 69m (230ft) tall and has 16 tiers, while its two flanking structures have 10 tiers and stand at 43m (141ft) high.

Café life in the Old Town is one of Dali's chief delights, but there are also a number of attractions well worth visiting. **Er Hai Lake**, the second-largest in Yunnan, is a 30-minute walk from town, and its main village, **Caicun**, is a maze of unpaved alleys and mud houses. From this point ferries cross the lake to more remote villages. On the eastern shore of the lake is the picturesque Bai village of **Wase**, and just offshore is **Little Putuo Island** (Xiao Putuo Dao), named for the the mythical mountain home of Guanyin, the Chinese Goddess of Compassion. There is a statue of the goddess, who is said to guard the lake's waters, in a temple on the island.

Rounding the northern tip of the lake, the road passes **Hudie Quan** (Butterfly Spring), once a charming pond shaded by an acacia tree and locally famed for its butterflies, but now an obligatory stop on the tour-bus lake circuit, generally filled with tourists and souvenir-sellers. Nearby **Zhoucheng** is an attractive Bai village that looks much as Dali must have three decades ago. The women still sport traditional red vests and bonnet-like headwear, and the buildings are also traditional, mostly in courtyard style, with upturned eaves, and fronted by cobbled streets.

For a walking tour of Dali and Er Hai Lake, see pp.218–19.

Lijiang's picturesque Old Town

Lijiang and around

The ethnic diversity and scenery for which Yunnan is famous reaches its zenith in the northwest, both in terms of culture and – literally – in terms of geography. The Naxi and Tibetan ethnic groups form the majority in these parts, and cherish their own strong cultural traditions and written languages. The landscapes are magnificent, with the surrounding Himalayan peaks reaching altitudes of over 6,000m (20,000ft).

The prime draw is the beguiling, if increasingly touristy, town of **Lijiang** ❹. With its backdrop of snow-capped mountains, rich local culture, twisting cobblestone lanes and vaulted stone footbridges crossing rushing canals of clear water, it's not hard to see why it has become such a popular tourist attraction – and now connected by air with Beijing and Shanghai.

The settlement here has flourished for centuries as a caravan stop on the road to Tibet. It was Kublai Khan who gave the town its name – which means 'beautiful river' – when his troops passed through here in 1253, and the Mongols also introduced Chinese music to the Naxi, giving birth to a musical tradition which still flourishes today.

The 750-year-old Naxi district of Old Lijiang is largely traffic-free and perfect for walking. Tiny food shops and small groceries are built into the fronts of the old Naxi homes, with carved wooden doors leading into central courtyards of intricate tile work. Massive wooden posts frame the scene, and stairways wind to the lattice-work balconies, while vaulted stone bridges cross swift-flowing streams of crystal-clear water. A must-see in this area is the **Mu Family**

Cultural Revival

In recent years Lijiang has seen a Naxi cultural revival which flourishes in the arts, particularly music. The 23 Tang-dynasty songs which Kublai Khan bequeathed to the Naxi were lost elsewhere in China but have survived here. Performances of this music, augmented with Naxi folk music, take place each evening at the **Naxi Orchestra Hall** (Naxi Yinle Ting; charge), opposite the Dongba Palace on Dong Da Jie.

Mansion Ⓐ (Mufu; 8.30am–6pm; charge), a re-creation of a Ming-style palace commemorating the rule of the Mu family, who governed Lijiang in the name of the Yuan, Ming and Qing emperors from 1254 until 1723.

A short walk north the Old City, following the stream, is the **Black Dragon Pool Park Ⓑ** (Heilongtan Gongyuan; daily 6.30am–8.30pm; charge). This park, where willow and

Zhongdian, in Yunnan's Tibetan northwest, has been fancifully renamed 'Shangri-la'

🚲 TOUR OF DALI

Dali's compact size and relative lack of traffic make it ideal for a day tour by bicycle. Both the ancient town and the surrounding countryside are wonderfully picturesque.

The tour starts at **Nanmen**, also called Tonghaimen, which is just one of four gateways – one for each of the cardinal points – piercing the well-preserved city walls of old Dali. Surmounted by an elegant double-tiered keep with classical upswept eaves, the gate has been recently restored and is easily accessible by well-maintained stone steps. Once atop the walls, a short stroll to the southwest bastion offers fine views of nearby **Yita Si** (Lone Pagoda Temple) to the west, while the keep itself offers spectacular views across the city and along Wenxian Lu towards Beimen (North Gate).

Dali's South Gate (Nanmen)

From Nanmen, head north along Wenxian Lu to the **Dali Museum** (Dali Bowuguan), set in a building that was once the minor palace of Du Wenxiu, the ethnic Hui Muslim leader of the great anti-Qing Panthay Rebellion (1856–73). Today it houses a collection of local, largely Bai-minority artefacts, as well as displays of local marble crafts.

Beyond Dali Museum, continue north past **Wuhualou**, the grey-marble Qing-dynasty 'Tower of Five Glories', to **Yu'er Gongyuan**, a small and tranquil public park favoured by pensioners and practitioners of *t'ai chi*. If you need a rest, stop over at **An Cafe Beag** at 215 Renmin Road en route – great all-day breakfasts as well as Chinese food.

Turn left (west) along Yu'er Lu, noting several traditional herb and spice shops on the south side of the narrow road, before leaving the walled city by **Ximen** (West Gate, also called Cangshanmen).

Tips

- Distance: 18km (11 miles)
- Time: A full day
- START: South Gate (Nanmen)
  END: Huguo Lu
- Points to note: Be sure to take water, sunscreen and a hat, particularly in summer, as it is easy to become dehydrated and sunburned. Food is not a problem, as Dali is full of small eateries and snack shops. Make sure to ask for a bicycle lock when renting a bike. It's always worth starting early to beat the rush, and give yourself time off in the middle of the day for lunch – and to avoid the heat.

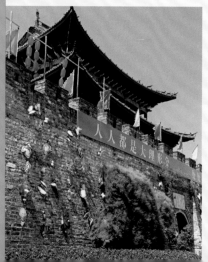

San Ta Si, the Three Pagodas

Turn right (north) along the wider and busier Yunnan-Xizang Lu, and cycle for around 2km (1¼ miles) to **San Ta Si Gongyuan**, or Three Pagodas Park.

San Ta Si, the famed Three Pagodas, are Dali's best-known sight, and draw a considerable number of visitors despite the high entry price. The tall, elegantly fluted towers are considered to be representative of the Nanzhao Kingdom that flourished here in around AD900, 400 years before the Mongol conquest and Yunnan's subsequent incorporation into China.

From San Ta Si head back south along Yunnan-Xizang Lu as far as the northwestern bastion of the Old City, then head east along the outside of the city walls, stopping at **Beimen** (North Gate, also called Anyuanmen), which marks the northern end of Fuxing Lu,

the walking street that leads directly through the Old Town centre and back to Nanmen. It's worth climbing the stairs to this keep, too, both for the views across the city, and for a refreshing cup of local green tea served at the small café set in the keep.

Leave Beimen and continue east along the city wall as far as the northeast bastion. Here turn northeast along the narrow road leading to **Er Hai Lake**, some 5km (3 miles) distant. Once at **Caicun village** on the lakeshore, it's possible to take a boat across the lake to **Wase village** on the east shore, visiting the pretty little temple on **Xiao Putuo Dao** or Little Putuo Island en route. The marble tomb of the rebel leader Du Wenxiu is tucked away in a small lane just south of Caicun – ask a local for **Du Wenxiu Ling**.

From Caicun head back to Dali Old City by the same route you came on, but at the northeastern bastion head south along the city walls to **Dongmen** (East Gate) and head west along Remin Lu to the junction with Wenxian Lu, which you crossed earlier in the day. Just north of here is **Huguo Lu**, the heart of the city's tourist area. Nearby, at 22 Remin Lu, **Bird Bar** is something of a Dali institution, with cool drinks and good food – a great place to relax after your tour.

Dali Tour

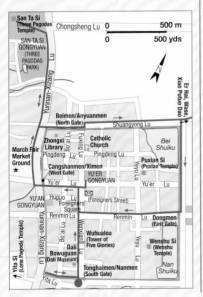

San Ta Si (Three Pagodas Temple)
Chongsheng Lu
0   500 m
0   500 yds

SAN TA SI GONGYUAN (THREE PAGODAS PARK)

Yunnan-Xizang Lu

N

Er Hai, Wase, Xiao Putuo Dao

Beimen/Anyuanmen (North Gate)

Shuangyong Lu

Zhongxi Library
Fuxing Lu
Catholic Church
Bei Shuiku
Pingdeng Lu
Pingdeng Lu
Puxian Si (Puxian Temple)

March Fair Market Ground ★

Cangshanmen/Ximen (West Gate)
YU'ER GONGYUAN
Yiyu Lu

Yu'er Lu
Yu'er Lu

YU'AN GONGYUAN
Huguo Lu
Foreigners' Square
(Foreigners' Street)

Renmin Lu
Renmin Lu
Dongmen (East Gate)

Yunnan-Xizang Lu
Bo'ai Lu
Wenxian Lu
Wuhualou (Tower of Five Glories)
Wenshu Si (Wenshu Temple)

Yita Si (Lone Pagoda Temple)
Dali Bowuguan (Dali Museum)
Tonghaimen/Nanmen (South Gate)
Nan Shuiku

Yita Lu

chestnut trees line pathways which meander around a small lake, is home to some architectural treasures, notably the 17th-century **Five Phoenix Hall** Ⓒ (Wufeng Lou). This is one of the best places in town to admire the magnificent view of Jade Dragon Snow Mountain, whose jagged snowy profile is reflected in the water of the lake. Close by the rear gate of the park is the **Dongba Research Institute** Ⓓ (Dongba Wenhua Yanjiushi; 8.30am–6pm; charge), with unique exhibits of the ritual clothing worn by shamans of the Naxi religion, as well as a collection of painted scrolls and manuscripts written in pictographic script.

For closer views of **Jade Dragon Snow Mountain** Ⓔ (Yulong Xue Shan), travel north to **Baishuitai**. From here a pony ride or cable car carries visitors up the steep slope to **Yunshanping**, an idyllic meadow at 3,300m (10,830ft). Further north, the spectacular 5,400m (17,720ft) Haba peak towers opposite Yulongxue Shan. The 16km (10-mile) narrow valley between the two massifs, cut by the surging waters of the Jinsha Jiang, is called **Tiger Leaping Gorge** Ⓕ (Hutiaoxia), so named because at its narrowest point a fleeing tiger is supposed to have escaped a hunter by leaping across the 30m (100ft) gap to safety. There can be few more spectacular sights in all of China.

The Far Northwest

The small town of **Zhongdian** ⑮, 200km (120 miles) north of Lijiang, is distinctively Tibetan. Now officially renamed 'Shangri La', the Old Town is located on the southern edge of Zhongdian, and is full of new restaurants and cafés, souvenir shops and rustic guesthouses. Muddy alleys have become cobbled lanes, and Tibetan folk dancing takes place around a central square in the evenings, with visitors enthusiastically joining the circle. On a hill behind the Old Town, a 23m (70ft) golden prayer wheel is pushed by locals, launching their prayers heavenwards. Beside the spiritual benefits, the spot offers a fine view over the Old Town.

About 5km (3 miles) north of town, in the village of Songzhanling, lies **Songsenling Monastery** (Sumtseling Gompa in Tibetan; daily 7am–4pm; charge), a sprawling complex of the Gelugpa (Yellow Hat) sect. The road from Zhongdian to Deqin consists of 190km (115 miles) of fantastic mountain scenery. Reaching altitudes of 4,000m (13,200ft), with sharp curves and precipitous drops, it is an incredible engineering feat and an unforgettable journey.

Southern Yunnan

Southern Yunnan, known as Xishuangbanna, is about as different from the northwest of the province as could possibly be imagined. Here China's international frontier marches with Burma and Thailand, Laos and Vietnam, and the climate is tropical. It's a region of hilly tree plantations and tropical fruits such as mangoes, bananas and coconuts.

Once a sleepy town lining the Mekong River (known in Chinese as the Lancang Jiang), the regional capital

Jinghong ⑯ is today a rapidly expanding city of close to half a million inhabitants. The main reason to visit is to explore the surrounding minority villages (bike trips are a good option), but the city itself is not without appeal.

The **Tropical Flower and Plants Garden** (Redai Huahuiyuan; daily 7.30am–6pm; charge) off Jinghong Xilu has more than 1,000 examples of Xishuangbanna's luxuriant native flora. About 1km (⅔ mile) southwest of the centre is the **National Minorities Park** (Mengbalanaxi Gongyuan; daily 8.30am–6pm, Wed and Sat until 11pm; charge), which offers tourist-oriented song-and-dance performances in a very pleasant setting.

The **Jinsha Night Market** (Jinsha Yeshichang), beneath the Xishuangbanna Bridge, is a lively place in the evenings, with numerous food stalls

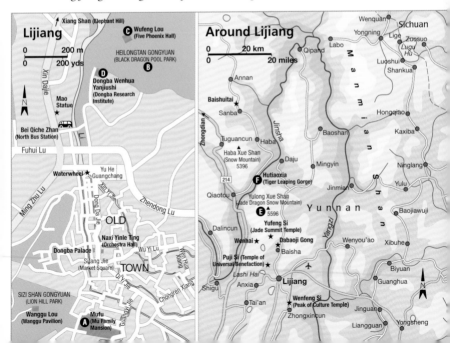

and even an outdoor massage area. Just north of Manting Park is **Wat Manting** (charge), a large Buddhist temple complete with traditional Thai-style sloping roofs.

Sanchahe Nature Reserve (Sanchahe Ziran Baohuqu), some 50km (30 miles) north of Jinghong, is one of Xishuangbanna's most popular attractions. The forest is home to a few wild elephants, and there is a cable-car ride through the treetops.

Ganlanba (also known as Menghan) is a nondescript town on the Mekong around an hour southeast of Jinghong, the heart of a fertile plain that has long been an important agricultural zone for the Dai people. The chief attraction is the **Dai Minority Park** (Daizu Yuan; 24 hours; charge). It is often crowded with tourists enjoying the daily shows of singing, dancing and water-splashing. The largest of the temples in the cultural village, **Chunman Dafo Si**, has a fine gold-leaf stupa.

The route south to **Mengla** traverses one of the wilder parts of **Xishuangbanna** (see left), an area which has retained some of its forest cover. A quiet road runs north from Mengla through picturesque scenery to Yaoqu; some 25km (16 miles) along the way is the **Bupan Aerial Walkway** (Bupan Wangtianshu Kongzhong Suodao), strung between the trees approximately 40m (130ft) above the ground, allowing for close-up views of the forest canopy.

A road heads west from Jinghong to the small town of **Damenglong** close to the Burmese border. The chief attraction in the vicinity is the **Bamboo Shoot Pagoda** (Manfeilong Sun Ta). Founded in 1204, it is the most celebrated stupa in Xishuangbanna, and is distinguished by a revered Buddha footprint.

The Dai Minority Park at Buddhist New Year

ACCOMMODATION

Fittingly, Chengdu, as one of China's largest and more cosmopolitan cities, has a fine selection of accommodation. The centre of the city and down towards the southern section are the best places to search.

Guizhou is less well endowed with hotels, but comfortable accommodation can be found in both Guiyang and Kaili.

Yunnan, with its huge influx of visitors over the last few years, enjoys a wide selection of excellent accommodation. Some of China's best boutique hotels can be found in this area.

Accommodation Price Categories

Prices are for a standard double room in peak season

$ = under Rmb300
$$ = Rmb300–600
$$$ = Rmb600–1,000
$$$$ = Over Rmb1,000

Chengdu

Kempinski Hotel
42 Renmin Nan Lu, Section 4
Tel: (028) 8526 9999
www.kempinski.com
Perfectly situated in the heart of Chengdu's dining and nightlife area, the 483-room all-modern Kempinski is five minutes south of the Central Business District by taxi. **$$$$**

Mix Hostel
23 Xinghui Xi Lu, Renjia Wan
Tel: (028) 8322 2271
www.mixhostel.com
With its cheery decor and very helpful staff, Mix has become a popular choice for budget travellers in Chengdu. The rooms are well appointed and clean – almost bearing out the hostel's claim that it has three-star standards at backpacker prices. **$**

Sheraton Chengdu Lido
15 Section 1, Renmin Zhong Lu
Tel: (028) 8676 8999
www.sheraton.com/chengdu
This luxurious and highly impressive hotel offers the most outstanding service and facilities in town, with attractive rooms, three restaurants and an indoor pool. **$$$**

Dali

Asia Star Hotel Dali
South Gate, Dali Old Town
Tel: (0872) 267 9999
Relatively luxurious accommodation just 15 minutes' walk from the Old Town. The well-appointed rooms have either mountain or lake views. **$$**

Jim's Tibetan Hotel
13 Yuxiao Lu, Yu Yuan Xiang 4
Tel: (0872) 267 7824
www.jims-tibetan-hotel.com
Jim's is probably the best-value accommodation in Dali and is located just outside the South Gate, within easy walking distance of the cafés and bars. The Tibetan Bai-themed rooms are tasteful and clean. **$**

Landscape Hotel
96 Yuer Lu
Tel: (0872) 266 6188
www.landscapehotel.com
A refurbished, historic Bai-minority house in the heart of the Old City is the setting for this atmospheric boutique hotel. It has a lovely

Mix Hostel , Chengdu

courtyard, which is illuminated with lanterns at night. **$$**

Emei Shan
Teddy Bear Hotel
43 Baoguo Lu
Tel: (0833) 559 0135
www.teddybear.com.cn
This hostel has good rooms, excellent food, and is the perfect spot to plan an assault on Sichuan's most famous mountain – the staff can help you plan the trip. **$**

Guiyang
Guizhou Park Hotel
66 Beijing Lu
Tel: (0851) 682 3888
This 400-room, four-star hotel, beside Quinling Park, has a bowling alley, disco and billiard room. Restaurants offer both Chinese and Western cuisine. **$$**

Jinghong
Crown Hotel
Jinghong Nan Lu
Tel: (0691) 212 8888
Good-value mid-range hotel, with a pool surrounded by palm trees, Dai-influenced architecture and attractive wooden floors. **$$**

Kaili
Gui Tai Hotel
Beijing Dong Lu
Tel: (0855) 826 9888
Located in the heart of the city, this hotel offers satellite TV and a complimentary breakfast including coffee, toast and jam, a combination not so common in China. **$**

Kunming
Camellia Hotel
96 Dongfeng Dong Lu
Tel: (0871) 316 3000
www.camelliahotelkunming.cn
Quiet, yet well-located, hotel close to the heart of the city. Rooms are basic, but clean and comfortable, and there is also dormitory accommodation for impecunious backpackers. Most of the staff speak at least some English and are very helpful. **$**

Kai Wah Plaza International Hotel
157 Beijing Lu
Tel: (0871) 356 2828
www.kaiwahplaza.com/en
A 525-room tower in the heart of the downtown area (not far from the railway station and around 15 minutes by taxi from the airport), the hotel has five executive floors and a good selection of de-luxe and superior rooms. **$$**

Kunming Green Lake Hotel
6 Cuihu Nan Lu
Tel: (0871) 515 8888
With a beautiful lakeside location, this former state guesthouse has been tastefully refurbished to retain much of its character. Though there is some room for improvement, it remains one of Kunming's more charming hotels and has a good location.

Lijiang
Banyan Tree Lijiang
Yuerong Lu, Shuhe,
Gucheng District
Tel: (0888) 533 1111
www.banyantree.com/en/lijiang
Situated north of town, this stylish resort property has 55 individual pavilions, a spa, swimming pool and a view of the Jade Dragon Snow Mountain. Tasteful, immaculate and exclusive. **$$$$**

First Bend Inn
43 Mishi Xiang, Xinyi Jie
Tel: (0888) 518 1688
This budget hotel in the centre of Lijiang's Old Town has plenty of character. The rooms are comfortable, and there's a lovely courtyard and helpful, informative staff, making it particularly good value. **$**

Grand Lijiang Hotel
Xinyi Jie
Tel: (0888) 512 0888
Located next to the waterwheel square on the way to Black Dagon Pool, the four-star Grand Lijiang is a modern, well-equipped hotel with fine views across to the mountains and the Old Town plus a pleasant restaurant beside the stream. **$$**

RESTAURANTS

Sichuanese food is famous for its fiery flavours, and is one of the most popular of Chinese cuisines. Chengdu, at the heart of Sichuan, perhaps more than any other city in China, has a strong sense of self-identity, reflected in the pride it takes in its food. Food in Guizhou is hot and spicy. In the towns and cities and at festivals, kebab, noodle and hotpot stalls provide cheap and interesting dining opportunities. Yunnanese cuisine features a diverse range of flavours, reflecting influences from Indo-China and Burma as well as Sichuan and the Hui Muslim community.

Chengdu

Cacaja Indian 印度菜菜餐厅
18 Binjiang Zhong Lu
Tel: (028) 8667 0399
This small, unobtrusive place situated next to the Binjiang Hotel serves some very good North Indian cuisine. There are also plenty of vegetarian dishes, including an excellent palak paneer. **$**

Gongguan Cai 公官菜
41 Qinghua Lu
Close to the northern entrance to Du Fu's Cottage, Gongguan Cai translates as 'official's food', and is a very well-respected place for quality Sichuan cuisine. **$$**

Huangcheng Laoma 皇城老媽
20 Erhuan Lu, Section 3
Tel: (028) 8513 9999
Quite possibly the king of Chengdu's hotpot restaurants – though the name means 'mother of the imperial city' – this four-storey restaurant not only takes hotpot cuisine to a new level, it also has impeccable Chengdu-themed decor. **$$**

Dali

An Caife Beag 休閒咖啡
215 Renmin Lu
Tel: (0872) 267 0783
This cosy café (the name is Gaelic, and translates as 'a small café') on lower Renmin Lu serves Dali's best breakfasts, and also has a selection of Chinese dishes. **$**

Guiyang

Miao Jia Meishi Yuan 苗家美石园
433 Baoshan Bei Lu
Tel: (0851) 675 1451
This Miao-minority establishment serves a heady mixture of hot and sour dishes along with a number of less spicy regular Chinese numbers. The spicy spareribs with deep-fried potatoes are an outstanding mix. **$$**

Siheyuan 四合院
79 Qianling Xi Lu
Tel: (0851) 682 5419
Siheyaun is a grand place to sample Guizhou's spicy Qian cuisine. The finely wrapped rice-flour pancakes known as Siwawa are a delight and an excellent example of the artistic side of Qian cuisine. **$**

Deep-fried tofu

Jinghong

Mei Mei's 美美咖啡
Manting Lu
Tel: (0691) 212 7324
An intimate café in the centre of town with internet access and books in English. Mei Mei's is the original backpackers' hangout, with all the reference material you could wish for on getting around Xishuangbanna, plus standard banana-pancake fare. **$**

Kaili

Bobo Simple Restaurant 美食家餐厅
Beijing Dong Lu
Tel: (0851) 826 0299
Bobo offers an extensive choice of Chinese cuisine and a great line-up of fresh juices and other beverages. The entrance is down a side street off the main road. **$**

Kunming

1910 La Gare du Sud 火车南站
8 Houxin Jie
Tel: (0871) 316 9486
Colonial-style restaurant serving Yunnan specialities and Chinese cuisine staples. An English menu is available. It's best to go by taxi (ask for *huoche nanzhan canting*), as it is difficult to find even with a map. **$$**

Salvador's 萨尔瓦多咖啡馆
76 Wenlin Jie, Wenhua Xiang
Tel: (0871) 536 3525
Situated on 'Culture Alley' in the university district, Salvador's is a foreign-run café and restaurant with excellent Tex-Mex cuisine, home-made ice cream and free internet. **$$**

Lijiang

Lamu's House of Tibet 西藏屋西餐馆
56 Jishan Xiang, Xinyi Jie
Tel: (0888) 511 5776
This long-time travellers' favourite serves a mixture of Naxi, Tibetan and Chinese dishes along with some Western standards, and is particularly fêted for its desserts. **$**

Sakura Café 樱花园
123 Cuiwen Xiang
Tel: (0888) 518 7619
The speciality here is Korean food, and both the hotpots and Korean barbecue are good. Japanese, Chinese and Western dishes are also served. Set by a picturesque canal. **$$**

ACTIVITIES AND TOURS

Sichuan, Guizhou and Yunnan offer endless possibilities for hikers. The holy mountain of Emei Shan makes for a fabulous hike and the wilds of western Sichuan will appeal to the more adventurous hiker and require proper preparation and equipment. Hikes between villages in Guizhou's east and south are also rewarding. In Yunnan, Xishuangbanna is perfect for treks between villages as well as more hardcore jungle treks, best organised through tour operators in Jinghong. Tours can be arranged through hotels, but it is possible to explore the area independently.

Adventure Activities

Camellia Hotel
96 Dongfeng Donglu, Kunming
Tel: (0871) 316 6388
www.camelliahotelkunming.cn
This excellent travel agent has years of experience and offers a vast range of tours.

Forest Café
23 Mengla Lu, Jinghong
Tel: (0691) 898 5122
www.forest-cafe.org
Prides itself on its eco-friendly treks into the countryside around Jinghong, with visits to many of the local minority groups.

Sichuan China Travel Services
Room 306, 15 Southern Section 3, 1st Ring Road, Chengdu
Tel: (028) 8889 8804

www.pandatour.com.cn
Comfortable three-day trips to the Wolong
Reserve to see the famous giant pandas.

Top China Travel
11 Binjiang Lu, Guilin
Tel: (0773) 288 5326
www.topchinatravel.com
Based in Guilin, Top China will organise
minority tours throughout Guizhou.

Xintuo Ecotourism
Qixing Jie, Lijiang
Tel: (0888) 510 6226
www.ecotourism.com.cn
Jointly owned by 24 Naxi families, Xintuo
specialises in introducing visitors to
the natural delights as well as the local
minority cultures of Northwest Yunnan.
Treks and mountain-bike tours to suit
your requirements.

FESTIVALS AND EVENTS

The southwest is the most ethnically diverse region in China. Reflecting this wide
cultural range, the area has a colourful array of festivals and events. Some of the
events are exclusive to just one locale or town, and dates vary – the best place to
check is the local branch of the China Travel Service (CTS or CITS). The Dong, Miao
and other minorities in Guizhou have a rich festival tradition, with events taking
place throughout the year, it's worth checking the websites mentioned below for
up-to-date information.

April
Third Month Fair
15th–21st days of the 3rd lunar month, Dali
Dragon dances and horse races accompany
a vast market during this boisterous fair. 👫

Water-Splashing Festival
Mid-April, Xishuangbanna
The Buddhist New Year celebration involves
lots of water-throwing. There are also
dragon-boat races and fireworks. 👫

July/August
Torch Festival
24th day of the 6th lunar month, various
locations
A Yi-minority festival celebrated with great
gusto in Dali, and to a lesser extent in
Lijiang. Elaborately decorated torches are
carried through the streets in the evening,
amidst much singing and merriment. 👫

October/November
Hungry Ghosts Festival
12th–14th days of the 7th lunar month,
Lijiang
This festival is observed all over China, but

is particularly colourful in Lijiang, with elaborate lanterns on display all over town. 👫

For details on the colourful Miao and Dong
festivals of Guizhou province, see p.51.

Water-splashing festival, Xishuangbanna

⭐ CHINESE MEDICINE

China has traditionally considered itself unique, a 'Middle Kingdom' at the centre of both the mundane and the spiritual worlds. While this is no longer quite so true, with China seeking to engage with, rather than cut itself off from, the wider world, past exclusivity inevitably continues to influence the Chinese mindset. A prime example of this can be seen in the fields of philosophy and medicine, where China has made unique and outstanding contributions.

Chinese religion has always tended to be eclectic and multi-faceted rather than dogmatic and exclusive. It is usually represented as a blend of the 'Three Teachings' of Confucianism, Buddhism and Daoism. In fact, all three teachings are more philosophical than religious when viewed according to Western notions.

To this 'big three' can be added other traditional Chinese theories that link an underlying philosophy with physical and mental well-being. These include

the concept of *qi*, or 'energy flow', which corresponds in some ways to the Western concept of 'vital essence'. It is essential to keep this in balance at all times, for example by avoiding surfeits of what are classified by the Chinese as 'heating' or 'cooling' foods *(see p.29)*.

Traditional Chinese medical theory asserts that the body has natural patterns of *qi* that circulate in channels. Symptoms of illness are believed to be the product of a disrupted, blocked or

A herbal medicine shop in Hong Kong's Western District

unbalanced flow of *qi*, and the idea is to relieve these imbalances through adjusting the circulation of *qi* by using a variety of techniques including herbal medicines, *t'ai chi* and *qigong*, massage and acupuncture.

Another significant element in traditional Chinese medicine and philosophy is the concept of *yin-yang*, or complementary opposites. This idea of balance lies at the heart of traditional Chinese medicine, and is a central principle of various forms of Chinese martial arts including both *t'ai chi* and *qigong*.

It is simple enough to make an appointment to visit a traditional practitioner for acupuncture or massage or other treatment. For people interested in learning more about Chinese medicine and the philosophy that underpins it, specialist operators offer a range of tours *(see below)*.

Tai chi in a Shanghai park

Chinese Medicine

Special-Interest Tours

China Connections Tours (www.china-tour.cn) do a 12-day 'Traditional Medicine', tour taking in Beijing and Shanghai with a focus on Chinese culture and medicine.

Beijing Xinhua International Tours (www.tour-beijing.com) operate martial-arts and spa tours.

Several UK operators, including **Abercrombie & Kent**, **Cox & Kings** and **Scott Dunn** do luxury packages with a Chinese spa theme offering traditional treatments.

Visit any Chinese park early in the morning to watch locals practising their daily t'ai chi and *qigong* routines.

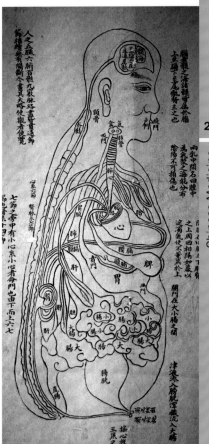

The body's flow of *qi* energy is mapped out in this traditional drawing

Silk Road and Tibet

The provinces of Gansu, Xinjiang, Qinghai and Tibet constitute China's vast and sparsely populated west, comprising almost half the national land area, yet with less than 5 percent of the total population. It is a region characterised by magnificent mountain and desert scenery, ethnic and cultural diversity, and fabulous historical attractions.

Lanzhou and Ürümqi

 Population: Lanzhou: 3.3 million; Ürümqi: 2.5 million

 Local dialling code: Lanzhou: 0931; Ürümqi: 0991

 Airport: Lanzhou Airport is 70km (44 miles) north of town. Ürümqi Airport is 16km (10miles) northwest of town.

 Trains: Lanzhou's main railway station sits at the southern end of Tianshui Nanlu. Some trains depart from the West Railway Station, off Xijin Xilu in the west of town. Ürümqi's main railway station is just southwest of the centre.

 Buses: There are several bus stations across Lanzhou. The main one is just north of the rail station on Pingliang Lu. Ürümqi's long-distance bus station is on Heilongjiang Lu, about 2km (1¼ miles) north of the railway station.

 Key areas: Lanzhou's busiest areas for both shopping and eating can be found all along Pingliang Lu and Tianshui Lu. In Ürümqi the area around Erdaoqiao Market in the southeast of the city has plenty of good restaurants plus interesting shops and stalls.

Western China is a land of harsh and beautiful extremes. To the north, the Silk Road provinces of Gansu and Xinjiang, where China blends with Central Asia and the Muslim world, are characterised by oasis towns linked by lonely highways across endless, empty tracts of desert. Temperatures, too, are extreme, with searing summer heat and harsh winter cold. Yet the oases, which mark the route of the former Silk Road, are unexpectedly green, fertile gems that break up the monotonous, sand-swept deserts and – in Xinjiang – circle the central Taklamakan like jewels on a necklace.

Ürümqi, the distant capital of Xinjiang, is further from the sea than any other city on earth. In the far west, the Karakoram and Pamir mountains form a definitive barrier between China and the Indian Subcontinent.

Further south, Tibet (Xizang) and Qinghai share the highest plateau in the world. As in Xinjiang, China proper seems a world away, and the Lamaist Buddhist faith of the Tibetans is everywhere apparent. Travelling to these distant – but increasingly accessible – realms is an experience not to be missed, as is a chance to visit the fabled cities of Lhasa and Kashgar.

Along the Silk Road

For centuries the main conduit for commerce and culture between China, Central Asia, India and Europe, the Silk Road passed through what was formerly known as Chinese Turkestan. Its eastern terminus was the great city of Chang'an, now Xi'an. From here the camel trains and pack mules marched west along the Gansu Corridor to the frontiers of Xinjiang, before skirting the central desert and arriving at last in Kashgar, the old oasis city beneath the mighty Pamirs before the crossing to Samarkand and Bukhara. It was a journey of several months which today can comfortably be accomplished in as many days, whether by rail or road – or by air in just a few hours.

Gansu

Gansu is an ancient Chinese province extending more than 1,000 km (625

The Yellow River near Lanzhou

miles) from east to west. The population is predominantly Han Chinese, but with substantial Hui Muslim and Tibetan minorities.

Lanzhou

The busy industrial city of **Lanzhou** ❶ in eastern Gansu is squeezed into a narrow valley between ranks of steep and rocky mountains astride the swift-flowing and powerful **Yellow River**. The main attraction is the dramatic setting, with the Yellow River surging through the city, accompanied by an unmistakable feel of Central Asia amid the Hui Muslim communities with their markets, cafés and restaurants. The river is best viewed from **Five Springs Hill Park** (Wuquan Shan Gongyuan; daily 6am–sunset) in the hills above the north bank. It's a long climb, but with temples, pavilions and teahouses to visit en route; alternatively, a cable car across the river climbs easily to the summit. The new **Gansu Provincial Museum** (Gansu Sheng Bowuguan; Tue–Sun 9am–5pm; charge), on Xijin Xilu in the west of the city, is well worth visiting for its collection of Silk Road artefacts.

Silk Road and Tibet

Entrance to the Mogao Caves

Elsewhere in Gansu

In the far south of the province at **Xiahe**, the magnificent **Labrang Monastery** ❷ (Labuleng Si; daily 9am–noon and 2.30–4.30pm; charge) is one of the largest and most active Tibetan lamaseries in China, with more than 1,000 resident monks. Beyond Xiahe, a wonderfully scenic route traverses high-altitude grasslands and Tibetan villages en route to Jiuzhaigou and Chengdu in Sichuan.

Southwest of Lanzhou are the **Thousand Buddha Temple and Caves** (Bingling Si Shiku; daily 8am–5pm; charge), with hundreds of statues and some of China's best-preserved Buddhist cave art.

From Lanzhou both road and rail follow the historic trade route northwest, flanked by the snow-peaked Qilian Mountains to the south and the arid wastes of the Gobi Desert to the north. A series of medium-sized oasis cities are tracked by the Great Wall west to **Jiayuguan** ❸, site of the 'First and Greatest Pass under Heaven', traditionally marking the end of China and the start of Central Asia. Here a magnificently restored fort, **Jiayuguan Chenglou** (daily

Monks at Labrang monastery, Xiahe

8.30am–7.30pm; charge), guards the pass between the Qilian Mountains to the south and the Mazong Range to the north. A short distance beyond the fort, the desert falls away sharply to the **Taolai River Gorge**, marking the end of the Great Wall.

A further 380km (237 miles) west, the sleepy town of **Dunhuang** makes a pleasant base for an exploration of the world-famous **Mogao Caves** ❹ (Mogao Ku; daily 8.30–11.30am, 2.30–6pm; charge). Cut into a desert cliffside, these tell the story of the great flowering of Buddhist art in China. They were created over a period of about 1,000 years, between AD366 and 1277. It is estimated that there are some

Desert Highlights

Near Mogao rise **Mingshashan**, the highest sand dunes in Asia, where visitors can ride camels, sand-surf, paraglide or drive quad bikes around the steep dunes. Beautiful, tiny and unexpected **Crescent Moon Lake** (Yueyaquan; daily dawn to dusk; charge) provides a tranquil setting in the midst of the desert.

45,000 sq m (484,000 sq ft) of mural paintings in the caves, as well as more than 2,000 painted sculptures.

Xinjiang

Xinjiang is China's largest province, accounting for fully one-sixth of the nation's territory – the size of France, Germany, Spain and the UK combined. In formal terms, it is called the **Xinjiang Uighur Autonomous Region**, home to China's Uighur Muslim people, as well as to a range of other predominantly Muslim minorities, including Kazakh, Kirghiz, Tajik, Uzbek and Hui.

West to Turpan

Beyond Dunhuang, the Silk Road continues west, across some 1,000km (620 miles) of bleak, stony desert, via **Hami**, the first oasis in Xinjiang, to **Turpan ❺**. This legendary oasis, set in the second-deepest depression in the world (after the Dead Sea), flourishes on water brought by underground channels from the watershed of distant mountains.

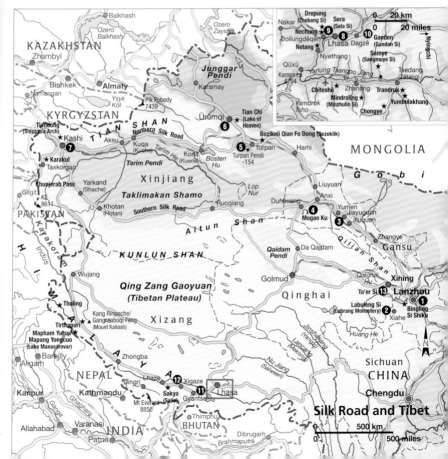

Silk Road and Tibet

The most remarkable sites in the area are the ruins of two ancient desert capitals. The city of **Jiaohe** (daily dawn–dusk; charge), 10km (6 miles) west of Turpan, was founded in the 2nd century BC and laid out in a grid. Destroyed at the end of the 14th century, its sand and brick still preserve the haunting outlines of a great city that stretched for a mile, with a Buddhist temple and headless statues at the centre. There are remains of underground dwellings, which offered protection from the elements – the heat is furnace-like in summer.

A second ancient city, **Gaochang** (daily dawn–dusk; charge), lies 46km (29 miles) east of Turpan. It has an imposing wall with a perimeter of 5km (3 miles). During the Tang dynasty, there were 30,000 inhabitants and more than 3,000 monks living here, but when Islam supplanted Buddhism here in the 13th century, the city was abandoned.

Ürümqi and the Tian Shan

Some 200km (125 miles) northwest of Turpan is the regional capital, **Ürümqi** ❻, a modern and predominantly Chinese city with the best hotels and restaurants in western China, but relatively little of interest in terms of sights. One exception is the excellent **Xinjiang Museum** (Xinjiang Bowuguan; Tue–Sun 10.30am–1pm and 4–8pm; charge), which houses Silk Road coins, earrings, tiles, silks and a fascinating collection of mummies, embalmed as long ago as the 13th century BC.

The **Tian Shan** or 'Mountains of Heaven' around Ürümqi are wonderfully scenic, and have two famous beauty spots. The celebrated **Heaven Lake** (Tian Chi), 120km (75 miles) east of the city, is one of the prettiest mountain lakes in the world, surrounded by Kazakh yurts, grazing sheep and snowy peaks, capped by the 5,444m (17,864ft) bulk of Mount Bogda. In the **Southern Mountains** (Nanshan), 75km (47 miles) south of Ürümqi, Kazakhs move their families on horseback and set up their yurts on the high pastures to graze their sheep.

Ruins at Gaochang

Magnificent scenery at Heaven Lake near Ürümqi

Into the Far West

South and west of Ürümqi, the modern railway and highway both track the old Silk Road west, via the modern oil town of **Korla** to the old oasis town of **Kuqa**, formerly a Buddhist Kingdom and an important staging post on the Silk Road. The area around this traditional Uighur town is rich in ancient pre-Islamic sites; to the northwest are the **Kizil Thousand Buddha Caves** (Kezier Qianfodong; daily; charge). Although relatively few are open to visitors, the murals still retain a numinous power to delight. To the north is **Subashi Ancient City** (Subashi Gucheng; daily; charge), evocative ruins that are all that survive of the ancient Buddhist Kingdom of Qiuci, which flourished between the 4th and 12th centuries AD.

A relatively short distance west, the industrial city of **Aksu** is of limited interest, but makes a good stopping point en route to Kashgar.

Kashgar

Kashgar, called **Kashi** ❼ by the Chinese, is, together with Samarkand and Bukhara, among the most evocative of all Silk Road place names. It is located in the far west of Xinjiang – closer to Tehran and Riyadh than to Beijing.

Today Kashgar is changing fast. Once ringed by crenellated walls and

> ### The Flaming Mountains
>
> Northeast of Turpan, the road skirts the **Flaming Mountains** (Huoyanshan in Chinese). Facing south, the slopes attract and store the sun's heat – temperatures here can reach as high as 55°C (131°F). On a sheer cliff in a gorge in these mountains perch the **Bezeklik Thousand Buddha Caves** (Bozikeli Qian Fo Dong; daily 8am-4.30pm; charge) with carvings and frescoes dating from the 5th century. Unfortunately, these beautiful grottoes have been plundered by archaeological looters from the West.

★ CULTURES OF THE SILK ROAD

The ancient Silk Road, which flourished for much of the first millennium AD and reached its zenith during the great Tang dynasty (618–907), served as a conduit not just for precious goods, but for religions, philosophy and scientific ideas. In spiritual terms, religious teachings from India, including Buddhism and Hinduism, spread eastwards, while from the Middle East the great monotheistic faiths of Judaism, Christianity and especially Islam arrived in distant Chang'an and Beijing.

Even today the Silk Road, or the area it once traversed, stands as a multi-faceted region of diverse cultures and civilisations, dazzling in its complexity. Somewhere around the frontiers of Gansu and Xinjiang 'China Proper' gives way to Central Asia, and the Chinese traditions of Buddhism, Confucianism and Daoism yield increasingly to Islam. And through the middle of this vast region, like a thread, lie the scattered communities of Chinese-speaking Hui Muslims, a merchant people born of Silk Road commerce who owe religious allegiance to Mecca, but political support to Beijing.

Muslim Xinjiang was conquered by the Qing as recently as 1877, although it had been claimed by successive Chinese dynasties, on and off, for almost two millennia, and was long a rebellious thorn in the side of Chinese rulers. It

An elderly Uighur man has his beard trimmed

The veil is a common sight in these westernmost regions of China

was less than 5 percent Han Chinese in 1949, peopled instead by groups of fiercely independent Central Asian Muslims, including the dominant Uighur, as well as Kazakh, Kirghiz and Tajiks.

Over the intervening six decades all this has changed, with the northwest firmly tied to China as 'autonomous regions', and Han Chinese making up fully 50 percent of the population. Yet despite this political reality, cultural distinctions persist, and even multiply. Many local Muslims, although having benefited from China's growing affluence and freedom, bitterly resent domination by Beijing and seek, if not the frankly unattainable goal of full independence, much fuller political and religious freedoms. This had led, in 2008 and 2009, to rioting and mayhem on the streets of Ürümqi and other centres – developments viewed by the Chinese authorities with a grave disquiet compounded by the emergence of independent states in former Soviet Central Asia, events which have raised Uighur hopes of an independent 'Uighuristan'.

Despite these profound changes, to travel along China's antique Silk Road today is still to journey between and across culture zones – if not time zones, as even distant Kashgar remains officially on Beijing time. It continues to be the case that, while Han Chinese may be numerically and politically ascendant, a great part of the richness of Chinese Central Asia lies in the continuing diversity of its peoples and traditions. Completely different to other parts of China, it makes for an unforgettable, vivid experience.

Cultures of the Silk Road

Brightly coloured silks at a Turpan market

Kashgar Sunday market

predominantly Uighur, it is becoming increasingly Chinese. Large parts of the Old City have been demolished in recent years, although the authorities have now belatedly recognised that the **Old Town** (Laocheng; daily; charge) is a valuable cultural asset and should be preserved, at least in part.

The city's cultural heart is the impressive 15th-century **Id Gah Mosque** (Aitika Qingzhensi; daily; charge for non-Muslims), reportedly China's largest mosque. Although paint is peeling off its central dome and two flanking minarets, the building still dominates its surroundings. To the north is an extremely lively bazaar street of barber shops, book and fur traders, blacksmiths, bakers, tailors and – directly by the mosque – dentists. The covered bazaar has just about anything for sale.

The most important weekly event is the **Sunday Market** (Xingqitian Shichang) held by the banks of the Tumen River. Tens of thousands of visitors and buyers and sellers come to this market from all around, giving it a very cosmopolitan atmosphere.

Heading south from Kashgar, the spectacular **Karakoram Highway** (Zhongba Gonglu) is the highest-altitude paved highway in the world, leading across the Karakoram Mountains via the **Khunjerab Pass** (4,693m/ 15,397ft) to Pakistan. Even if you're not going all the way, a drive to magnificent **Lake Karakul**, located high in the mountains at the foot of **Muztagh Ata** (7,546m/24,760ft) makes for an incomparable day trip.

Tibet and Qinghai

Tibet – or Xizang, as it is called in Chinese – is a uniquely different and exhilarating destination, with its own culture, history and extraordinary scenery marking it out as a separate and distinct entity from the rest of China and just about anywhere else in the world. Qinghai, much of which was historically part of Tibet, is among the poorest and least visited of Chinese provinces, but is starkly beautiful in its isolation.

Lhasa

The only sizeable city in Tibet, and the centre of Tibetan Buddhism, is the capital, **Lhasa** ❽ (population 1,100,000), located at a dizzying altitude of 3,680m (12,070ft). While its name conjures up mysterious and romantic images, much of Lhasa has assumed the appearance of a Chinese city, with the ubiquitous concrete buildings and increasingly heavy traffic found elsewhere in China. Yet, despite the perhaps inevitable changes, the city still retains some remarkable sites, and a considerable power to impress.

Crowned by golden roofs visible from far and wide, the **Potala** (Budala Gong; daily 9am–6pm; charge) is a huge and dramatic building, the symbol of Tibet and residence of the Dalai Lamas from its construction in the 1640s until 1959. The section known as the **White Palace** (Potrang Karpo) was built first; the smaller **Red Palace** (Potrang Marpo), which houses almost all the items of interest, was completed 50 years later. The 13 floors hold almost 1,000 rooms, with ceilings supported by more than 15,000 columns. There is a tremendous view down into the valley and the Old City from the roof of the Red Palace.

Holiest of all Tibetan religious sites, the **Jokhang** (Dazhao Si; daily 8am–8pm; charge) is at the epicentre of the Tibetan world and the heart of Lhasa, the destination for devout pilgrims from across the land. The main building, built on a mandala foundation, dates from the 7th century, when it was built as a shrine for a Buddha statue that the Chinese princess Wen Cheng brought to Lhasa as a wedding gift from the Chinese emperor.

About 7km (4 miles) west of the city centre in pleasant grounds, the **Norbulingka** (Luobulinka; daily 9am–12.30pm, 2.30–6pm; charge) was built for the seventh Dalai Lama in the second half of the 18th century. It later served as a summer residence for the Tibetan rulers until 1959. On the top floor of the building, which is decorated with numerous wall murals, is an audience hall with paintings from the history of the Tibetan people. Also open are the meditation room and bedroom of the Dalai Lama.

Around Lhasa

Just 5km (3 miles) north of central Lhasa, at the foot of the chain of

A pilgrim holds a butter lamp in the Jokhang

in the world at the height of its power, nearly 10,000 monks are said to have lived within its walls.

Ganden Monastery ❿ (Gandan Si; daily 9am–noon, 2–4pm; charge), 40km (25 miles) northeast of Lhasa, was founded in 1409. It once housed 5,000 monks, making the almost total destruction of the site during the Cultural Revolution even more tragic. Only in 1985 was the reconstruction of the monastery finally completed; since then, several hundred monks have returned, and it is now one of the most popular tourist attractions in Tibet.

The Road to Nepal

The journey from Lhasa, via Gyantse and Shigatse to the high Himalayas and then over the border into Nepal, is a great travel adventure, taking in some of Tibet's finest scenery and its largest monasteries.

The sizeable town of **Gyantse** ⓫ lies by the northern bank of the Nyangchu River, some 265km (165 miles) south-west of Lhasa. The most important

mountains dominating the Kyichu valley, **Sera Monastery** ❾ (Sela Si; daily 9am–noon, 2–4pm; charge) was founded in 1419. During its most active period, almost 5,000 monks lived here, and it had a brilliant reputation because of its famous academy. Today, Sera is home to around 300 monks.

To the west of town is **Drepung Monastery** (Zhebang Si; daily 9am–6pm; charge), built in 1416 and for a long time the political headquarters of the Buddhist Yellow Hat sect. The predecessors of the Great Fifth Dalai Lama lived here before moving to the Potala. Probably the largest monastery

The magnificent Potala palace dominates the centre of Lhasa

monastery here is **Palkhor Chode** (Baiju Si; Mon–Sat 9am–noon, 3–6pm; charge). The 32m (105ft) **Kumbum Dagoba** in the centre of the complex is a unique example of Tibetan architectural skill. Built in the shape of a three-dimensional mandala, it symbolises Mount Meru; the central structure at the tip is a chapel for the original Buddha. The centre of Gyantse has largely retained its attractive Tibetan architecture.

Shigatse ⓬ (also spelled Xigaze), 360km (224 miles) west of Lhasa on the southern bank of Yarlung Tsangpo, is Tibet's second city and the seat of the Panchen Lama, the second head of Tibetan Buddhism. **Tashilhunpo Monastery** (Zhashilunbu Si; daily 9am–noon, 3.30–5pm; charge) is one of the most impressive religious centres in Tibet. The site dates from the 15th century but was substantially expanded during the 17th and 18th centuries. Nearly 4,000 monks once lived here; today, there are around 600.

The last town before the Nepalese border is **Dingri**, a small settlement dominated by the ruins of an old fortress destroyed during an 18th-century Nepalese invasion. There are views south to the Himalayas. From here it's a five-hour drive to the frontier at Zhangmu – the last stretch descending off the edge of the Tibetan Plateau into an ever-deepening, ever-greener gorge.

Qinghai

Occupying the northeastern part of the Tibetan Plateau at an average altitude of 4,000m (13,100ft), remote **Qinghai** is one of China's least visited provinces.

Looking south to the Himalayas from Dingri

The largest city, **Xining**, is a useful base and also home to the **Dongguan Great Mosque** (Dongguan Qingzhen Dasi; daily 8am–8pm; charge to non-Muslims), with an intriguing blend of Arabic and Chinese architectural styles, with green-tiled domed towers flanked by Chinese-style archways.

Kumbum Monastery ⓭ (Ta'er Si; daily 8am–6pm; charge), 25km (15 miles) southeast of Xining, is one of the most important Tibetan religious centres outside of the Tibetan heartlands. Construction began in 1560, but many of its once-exquisite halls bore the brunt of legalised vandalism from Red Guards during the Cultural Revolution. Extensive restoration work has resulted in the complex returning to fully functioning monastic life, with several hundred resident monks.

The immense **Qinghai Hu** is China's biggest lake. Famous for its birdlife, it forms part of the **Qinghai Lake Natural Protection Zone**, which limits visitors to two main viewing areas (daily 9am–5pm; charge).

ACCOMMODATION

Towns are few and far between across these far-flung areas of western China, and good accommodation is therefore limited to the bigger towns and cities – where there is a good supply of comfortable and characterful hotels.

Dunhuang

Silk Road Dunhuang Hotel
Dunyue Lu
Tel: (0937) 888 2088
www.the-silk-road.com
Well-appointed hotel with rooms in traditional Silk Road caravanserai style. **$$$–$$$$**

Kashgar

Qianhai Hotel
48 Renmin Xi Lu
Tel: (0998) 282 2922
All rooms are air-conditioned, an absolute must in the hot summer season. Facilities include two pretty good restaurants and a gym. **$$**

Seman Hotel
337 Seman Lu
Tel: (0998) 258 2150
In the grounds of the old Russian Consulate, the Seman continues to radiate a little 19th-century 'Great Game' ambience. **$–$$$**

Lanzhou

JJ Sun Hotel
589 Donggang Xi Lu
Tel: (0931) 880 5511
www.jinjianghotels.com

A 24-storey, three-star hotel in the heart of the city's commercial district. All rooms have cable TV and internet access. **$$$**

Lanzhou Legend Hotel
529 Tianshui Lu
Tel: (0931) 853 2888
www.lanzhoulegendhotel.com
Handy for both the train and long-distance bus stations. Facilities include a choice of several good restaurants. **$$$**

Lhasa

Brahmaputra Grand Hotel
Yangcheng Plaza, Gongbutand Lu
Tel: (0891) 630 9999
www.tibethotel.cn
Advertises itself as the only museum hotel in the world, and it's not hard to see why: everywhere you look there are beautiful Tibetan crafts and antiques. **$$$**

Four Points by Sheraton Lhasa
10 Bo Linka Lu
Tel: (0891) 634 8888
www.starwoodhotels.com
Tibet's finest hotel, at least for the moment. Facilities include humidifiers in all guest rooms, a boon in Lhasa's dry climate. **$$$$$**

House of Shambhala
7 Jiri Er Xiang
Tel: (0891) 632 6533
www.houseofshambhala.com
In the heart of Old Lhasa, this boutique hotel in an old Tibetan residence offers good rooms and very friendly staff. **$$$**

Kyichu Hotel
19 Beijing Zhong Lu

Tel: (0891) 633 1541
www.hotelkyichu.com
The family-run Kyichu is well situated between the Jokhang Temple and Potala Palace. Friendly English-speaking staff. **$$**

Turpan
Grand Turpan Hotel
20 Gaochang Lu
Tel: (0995) 855 3668
A comfortable budget option; the guest rooms in the newer wing are large, with mini-bar, satellite television and internet access. **$$**

Oasis Hotel
41 Qingnian Bei Lu
Tel: (0995) 852 2491
www.the-silk-road.com
Wonderful Central Asian-style rooms feature in this highly recommended hotel. **$$–$$$**

Ürümqi
Bogeda Hotel
10 Guangming Lu
Tel: (0991) 886 3910
Clean, centrally located and within walking distance of City Square and the bustling area around Zhongshan Lu and Minzhu Lu. **$$**

Hoi Tak Hotel
1 Dong Feng Lu
Tel: (0991) 232 2828
www.hoitakhotel.com

Ürümqi's best accommodation provides wonderful views of the Tian Shan Mountains from its upper floors. Amenities include snooker tables, sauna and whirlpool. **$$$$–$$$$$**

Xiahe
Labrang Baoma Hotel
Renmin Xijie
Tel: (0941) 712 1078
www.labranghotel.com
A friendly Tibetan-oriented establishment, the Labrang Baoma has pleasantly decorated rooms, most of which have en suite baths. **$**

Xining
Huitong Jiangguo Hotel
1 Qiyi Lu
Tel: (0971) 816 3888
Convenient for the railway station, this comfortable mid-range hotel offers bright, airy rooms and staff that tries its best to accommodate foreign guests. **$$**

Qinghai Hotel
20 Huanghe Lu
Tel: (0971) 614 8999
www.qhhotel.com
The city's largest hotel, with 395 air-conditioned rooms, all with satellite TV and internet connections. Other amenities include a gym, sauna and beauty salon. **$$$**

RESTAURANTS

Lanzhou is rightly famous for its beef noodles and its imaginative blend of Han, Hui and Uighur cooking styles. Uighur fare, available all over Xinjiang, is typified by flatbreads, locally- grown fruits, lamb dishes and noodle stews. Tibetan food is not renowned for its variety, but simple dishes like *momo* (meat-filled dumplings) will keep your hunger at bay.

Dunhuang
Feng Yi Ting 敦煌山莊
Silk Road Dunhuang Hotel, Dunyue Lu
Tel: (0937) 888 2088
The Chamber of Grandeur, as Feng Yi Ting translates, serves some fine Cantonese and

Sichuan specialities. In the high season traditional dancers perform nightly next to the restaurant. **$$–$$$**

Shirley's Café 咖啡厅
Mingshan Lu

A Lanzhou resident

One of a number of good cafés on Mingshan Lu. Good dumplings and a variety of Western dishes; their apple pie is recommended. **$**

Kashgar
Lao Chayuan Jiudian 老茶苑酒店
251 Renmin Xi Lu
Tel: (0998) 282 4467
A variety of Uighur cuisine including *polo* (a rice speciality), lamb kebabs and *laghman* (noodles in a thick stew). **$**

Norling Restaurant 西藏式旅馆
Kyichu Hotel, 19 Beijing Zhong Lu
Tel: (0891) 633 1541
Choose the pleasant garden terrace at the Norling to sample a wide range of good North Indian, Nepalese and Tibetan dishes. **$**

Lanzhou
Fengshan Jiudian 风山酒店
Nongmin Xiang
Local Gansu cuisine, including some excellent desserts such as steamed lily or stuffed melon. Located behind the Lanzhou Hotel and close to the CITS office. **$**

Mingde Gong 明德宫
191 Jiuquan Lu
Tel: (0931) 466 8588
Lanzhou's famous *Lanzhou lamian* (beef noodles) and other Gansu dishes are a speciality of this delightful four-storey restaurant. **$$**

Lhasa
House of Shambhala 藏式传统宾馆和餐厅
7 Jiri Er Xiang
Tel: (0891) 632 6533
This lovely little restaurant in an old building once owned by a Tibetan general serves up dishes from Tibet, Nepal and India, plus a few Western favourites. **$$$**

Namtso Restaurant 纳木错餐厅
8 Beijing Dong Lu
Tel: (0891) 633 0489
A diverse menu offers everything from yak burgers to chicken sizzlers and vegetarian lasagne at this very good rooftop restaurant. **$**

Turpan
John's Information Café 约翰信息咖啡厅
2 Qingnian Lu
Tel: (0995) 852 4237
John's is always good for a hearty breakfast, and the Chinese and Western standards provide relief from the rather fatty local Uighur cuisine. **$**

Xin Shiji 新世纪
Xinzhan Dingzi Lukou
Tel: (0995) 855 1199
Famed for its 'cook your own' kebabs and *sangshen jiu* (mulberry wine), the Xin Shiji is a good place to sample a Uighur banquet. **$$**

Ürümqi
Fubar Ürümqi 乌鲁木齐市
40 Gongyuan Beijie
Tel: (0991) 584 4498
An excellent range of pastas, pizzas and burgers. The management are a great source of information on travel in Xinjiang. **$$**

Kashgari's 新疆大酒店
Xinjiang Grand Hotel, 168 Xinhua Bei Lu
Tel: (0991) 281 8788
You'll find Uighur dishes such as *polo* (a rice speciality), lamb kebabs, *nang* flatbread and *samsa* (samosa) in this hotel restaurant.
$$-$$$

Xiahe
Tsewong's Café 咖啡厅
Renmin Xijie
Tel: (0941) 712 2804
Respected for its Western food, Tsewong's is also renowned for its coffee. Pizzas are cooked in a real wood-fired pizza oven. **$**

SPORTS, ACTIVITIES AND TOURS

Either mountain-trekking or desert-trekking are the favoured activities in both Gansu and Xinjiang. In Dunhuang there are plenty of opportunities for camel treks. Permits are generally needed for trekking in Tibet, but if you have the patience for obtaining them then there are some wonderful trails.

Gansu
John's Information Cafe
22 Mingshan Lu (Next to Feitian Hotel)
Tel: (0937) 882 7000
John Hu has been helping travellers on the Silk Road for many years. He has other branches in Kashgar, Turpan and Lhasa.

Xinjiang
Kashgar and Ürümqi tour companies can arrange 4–6-day mountain treks in the area around Lake Karakul (3,900m/12,795ft) and Muztagh Ata (7,546m/24,760ft) in the Karakoram Mountains. Numerous companies in Kashgar and Khotan will arrange camel-trekking tours in the Taklamakan Desert lasting from one to three days, longer by arrangement.

Karakoram Café
87 Seman Lu (opposite the Chini Bagh Hotel)
Tel: (0998) 342 2888
This Kashgar office of the Crown Inn Hotel at Tashkorgan on the Karakoram Highway can arrange trips into the Karakoram Mountains, as well as desert adventures across the Taklamakan.

Listings

FESTIVALS AND EVENTS

Labrang Monastery, at Xiahe in Gansu, is one of the six great monasteries of the Tibetan Yellow Hat sect, and is the most important Tibetan monastery in China outside the Tibetan Autonomous region. All major Tibetan festivals are held here each year. In Xinjiang and other predominantly Muslim areas, two main Islamic festivals are celebrated: Id al-Fitr (Festival of the Breaking of the Fast), held at the end of Ramadan, and Id al-Adha (Festival of the Sacrifice).

February/March
Losar (Tibetan New Year) and Monlam Prayer Festival
Gansu, Qinghai and Tibet
A period of feasting, party-going and making offerings at temples, Losar offers the perfect opportunity to see Tibetans really let their hair down. It is immediately followed by Monlam. In Lhasa the Jokhang Temple's Maitreya image is paraded around the town.

May/June
Gyantse Horse Racing Festival
Gyantse, Tibet
Apart from the horse racing there are archery tournaments, ball games and folk singing.

PRACTICAL ADVICE

Accommodation

As tourism surges in China, so the range and standard of accommodation for travellers are improving. Popular tourist areas will have a wide range of options for every budget, from luxurious five-stars to backpacker hostels, while places off the beaten track will obviously have less choice, and accommodation may be of a poor standard. In the peak months of May, September and October and particularly during Chinese New Year (a week or two in January or February) pre-booking your accommodation is advised. Most hotels remain open in the low season, though facilities such as swimming pools or tours may be unavailable.

HOTELS

Chinese hotels range from first-class to grimly spartan. The newest establishments, often built with foreign cooperation and with foreign management, bear a close resemblance to their counterparts in Europe or America, although service standards frequently fall short. Chain hotels such as Holiday Inn have recently entered the market, as have domestic imitators such as Bestay Hotel Express.

The prices of better hotels are generally in line with those in the West, though the star-rating system is not always reliable (and not always displayed). A hotel rated with three or more stars should have 24-hour hot water, television in every room as well as a bookstore, gym, western restaurant and foreign exchange facilities. Even cheaper hotels should have air conditioning, though bathroom facilities are often not up to Western standards. Many Chinese hotels do not offer

Beijing is well supplied with 5-star hotels

Western-style double rooms: the choice is between a twin room, ie with two single beds, or a suite. Suites will have a bed large enough for two people, though they are often much more expensive than twin rooms.

Websites ctrip.com and www.elong.net can be used to book hotels in advance, though the best prices can often be achieved by bargaining for a room in person at the front desk. With the exception of most chain hotels, the rack rate can always be bargained down – often considerably during low season or for longer stays.

Noise pollution can be a big problem, so ensure your room does not abut a construction site or is on a floor that is being renovated. It's unlikely hotel staff will inform you of such problems in advance, so you may want to check your room and facilities before you pay. Tap water will not usually be potable and paper should not be put into the toilet – there will be a bin next to the toilet for paper. All hotels are legally permitted to accept foreign guests, but some may lack the computer facilities to register passport information correctly.

In the larger Chinese-managed hotels there is a service desk on each floor with a staff member who often speaks some English, keeps room keys, handles the laundry, deals with phone problems and sells cigarettes, snacks, drinks and postcards. Postal and tour desks, a foreign-exchange facility and gift shops are usually located on the ground floor.

Rates at more expensive hotels are subject to 10–15 percent service surcharge. Check-out time is at noon.

A guesthouse in well-preserved Pingyao

BUDGET ACCOMMODATION

Budget options will not usually be presented to foreign tourists at tourist information centres or advertised on the internet. We have attempted to include a range of accomodation, including budget options, in this guidebook, but others can be found by asking taxi drivers, friendly locals or through your own exploration.

The cheapest accommodation option is usually dormitory rooms in small hotels within walking distance of train and bus stations. These often cost less than Rmb100 a night, and foreign guests will often have the room to themselves. Facilities will be very basic, and it is highly unlikely staff will speak English.

Hostelling International hostels have arrived in many major Chinese cities and can be booked online at www.iyhf.org. Staff will speak some

A mountain guesthouse in the Himalayas

English, and the facilities and cleanliness is usually good. Membership cards grant small discounts.

Some universities offer dormitory accommodation to travellers. Campus restaurants will certainly be cheap, and foreign guests may attract a lot of friendly attention. University gates often close early.

OTHER ACCOMMODATION

It is difficult for foreigners to find accommodation outside of hotels and guesthouses, although some universities and institutes have guesthouses where foreign visitors can find good, cheap lodging. If you are going on a long trip or hike in the countryside, especially in Tibet or in areas around the sacred mountains of China, you will come across some very basic travellers' lodgings where it is advisable to take your own sleeping bag. These guesthouses (*zhaodaisuo*) or hostels (*lüguan*) may have a telephone for booking but rarely advertise. It

is advisable to carry your own sleeping bag. On remote mountains there may be accommodation available at temples, usually extremely basic.

"Couchsurfing" is a growing trend in China. Travellers can connect with hosts who provide free accommodation in their homes – see www.couch-surfing.org. Before making contact, hosts and travellers set up profiles on the site including their details and preferences – such as interests, languages spoken, if they smoke etc.

There are various homestay organisations, such as chinahomestay.org, usually in big cities such as Beijing, that can organise for a foreign guest to stay with a vetted Chinese family. Users report mixed experiences however so caution is advised.

Camping

China does not have Western-style campsites, although tourism authorities are taking an interest in the industry, so check the internet for up-to-date information. Some companies offer camping holidays and expeditions. The China Culture Center (www.chinaculturecenter. org) organises trips to historically significant sights, sometimes with overnight stays. Beijing U-DO adventure (www.udoadventure.com) offers programmes of hiking, camping and-mountain climbing around China.

Wild camping is possible in the more remote areas so long as you stay far enough away from villages and fields. Generally it's best to try not to attract attention as local police may try to move campers on or try to extract bribes.

Transport

GETTING TO CHINA

By air

There are numerous non-stop flights from London to Beijing, Shanghai and Hong Kong, taking around 10–12 hours. From North America, a non-stop flight from Los Angeles or Vancouver to Beijing takes around 13 hours. New York has non-stop flights to Beijing, Shanghai and Hong Kong.

Airlines providing regular flights to China include: Cathay Pacific www. cathaypacific.com; British Airways www.britishairways.com; Lufthansa www.lufthansa.com; Air China www. airchina.co.uk; Virgin Atlantic www. virgin-atlantic.com; United www. united.com; and Delta www.delta.com.

The best prices can sometimes be obtained by approaching the airways directly. Otherwise, try a flight agent such as Ebookers www.ebookers.com.

By rail

The Trans-Siberian Railway provides one of the world's great train journeys. Two routes cover the ground between Moscow and Beijing. Travellers require a Russian visa as well as a Mongolian visa if taking the trans-Mongolian route. For packages: Trans-Siberian Experience www. trans-siberian.co.uk; Monkey Business (Beijing) www.monkeyshrine. com. Ticket agents and consolidators include: Orbitz www.orbitz.com; Travelocity www.travelocity.com; and Air Brokers www.airbrokers.com.

It is also possible to enter China by rail from Kazakhstan and Vietnam, but you'll need to arrange visas in advance.

GETTING AROUND CHINA

China's extensive rail network is often the most convenient and cost-effective

Beijing Capital Airport

way to travel. Trains run on time and are safe, and major routes have clean and comfortable carriages. The rapid growth of the air-travel industry has seen many cities construct an airport, some even with international connections. For longer journeys, a flight can be a valid and inexpensive option. Long-distance buses or taxis (some may be hired for a day) are readily available, and speedy new highways make for short journeys.

Domestic flights

Air service inside China is handled by several domestic airlines, and all of China's major cities are connected by domestic flights. The air fleet is rapidly expanding, but delays are still common. On-board service on domestic flights varies greatly. Buying a return ticket on some routes is difficult, except to cities such as Beijing and Shanghai. For shorter journeys within China, the train is generally more enjoyable than travelling by plane, and saves the airport tax of Rmb50 that is levied at all domestic airports.

Air China (global sales tel: (400) 810 0999: www.airchina.com) flies to more than 200 destinations within China; other major domestic airlines are China Eastern Airlines (010) 6468 1166; www.flychinaeastern.com) and China Southern Airlines (tel: 955399; www.flychinasouthern.com), both of which operate on around 120 domestic routes.

For domestic departures you need to check in about 30 minutes before the flight, although Shanghai demands arrival one hour in advance.

High-speed catamarans operate between Hong Kong and Macau

Tickets can be bought with great convenience from small ticket offices throughout cities and towns – look out for signage that features pictures of trains and planes.

Ferries

Most travellers need not make use of sea connections within China, though there are regular ferry and boat connections between large coastal cities. These include: Shanghai–Dalian, Dalian–Tianjin, Shanghai–Qingdao, Shanghai–Guangzhou, Beihai–Guangzhou, Shenzhen–Zhuhai and Zhuhai–Hong Kong. Tickets can be bought from ferry terminals or via CITS (www.cits.cn).

In terms of river boats, the passenger ferries along the Yangzi are now eclipsed by the vastly improved road network, although some services do still operate (notably between Chongqing and Yichang – the same stretch used by the tourist cruise boats). Ferries are an important means of transport in many cities, too. For practical details on Yangzi cruises, *see pp.23–5 and p.159*.

Trains

The Chinese rail network extends more than 80,000km (50,000 miles) into the nation's furthest reaches, including Tibet and Xinjiang. Average train speed is not very high, although increasing rapidly due to modernisation and investment programmes. The new D trains are high-speed bullet trains, which are much quicker but up to 50 percent more expensive than T express trains.

Demand for train tickets is usually high, so, wherever you want to travel to, it is advisable to buy your ticket as soon as reservations open. This varies between types of train and destinations. The usual maximum advance period is 10 days, but may be as long as 20 days for Z trains (high-speed long-distance trains), or as short as three days for local services. During the main travel season (Chinese New Year, and the 1 May and 1 October holiday periods; *see also Public Holidays, p.14*) it becomes nearly impossible to buy tickets to and from major cities.

There are special ticket counters for foreigners at railway stations. Tickets can also be bought from the same, numerous small ticket offices that sell domestic-travel plane tickets.

There is no first or second class on Chinese trains, but four categories or classes: *ruanwo* or soft-sleeper, *ruanzuo* or soft-seat, *yingwo* or hard-sleeper, and *yingzuo* or hard-seat. The soft-seat class is usually only available for short journeys.

Long-distance trains normally only have soft-sleeper or hard-sleeper facilities. The soft-sleeper class has four-bed compartments with soft beds, and is recommended, particularly for long journeys. The hard-sleeper class has open, six-bed compartments. The beds are not really hard, but are cramped and not very comfortable. While you can reserve a place for the first three classes (you always buy a ticket with a place number), this is not always essential for the hard-seat category.

There are dining cars on long-distance trains, often much less crowded than hard seats, that can be enjoyed for the price of a meal.

A useful English-language train schedule can be found at www.travelchinaguide.com. More comprehensive English-language rail information

A hard-seat train carriage

is available at www.chinatt.org, also offering a full national timetable available for a small fee. For more on train travel, *see p.154*.

Long-distance buses

Though China's railway network is extensive, long-distance buses fill in the gaps and are an alternative when train tickets have sold out. Buses are usually cheaper than rail travel and when traversing major highways can be almost as quick. Some overnight buses even have bunk beds. Often ticket prices for direct travel are higher. Otherwise the vehicle will stop to pick up extra passengers on the way, increasing the journey time considerably.

Tickets

The small ticket offices that sell plane and train tickets do not supply long-distance bus tickets, so the usual

method is to head to the town's long-distance bus station, up to three to five days in advance.

Cycling

The capital of China is inextricably linked with the bicycle, and with good reason. Flat, sprawling and frequently with one-third of a road assigned to cyclists, Beijing is a bike-rider's paradise. Many other Chinese cities are also ideal for those with two wheels and a strong pair of legs. Bicycles can often be hired at hotels or tourist sights, and some cities have pick-up and drop-off spots at various locations for rented bikes. Bicycle-repair stalls are widespread in towns and cities, so a flat tyre is nothing to worry about.

If hiring is not a possibility, the low price of bicycles (road bikes from Rmb300, mountain bikes from Rmb500) means that buying and reselling later is a definite possibility.

Safety wear is harder to find, however, and China's chaotic road conditions – cars can turn right even at a red light – mean that alertness is required at all times. Bicycles in China usually do not usually come fitted with lights.

With their spectacular sceneries, variety of landscapes and minority villages, Sichuan and Yunnan provinces are certainly among the most popular areas for cycling tours.

Odyssey Cycling (www.odyssey cycling.com) has been operating for over 20 years and offers cycling tours, mostly within southern China.

For cycling tours throughout China, travelogues and comprehensive

A Hong Kong tram

Bicycles are far less ubiquitous than they were 20 years ago in China's cities

information on cycling, see Bike China (www.bikechina.com).

Driving

China is not an easy country for visitors to obtain driving licences and, although road rules generally match those found in the West, driving conditions are often dangerous. Taxis and chauffeur-driven cars are the usual choice, both readily available through hotels. If you don't want to hire a car for the whole day, it's often possible to arrange for a taxi by the hour.

Regulations

An international driving licence is not valid for use in China. A three-month temporary licence can be obtained after attending lessons in Chinese road-safety regulations. Non-resident drivers in China report that the rules are confusing, however, and not always applied evenly. Obtaining a driving licence for Hong Kong and using that to acquire a permanent mainland China driving licence is one possibility.

Companies such as FESCO (www.fescochina.com) and Beijing Expats Service (www.expatslife) have experience helping foreigners obtain driving licences for use in China and can provide up-to-date information on the latest regulations.

Vehicle hire

Though self-driving in China is complex for visitors, drivers can often be hired for reasonable prices, and some may even speak basic English.

First Choice Car Rental Service in Beijing (tel: (138) 1015 6525; English) provides short- or long-term car rentals and English-speaking drivers. Prices start from Rmb6,000 per month; www.fcars.cn.

Hertz

This international car-rental firm currently has locations in Beijing and Shanghai. Tel: (800) 988 1336; www.hertz.com.

Accessibility

Only in recent years have the needs of disabled people received attention in China. Regulations regarding rooms and other facilities for the disabled must be met by new hotels. In general, though, towns, institutions, public transport and sights offer little accessibility.

Travelling in a group for the disabled certainly reduces these problems considerably. The China National Tourist Offices and CITS have information about special trips for the disabled.

Health and Safety

VACCINATIONS

A clinic specialising in travel medicine should be visited at least four weeks prior to travel to China in order to allow time for vaccines to take effect. China requires travellers arriving from countries where yellow fever is present to have proof of vaccination.

Vaccinations recommended by the WHO for travellers to China include hepatitis A and B, typhoid (for rural areas), rabies, Japanese encephalitis (advisable for rural areas in general) and polio (for Xinjiang). Routine shots for measles and mumps etc should be up to date.

The Center for Disease Control and Prevention (www.cdc.org) provides updates on disease outbreaks in China.

Hepatitis A

A viral infection of the liver transmitted by faecal-contaminated food or drink, or through direct person-to-person contact.

An effective vaccine is available and highly recommended, especially for those who plan to travel repeatedly or at length in China.

Workers in hard hats

Hepatitis B

Hepatitis B is a viral infection of the liver transmitted through the exchange of blood or blood-derived fluids, or through sexual activity with an infected person. Unscreened blood and unsterilised needles, or contact with potentially infected people with open skin lesions, are sources of infection. Inoculations for this type of hepatitis should be started six months prior to travel.

Malaria

Risk: little or no risk in urban areas and popular tourist destinations; there is no risk in provinces bordering

---

Emergency Contacts

The following telephone numbers can be used in case of an emergency. An English-speaking operator is not guaranteed, so for medical emergencies consider International SOS (tel: (10) 6462 9100). Ambulances are not always reliable, so it's often quicker to take a taxi directly to hospital.

Ambulance: 120
Fire service: 119
Police: 110
Traffic police: 122
International assistance: 115

Mongolia or in Heilongjiang, Ningxia, Qinghai, Hong Kong or Macau. Travellers in risk areas should avoid being bitten by mosquitoes: use mosquito repellents, wear long-sleeved shirts and long trousers, and ask at your hotel for a mosquito net or an electronic mosquito repellent device (*quwenqi*) or coil (*wenxiang*). Taking drugs to prevent malaria is recommended only for travellers to rural areas and those who expect to have outdoor exposure during evening hours.

Typhoid fever

A bacterial infection transmitted by contaminated food and/or water, or directly between people. Be cautious in selecting food and water. Drinking bottled or boiled water and eating only well-cooked food lowers the risk of infection.

Medical services

There is a big difference in China between urban and rural medical services. If travelling in the country-side, there may be no appropriate medical services beyond primary healthcare – although this is generally good in China. Some hospitals in large cities have special sections for foreigners where English is spoken. Payment must be made on the spot for treatment, medicine and trans-port. There is a risk of overcharging whereby patients are sold unnecessary extras, such as a private room. If planning to visit areas out-side Beijing, Shanghai, Guangzhou and Hong Kong, consider taking out emergency evacuation insurance.

Pharmacies are widespread, open late and often have an English-Chinese medical dictionary to hand and staff are usually very helpful.

A traditional medicine practitioner

Australia
21 Dongzhimenwai Dajie, Chaoyang
Tel: (10) 5140 4111
www.china.embassy.gov.au

Canada
19 Dongzhimenwai Dajie, Chaoyang
Tel: (10) 5439 4000
www.beijing.gc.ca

Ireland
3 Ritan Dong Lu, Chaoyang
Tel: (10) 6532 2691
www.embassyofireland.cn

New Zealand
1 Ritan Dong Er Jie, Chaoyang
Tel: (10) 8532 7000
www.nzembassy.com/china

South Africa
5 Dongzhimenwai Dajie, Chaoyang
Tel: (10) 6535 0171
Email: safrican@163bj.com

United Kingdom
11 Guanghua Lu, Jianguomenwai
Tel: (10) 5192 4000
ukinchina.fco.gov.uk/en

United States
55 Anjialou Lu, Chaoyang
Tel: (10) 8531 3000
beijing.usembassy-china.org.cn

International SOS
Tel: (10) 6462 9100, 24hrs, emergencies only; www.internationalsos.com.

Natural hazards
After-sun lotion is difficult to find in China, so consider buying some before you arrive. Using a hat or parasol is advisable on summer days.

Bedbugs can be a problem. Itching can be calmed with an antihistamine. Several deaths occur in China each year from wasp or hornet stings, so take care not to disturb nests.

Fire safety can be poor in China, so check your escape routes in hotels and especially crowded buildings.

FOOD AND DRINK
Most tap water in China is not potable. Ensure water has been boiled properly or drink only bottled water.

Travellers' diarrhoea
Take care with food and drink bought from street vendors. Food is often cooked early in the morning and may have been sitting in the open for some time. Stick to freshly prepared food and check the preparation area is clean. Avoid raw or undercooked meat and seafood and raw fruit unless you wash or peel it yourself. If diarrhoea is prolonged, seek advice from a local doctor. If the condition persists, consider heading to hospital to be treated for a possible parasitic infection.

CRIME
China is generally a safe country to travel within. Violent crime is low. The biggest threat is from pickpockets on crowded public transport. Scams include a friendly stranger inviting foreigner travellers to a teahouse or restaurant which then charges extortionate rates, and widespread fake goods such as antiques and designer-label goods.

Security guards are a common sight in Chinese cities but are paid low wages and may be unwilling to help someone in trouble. Call the police in an emergency. Note that China has very strict drug laws, including the death penalty for drug-dealing.

Money and Budgeting

CURRENCY

The Chinese currency is called renminbi (people's currency) and is often abbreviated Rmb. The basic unit is the yuan (colloquially, *kuai*). Ten jiao (colloquially, *mao*) make one yuan; ten fen make one jiao. Thus, 100 fen make one yuan. Notes are currently issued for 1, 2, 5, 10, 20, 50 and 100 yuan. Coins come in 1 yuan, 5 jiao, 1 jiao and 5 fen.

In late 2010, the exchange rate for the renminbi (Rmb) stood at:

1 US$ = 6.74 ('pegged' rate)
1 GB£ = 10.4
1 Euro = 8.7

Major currencies are accepted in banks and hotels.

Hong Kong and Macau have retained their separate currencies, the Hong Kong dollar (HKD) and pataca (MOP) respectively. HK$1 is equal to Rmb 0.87.

Special permits are required to take Rmb20,000 or US$5,000 equivalent of foreign currency out of the country. The renminbi is not freely traded and so may be difficult to convert outside of China.

Foreign currency of up to US$500 equivalent may be bought per day unless with proof of exchange from Rmb, so keep the exchange receipts when you convert foreign currency to yuan.

CASH AND CARDS

Global network-connected ATM machines (Cirrus, Plus, Visa) can be found in major cities and tourist towns – try branches of the Bank of China, major hotels and department stores. Citibank also has a presence in Beijing, Shanghai and Guangzhou,

Chinese yuan. Coins are very low denomination and are rarely used

Budgeting Costs

Top-class/boutique hotel: £100/US$150 for a double
Standard-class hotel: £40/US$60 for a double
Motel: £30/US$45 for a double
Youth hostel: £20/US$30 per person

Domestic flight (one-way): Beijing–Shanghai £120/US$180
Intercity coach ticket (one-way): Beijing–Shanghai £14/US$22
Intercity train ticket (one-way): Beijing–Shanghai £34/US$52
Car hire: £22/US$34
Petrol: Rmb6.5 (£0.70p / US£1) per litre
10-minute taxi ride: £1.50/US$2.20
Airport shuttle bus: Rmb20
Short bus ride: Rmb1
Three-day travel pass: £1/US$1.50
Local-style breakfast: £1/US$1.50

Lunch in a café: £2.50/US$3.70
Coffee/tea in a café: £2/US$3
Main course, budget restaurant: £2/US$3
Main course, moderate restaurant: £4/US$6
Main course, expensive restaurant: £10/US$15
Bottle of wine in a restaurant: £10/US$15
Beer in a pub: £2/US$3

Museum admission: £2/US$3
Daytrip to ticketed scenic area: £12/US$18
Skiing, two hours: £12/US$18
Swimming pool entry: £3/US$4.40
Bicycle rental per day: £6/US$8.80
Theatre/concert ticket: £8/US$12 and up
Item of handmade porcelain: £8/US$12
Nightclub entry: £5/US$7.40

and its ATMs usually accept lots of different cards. The Chinese bank will usually make a small charge for withdrawals using foreign cards.

Many places frequented by foreigners take the usual credit cards such as American Express, Visa, Diners Club and MasterCard. Don't expect to use them much outside of the major cities, however. Train and bus tickets must be purchased in cash, but plane tickets can be bought with credit cards.

Traveller's cheques are recognised at money-exchange counters in hotels, banks and some shops.

TIPPING

Tipping is not customary in mainland China and may result in confusion or even offence. Tour guides and hotel staff used to serving westerners will be aware of the practice and almost certainly happy to accept tips, however. Only the more expensive restaurants add a service charge to the bill. Tipping bar staff early in the evening may lead to better service.

TAX

VAT should be paid on most goods and services. In reality, retailers often only pay tax on goods if the customer asks for a tax-paid receipt known as a *fapiao*. To encourage more customers to do so, *fapiao* often have a scratch-off area offering the possibility of small cash prizes. Some vistors tip taxi drivers by rounding up the fare, but on the whole this is not expected.

Haggling for souvenirs

BUDGETING FOR YOUR TRIP

Though transport, food and – to a lesser degree – accommodation are generally cheaper in China than in the West, ticket prices at major tourist sights, upmarket hotels and tours aimed at foreigners can be quite expensive. Goods and services are considerably more expensive in major cities than in rural areas, so the prices below should be considered a guide.

For a budget, backpacker-style holiday you will need to set aside around Rmb800 (£80/US$120) per person per week. A standard family holiday for four will cost around Rmb4,000 (£400/US$600) per week. A luxury, no-expense-spared break can cost over Rmb10,000 (£1,000/US$1,500) per person per week. Refer to the Budgeting Costs panel, opposite, for more information.

Money-Saving Tips

- Never be embarrassed to bargain for goods and services in China.
- Foreigners may be charged more than locals, so check prices carefully. Tours and services aimed at foreigners usually come with premium prices.
- If you are prepared to compromise on comfort and privacy, hard-sleeper (*yingwo*) is generally acceptable for overnight train journeys, and costs around half the amount of soft-sleeper

(*ruanwo*). It's also generally more fun, as you are more likely to meet people.
- Internet cafés and "phone bars" (for long-distance and international calls) are usually much cheaper than the overpriced services provided by hotels.
- Eating in hotel restaurants can be expensive. Most Chinese cities have "food streets" offering some of the most competitive prices – and the food is often better, too.

Responsible Travel

ECOTOURISM

Many tourist destinations in China attract huge numbers of visitors, and this can lead to destruction of the natural environment. Media reports help to raise public awareness, but many tourist operators simply slap an 'ecotourism' label on their services with minimal efforts made to live up to green promises and no official supervision. International certification from Green Globe (www.greenglobe. com), now making inroads into China, can provide credibility.

A good example of an eco-friendly organisation is the **Wenhai Ecolodge** (www.northwestyunnan.com) near Lijiang, owned by a village cooperative of 56 families. Manure is converted into gas, and solar panels provide power. Guides arrange trekking to minority villages. Another example is **Nanling Park** (http://english. eco-nanling.com), protecting an area of ancient forest on the Guangdong/ Hunan; accommodation is at the Orange House hotel or campsite.

ETHICAL TOURISM

In ethnic-minority areas, major hotels are often not run by local people. Patronising smaller lodges or guest-houses and using local guides should ensure your money has a better chance of remaining in the local community.

In terms of etiquette, minorities have widely different traditions, so travellers should educate themselves on local customs in the areas they visit. Note that Buddhist monks may object to having

their photo taken, and avoid touching religious artefacts in monasteries.

VOLUNTEERING/CHARITIES

Volunteer opportunities for foreigners in China are quite limited. Many involve teaching English. Non-profit Global Aware (www.globeaware. org) runs a project in the outskirts of Beijing teaching English to children of migrant workers and helping to maintain the schools. Cross Cultural Solutions (www.crossculturalsolutions. org), another non-profit organisation, currently manages a project in Xi'an enabling volunteers to help orphans and children with disabilities.

THINGS TO AVOID

Many wildlife products legally sold in China may be illegal to take out of the country. These include ivory and traditional medicines containing animal parts. Avoid restaurants that serve meat from engangered species. See www.wwfchina.org.

Green tourism is growing in China

Family Holidays

PRACTICALITIES

The Chinese are very fond of children, so travelling with a family in China can be a great pleasure. It's common that strangers will want to touch or even pick up young children, friendly gestures that may become irritating – a polite but firm refusal may become necessary. Always make sure your children carry identification and contact information, perhaps a hotel card.

Supplies for babies such as nappies and baby food are available in supermarkets and pharmacies such as Watsons, common in major shopping centres. Nappy-changing facilities are almost unheard of, but there is no cultural problem with using either male or female toilets for this purpose. Cleanliness may be an issue however, so bring your own toilet paper and baby wipes.

Child seats are rarely used and difficult to buy within China. Leyou (www.leyou.com) stocks child seats at their store in Wangjiao Shopping Centre (tel: (010) 6558-6558), Beijing.

ACCOMMODATION

Chinese hotels will usually have no problem accommodating children, though facilities may be basic. Children under 12 generally stay in their parents' room at no extra cost. Child safety may be an issue, particularly around swimming pools or play areas.

FOOD AND DRINK

Chinese restaurants welcome children, though may not have high-chairs for babies. Chopsticks come only in adult

Travelling with kids can be rewarding in China

sizes, so a more child-friendly option may be asking for a plastic spoon. Typical Chinese food may seem strange to children, though old favourites such as noodles, dumplings and pancakes should be acceptable. Restaurants will usually be happy to make dishes with less chilli, salt and MSG on request. Most Chinese restaurants do not observe a no-smoking policy, though larger places often have a non-smoking area. Fast-food restaurants such as McDonald's are common in large cities.

ACTIVITIES

Child-friendly sights are indicated by the 🛍 symbol throughout the book. Many parks have children's activity areas with simple games and rides. Theme parks have more advanced activities. Safety precautions at scenic sights and sports areas may be lacking, so ensure teenagers are not at risk if you allow them to go off on their own.

SETTING THE SCENE

History

THE EARLIEST DYNASTIES

The confluence of mythology and history in China took place around 4,000 years ago during the semi-legendary Xia dynasty. During the second of the quasi-legendary dynasties, the Shang (from about the 16th to 11th centuries BC), the Chinese developed an interest in art. Careful geometric designs as well as dragon and bird motifs adorned bowls and implements. Among the advances of the era were the introduction of astronomical calculations, the use of cowrie shells as a unit of exchange, the construction of palaces and temples, and the introduction of chopsticks.

THE ZHOU DYNASTY

The Zhou had long been vassals of the Shang, but eventually grew strong enough to defeat them in warfare in the 11th century BC. They continued to hold sway for around 600 years. During this time, Chinese boundaries were expanded, land reform was instituted and towns were built.

In the later years of the Zhou era, two of China's most influential thinkers emerged. China's supreme sage, Kong Fuzi, better known internationally as Confucius, was born in 551BC in what is now Shandong province. So profound was his influence that 11 Chinese emperors made pilgrimages to the birthplace of the Great Teacher. His contemporary, the philosopher Laozi is credited with founding Daoism, emphasising nature, intuition and the cosmic flow known as 'the Way'.

After the death of Confucius, China entered a period of upheaval known as the 'Warring States' period (475–221BC). Social and economic advances in these times included the introduction of iron, the development of infantry armies, the circulation of currency and the advent of private landownership, as well as the expansion of cities.

THE CHINESE EMPIRE

Under the Qin dynasty, China is considered to have been unified for the first time. Qin Shi Huangdi (221–206BC) organised his empire along strict lines. Land was divided into provinces and prefectures, with power vested in a central government staffed by highly educated bureaucrats. Disapproved books were burnt

Confucius statue, Beijing

and dissidents were either executed or exiled. Canals, roads and the Great Wall were built under the auspices of an extensive public-works programme staffed mostly by conscripts. Official decrees standardised weights and measures and even the axle dimensions of all wagons. You can visit a site of the Qin dynasty today at Xi'an, where the first emperor's terracotta army was unearthed in 1974.

The Han dynasty (206BC–AD220), which followed the Qin, consolidated the imperial order. Civil servants were selected by exams, the centralised government standardised currency, and the 'Silk Road' across Central Asia opened up intercontinental trade. Marauding Huns were vanquished, and Chinese sovereignty was extended almost to today's frontiers.

A golden age began, and a university was established in the capital city, Chang'an (now Xi'an). Intellectuals, who had been harried by the Qin, were now encouraged in their creative endeavours, and with the invention of paper, the influence of their writings became more widespread. Trade and industry developed and communication systems improved. Sculpture, ceramics and silk manufacture flourished. The arrival of Buddhism, entering from India via Tibet, was to have an enduring effect on Chinese life and art.

THE THREE KINGDOMS

Like dynasties before and after, the Han succession ended around AD220 in a new struggle for power and anarchy. As a result, the nation was split into three competing kingdoms. The era of the Three Kingdoms lasted only

The terracotta army, near Xi'an

about half a century, but it had as a legacy some thrilling tales of derring-do that later inspired various plays and a classic Ming-dynasty novel. Three rival states held power under almost constant threat from usurpers at home and abroad. Regionalism and class distinction re-emerged. Many people moved south and the Yangzi (Yangtze) Valley became the leading centre of Chinese culture.

Reunification and economic advance were achieved under the vigorous but short-lived Sui dynasty in the latter part of the 6th century.

THE GLORY OF THE TANG

In the realm of culture, no era of Chinese history has surpassed the Tang dynasty (618–907), during which poetry and art reached a brilliant apex. China's Imperial Academy of Letters was founded, about 900 years before any such institution was established in

Tea-drinking, thought to have originated in China during the 3rd century AD

subtle brushwork of calligraphy. Sculptors excelled in portraying lifelike human, animal and religious figures.

However, by the beginning of the 10th century, the Tang rulers had lost their control of the country. Revenues from tax collection dwindled, ambitious palace eunuchs plotted, reform schemes failed and rebellious forces threatened. In 907 the last of the Tang monarchs abdicated.

THE SONG BRING STABILITY

The next half-century is known as the era of 'The Five Dynasties and the Ten Kingdoms'. This transitional period was marred by political and military infighting, and by rivalry, intrigue and cruelty. Then, a general named Zhaokuangyin came onto the scene and founded the Song dynasty (960–1280), which ensured Chinese cultural supremacy for the next three centuries.

The number of cities in China increased dramatically under the Song, particularly in the Yangzi Valley and in the southeast. Where there were cities, there were scholars, artists and artisans. Moveable type revolutionised printing, books became more common and literacy increased; Chinese scientists published works on botany, astronomy, mathematics and geography. Emperors appointed court painters, and glazed porcelain was received abroad with admiration and awe.

But while art and scholarship continued to thrive, the political and military situation deteriorated. Foreign invaders chipped away at the empire. Taxpayers groaned under the burden of the army and the tribute paid to foreign rivals, and complained

Europe. The first known printed book, a Buddhist scripture, was published in China in 868.

The capital city, Chang'an, had a population of more than a million, and was probably the largest city on Earth at that time. In Chang'an, extravagant palaces and temples were interspersed with markets stocked with exotica from as far away as Byzantium. Foreign traders journeyed here to purchase silk, porcelain and spices and, by so doing, introduced the Chinese to foreign ideas.

Scholars, poets and artists all achieved prominence. Encyclopaedias were compiled, and poetry evolved a metrical system and lines that rhymed. As Buddhism gained strength and took on a Chinese character, it inspired the construction of great temples and pagodas adorned with frescoes and statues. Artists painted sensitive landscapes and perfected the about the luxuries of palace life. Disaster was inevitable: invaders from Manchuria forced the Song to retreat to the south. And the Mongol invaders, headed by Genghis Khan, swept across China, bringing the country under foreign rule for the first time.

UNDER MONGOL RULE

The new era, known as the Yuan dynasty (1279–1368), lasted less than a century. Creativity declined, but the new ruler of China, Kublai Khan (grandson of the great Genghis Khan), had an open mind and a generally humane attitude. He appointed Chinese bureaucrats and scholars to help rule the country. Historians generally conclude that Kublai Khan became an 'almost authentic' Chinese emperor, and that the conquerors changed more profoundly than the conquered.

The capital of the new empire was built on the site of present-day Beijing and was called Dadu, or 'Kanbalu' in the words of that most renowned of medieval travellers, Marco Polo. His

The coronation of Kublai Khan

account of the vast new capital is filled with admiration for the palaces and bazaars and the profusion of shade trees. He regards with wonder the Great Khan's religious tolerance, generosity and admirable taste in wives. He reports all manner of innovations, not least the invention of paper money.

With the death of Kublai Khan in 1294, the Mongols started to lose their grip. The emperor's successors lacked his vision and vigour. Insurrection was in the air, met by oppression and resulting in ever more sustained resistance. Finally, an uprising led by a peasant general, Zhuyuanzhang, routed the Yuan rulers. In 1368 the victor assumed the throne of the Middle Kingdom, founding yet another great dynasty, the Ming.

THE BRILLIANCE OF THE MING

In Chinese, the word Ming is written as a composite of the characters for 'sun' and 'moon', which are combined to mean 'brilliant' or 'glorious'. In fact, the dynasty (1368–1644) didn't quite live up to its name. Beauty was achieved in architecture, sculpture and the decorative arts. But literature, now serving an ever-wider audience, produced few masterworks, and philosophy saw no new developments. Science, which had been far more advanced than in Europe, was so gravely neglected that China became a technological backwater.

Conservatism and hostility to foreign ideas, however, could not be absolutely maintained. During the Ming era, China imported tobacco, pineapples and peanuts. The first

Christian missionaries came to China with the arrival at Guangzhou, in 1516, of Portuguese ships. Thanks to the emancipated Confucian tradition, they were usually welcomed, although they hardly achieved mass conversions. From the Jesuits the Chinese learnt European mathematics and astronomy.

At first the Ming headquarters were moved south to the Yangzi River port of Nanjing, the 'Southern Capital', but at the beginning of the 15th century the capital returned to what was now renamed Beijing, the 'Northern Capital'. Here Ming architects and artisans produced some of China's most elegant palaces, temples and parks, including the Forbidden City and Temple of Heaven, masterpieces that survive today.

The move northwards made the supervision of defence efforts on the ever-sensitive borders of the empire easier. The Ming rulers oversaw the construction and renovation of the sections of the Great Wall that millions of tourists visit today, but even this eventually proved incapable of keeping out enemies. By the 17th century, after repeated forays, infiltrations and invasions, forces from Manchuria capitalised on domestic upheavals in China to take power in Beijing, almost by default. But consolidating control over the rest of the country was a long and brutal business.

THE GREAT QING

The new dynasty was called the Qing, and it would hold power until modern times (1644–1911). The Manchu adopted all the refinements of Chinese civilisation, and installed a regime so conservative that it began to hold back progress. One of the most dynamic emperors was Kangxi, who reigned at almost the same time as Louis XIV of France. He presided over an era of prosperity and positive achievement, rebuilding Beijing, encouraging scholarship and expanding the empire to its greatest area.

Under Emperor Qianlong, Kangxi's grandson, conflict arose between Europe's empires and the Middle Kingdom. King George III of Britain sent an emissary to negotiate diplomatic and trade relations. The emperor flatly turned him down but thanked him for showing such 'submissive loyalty in sending this tribute mission'. No insult appears to have been intended, even though the message referred to Britain as 'the lonely remoteness of your island, cut off from the world by intervening wastes of sea'. China sincerely believed itself to be the centre of the world: it

Figure of Emperor Zhu Di at the Ming Tombs

had nothing to learn or gain from so-called foreign devils. But such sublime self-assurance was to be short-lived.

The soaring demand in Europe for Chinese tea, silk and porcelain brought increasing pressure for freer trade. However, the Chinese were stubborn. Needing no commodities, they would accept only silver bullion in exchange for goods, thus undermining Britain's balance of payments. Then, at about the turn of the 19th century, wily foreign traders thought of an alternative medium of payment – opium. Tons of the drug were brought into China from India.

In 1839 the Chinese government finally cracked down on this drain on the treasury, which was also causing mass addiction among the Chinese. Some 20,000 chests of opium were confiscated from British merchants in Guangzhou (Canton), and a Qing imperial edict was issued that terminated trade between China and Britain. Retaliation came a year later in the first of the Opium Wars, which culminated in a series of 'unequal treaties' forced on an increasingly weak Manchu regime. Under the 1842 Treaty of Nanjing, China was obliged to pay an indemnity to Britain, to open major ports to foreign political and economic penetration, and to surrender Hong Kong to Britain.

Infinitely more costly in human terms was the Taiping Rebellion, which began in 1850 as a peasant revolt. There was a struggle between the Qing dynasty and rebels determined to overthrow such traditional values as respect for religion, private property and male supremacy. The

Opium Wars satirised, 19th-century style

revolt lasted 14 years and cost more lives than World War I. The Qing finally won, but the regime and the nation were fatally weakened.

WAR WITH JAPAN AND THE WEST

This became patently clear during the Sino-Japanese War of 1894–5, in which the inadequacy of the Chinese army was starkly displayed. Japan and Western powers were dismantling the Chinese Empire. Demands for reform won the support of the emperor, but his notoriously scheming aunt, the Empress Dowager Cixi, edged him off the throne. Soon after, Cixi had the chance to exploit the Boxer Rebellion (1900), a revolt against foreign influence. It was finally put down by the intervention of all the Great Powers, which joined together in an unprecedented alliance. China was

French troops fighting against Taiping rebels

saddled with the payment of a humiliating indemnity and a further loss of respect.

The elderly empress died in 1908, one day after the mysterious death of her nephew, the unseated emperor. The heir apparent was a two-year-old prince, Puyi – hardly the leader the dynasty and the nation needed in the face of civil disorder and foreign threats. Less than three years later, an army uprising took place in Wuhan and quickly won widespread support. The success of the revolution surprised many observers. It came so suddenly that Dr Sun Yat-sen, the inveterate revolutionary who had led several earlier insurrections, was still abroad at the time. He returned in triumph to accept the presidency of the Chinese Republic. The Manchu dynasty and its child-emperor surrendered in 1911.

But the path of the new republic was strewn with dangers. A warlord seized power in Beijing, hoping to restore the monarchy. A harried Sun Yat-sen then moved his Guomindang or Nationalist Party south to Guangzhou. Towards the end of hostilities, China entered World War I on the side of the Allies. But the 1919 Versailles Peace Conference proved a bitter disappointment when Japan, and not China, won control over Germany's former holdings in Shandong province. Frustration inspired protest demonstrations. The targets of increasingly widespread bitterness were the foreign powers and the regime in Beijing, as agitation for drastic social reforms caught the imagination of students and factory workers.

In 1921, the nascent Communist Party of China held its first national congress in Shanghai. A cautious Communist alliance was arranged with the Guomindang in 1924. Disappointed with the Western powers, Sun Yat-sen turned for support to the leaders of the young Soviet regime. The Kremlin obliged by sending political and military advisors. In turn, Dr Sun dispatched his 37-year-old follower, Chiang Kai-shek, as head of a mission to Moscow. Dr Sun, who rallied the Chinese with his Three Principles – Nationalism, Democracy and the People's Livelihood – died in 1925. His successor, Chiang Kai-shek, took over the campaign, moving the capital to Nanjing.

In 1927 Chiang turned on the Communists as well as on leftists within his own party, unleashing a bloody purge. The Communists, who had already organised the support of millions of peasants, gathered strength in the south. But, facing increasing military pressure, they set out on the epic Long March to north-west China, a distance of some 10,000 perilous kilometres (over 6,200 miles). During one of history's greatest strategic retreats, one of the founders of the Chinese Communist Party, Mao Zedong, was chosen as party leader. It was a mandate he would retain for the rest of his life.

THE BITTER YEARS OF WAR

In 1931 Manchuria was seized by Japan and proclaimed as the 'independent' state of Manchukuo. This was to be a fatal prologue to World War II. Over the next few years Japanese troops advanced into several other areas of northern China. The Japanese juggernaut crushed all the resistance in the big coastal cities as well as in Beijing and Nanjing. The retreat ended in 1938 with the nationalist government dug in behind the gorges of the Yangzi River, in the last-ditch capital of Chongqing.

Even before entering World War II, the US was supporting the armies of Chiang Kai-shek with food, fuel and transport. However, once in the field, the Americans soon became disheartened with the confusion, corruption and stalling. Chiang, they believed, was hoarding everything from rice to aircraft in the struggle against the Chinese Communists and leaving the Allies to worry about the Japanese.

When Japan surrendered in 1945, Chiang Kai-shek could share the victory toasts as one of the Allies. But he was already losing the battle of his lifetime – for China. By V-J Day (15 August), when Japan officially surrendered, the Chinese Communists controlled an area inhabited by nearly one-quarter of the nation's population. At first the Americans tried to mediate between the Communists and the nationalists, even while continuing to supply the nationalists. But any chances for post-war cooperation between right and left were wrecked in a matter of months. China was sinking into civil war.

Despite early setbacks, the Communist armies became an overwhelming force. They were greeted as liberators by the peasants and met only desultory resistance in most cities. The nationalists, in despair, fell back and finally fled, moving the government and countless national treasures to the island of Taiwan, pledging to return one day.

In Tiananmen Square in Beijing on 1 October 1949, Chairman Mao

Dr Sun Yat-sen

Zedong proclaimed the People's Republic of China. After thousands of years of empire and a few decades of violent transition, the most populous country in the world was committed to Communism.

IMPOSING THE NEW ORDER

Before any grandiose plans could be implemented, China's fledgling rulers had to rebuild society and a crippled economy. Agrarian reform was the first revolutionary innovation, followed by organisation of the cities under Party control.

Hardly had the groundwork been laid than China entered the Korean War, sending 'volunteers' to fight against American-led United Nations forces. Relations between the US and China suffered, but Beijing's ties with Moscow prospered in comradely harmony. The world's first Communist state, the USSR, shipped technical advisors and roubles to China, and many new institutions were set up along Soviet lines. As in Russia, the

farms were collectivised and heavy industry took economic precedence.

Mao Zedong's 'Great Leap Forward' (1959) was designed as a crash programme of economic growth, but it kept the country in turmoil and brought disastrous results. At about the time the Leap was suddenly reversed, relations between China and the Soviet Union plunged from polite to frosty to hostile. China cut off relations with the world and tested its own nuclear bomb.

From 1966 to 1976, China was convulsed by the Great Proletarian Cultural Revolution. This was Mao's attempt to put an end to bureaucratic stagnation and reassert his control over the Chinese Revolution. He saw students as his activists and encouraged them to turn on their teachers. The most chaotic phase lasted from May 1966 until late 1967. Students organised 'Red Guard' units all over China. Mao's slogan that 'It is right to rebel' propelled their campaign to destroy remnants of the old society. Brandishing Mao's Little Red Book of quotations, they destroyed temples and historic sites, and broke into homes to destroy books and art. Much of China's cultural heritage was destroyed. Party leaders and other 'counter-revolutionary' forces were denounced and subjected to mass trials.

Changes came in quick succession in the 1970s. In 1971 China was admitted to the United Nations. In 1972, the US president, Richard Nixon, visited China, thus paving the way to normalising relations between the two countries. In early 1976 the

The Sino-Japanese war preceded, then merged with, World War II

Revolutionary Mao Zedong billboard, Yan'an

widely admired prime minister, Zhou Enlai, died. Eight months later, in September, Chairman Mao died.

THE REPUBLIC AFTER MAO

In 1978 Deng Xiaoping became China's paramount leader and inaugurated what he called a 'second revolution'. He stressed the 'Four Modernisations' – in agriculture, industry, national defence, and science and technology – for Chinese development. Mao had considered politics the key to China's progress. Deng put his faith in economic advances.

Relations with the United States were normalised in 1979. Deng travelled to the US and met President Jimmy Carter and business leaders. Deng's policy of 'opening' China to the outside was a recognition that the country needed technological expertise and capital from elsewhere.

To modernise agriculture, Deng disbanded Mao's communes, which had proved over the decades to be a disaster. Farmers could now sell surplus vegetables, fruit, fish or poultry in private markets and keep the profits. As a result, rural agricultural production more than doubled in the 1980s. Deng began reforming industry in China by upgrading technology and managerial systems, implementing price reforms, promoting foreign trade and investment, revamping the banking system and encouraging private business.

TIANANMEN PROTESTS

In April 1989, Tiananmen Square became the focus of the world's media, as students and workers aired their grievances against the government after reformer Hu Yaobang's death. Angered by widespread corruption, they demanded democratic reform. As the number of protesters swelled to a million, martial law was imposed, and, on the night of 3 June and early hours of 4 June, the army stormed Tiananmen Square. Although debate continues concerning bloodshed in the square itself, at least 300 people are believed to have died in surrounding streets. The incident provoked international outrage and also showed that China's leadership would not tolerate political challenge.

CONTEMPORARY CHINA

Despite crushing the democracy movement, the government knew that its survival depended on both absolute power and the continuing success of its economic reform. The 1990s were a decade of high economic growth as well as tension between China and other nations, as Deng's successor, Jiang Zemin, grappled with China's new role in the international community.

Hu Jintao, president since 2003, has overseen years of prosperity

Hong Kong returned to China in 1997 and Macau in 1999. Attention turned to Taiwan, which Beijing hoped to woo back to the fold, promising 'one country, two systems'. Taiwan has resisted reunification while shying away from declaring independence.

US–China relations have improved since September 11, 2001. In 2001 China joined the World Trade Organisation, and in 2003 Hu Jintao succeeded Jiang Zemin as president and Wen Jiabao replaced Zhu Rongji as premier, completing the shift to a younger leadership.

Today China is one of the world's top exporters and is attracting huge amounts of foreign investment. In turn, it is investing billions of dollars abroad. Yet the rise of private Chinese enterprise and the demise of state-run industries has also carried a heavy social cost in unemployment and

rising inequalities. Many people in the cities of the eastern coastal regions and the south have become wealthy, but progress has been slow to reach the countryside, and the rich–poor divide has widened. The nation's economic miracle is also taking a heavy toll on the environment with the uncontrolled expansion of industry, an explosion in car ownership and rising power consumption mostly fuelled by high-pollution coal-fired power stations.

Yet, despite all these problems, the average Chinese citizen – even those from ethnic-minority groups such as the Tibetan and the Uighur – are undoubtedly richer and more free today than they have been at any time in China's long history. China is united, strong and generally enjoys high international prestige. No doubt there is a way to go – but China has indeed 'stood up', and is today a burgeoning superpower.

Historical Landmarks

21st–16th Centuries BC
Xia dynasty: the first Chinese state.

16th–11th Centuries BC
Shang dynasty. Bronze casting.

11th–5th Centuries BC
Zhou dynasty. Chang'an becomes capital.

771BC
Zhou capital moved to Luoyang.

551BC
Birth of Confucius.

475–221BC
Conflict between the 'Warring States'.

221–206BC
Qin dynasty. Construction of the Great Wall.

206BC–AD220
Han dynasty. International trade along the Silk Road.

220–581
Three Kingdoms period.

581–618
Sui dynasty. Printing invented. Grand Canal construction begins.

618–907
Tang dynasty. Invention of gunpowder and porcelain.

907–60
'Five Dynasties and Ten Kingdoms'.

960–1280
Song dynasty. Movable-type printing and paper money.

1279–1368
Yuan (Mongol) dynasty. Beijing (Dadu) becomes capital. Marco Polo in China.

1368–1644
Ming dynasty. Beijing Imperial Palace built.

1644–1911
Qing dynasty (Manchu).

1911
Republic of China founded by Sun Yat-sen.

1934–5
The Long March.

1938–45
Japanese invasion and World War II.

1945–49
Civil War ends in Communist victory.

1949
Mao proclaims the People's Republic.

1966–76
Cultural Revolution.

1976
Mao dies; Tangshan earthquake.

1978
Deng Xiaoping becomes leader; economic reforms begin, with openness to the West.

1989
Tiananmen Square demonstrations.

1997
Deng Xiaoping dies; Hong Kong reverts from British to Chinese rule.

2001
China joins the World Trade Organisation.

2003
Hu Jintao becomes president.

2008
Beijing hosts the Olympics; riots in Tibet; powerful earthquake hits Sichuan.

2009
Xinjiang riots.

2010
China becomes the world's biggest exporter.

Culture

With a population of around 1,350,000,000 in 2010, China has the largest population in the world – though it due to be overtaken by India around 2025. The Chinese authorities officially recognise 56 different ethnic groups, the largest of which is the Han, who constitute about 92 percent of the total population. Other major groups are the Zhuang (16 million), the Manchu (10 million), the Hui (9 million) and the Miao (8 million). In the sparsely settled west of the country, Uighurs number 7 million, Tibetans 5 million and Mongols 5 million. The Han – that is, the people whom Westerners generally consider to be 'Chinese' – traditionally lived in the east and south, but internal migration in the last 60 years has seen the Han spread throughout this vast country, so that today they predominate just about everywhere.

The Chinese today have more opportunities than they have ever had: more freedom to move around and travel overseas, more opportunities to seek better jobs and better education, and more chances to work and save money for a better future. The outlook has never been so good for so many people. But at the same time, inevitably, huge problems exist. A widening gap separates rich from poor. In the cities, many people make relatively good money, but free access to schools, hospitals and housing, as well as other services which were taken for granted a generation ago, are increasingly threatened by privatisation, as China's Brave New World of market economics sweeps away the socialist past.

Hui Muslims at Xi'an's Great Mosque

POPULATION PROBLEMS

In 1979, the government began a one-child-per-family programme. In urban areas, the programme has been mostly successful, but less so in rural areas, where traditions die hard and larger families are needed for farming. Skewing all population statistics, however, is the preference for male heirs. In China, family lines are passed on through the male child. Partly because of this, and because male offspring are more likely to support ageing parents, especially in rural areas, sons are

Schoolkids in Pingyao

Contemporary China is the scene of a huge population movement, as tens of millions of migrant workers, lured by the sudden promise of wealth, have abandoned the still poor villages and towns of their home provinces in China's interior and western regions and headed for the coastal cities in search of opportunities. Yet accompanying this freedom of movement is a growing lack of security. Migrant workers are rarely eligible for national health insurance, cannot afford private insurance, and their employers seldom provide it. Hospitals routinely turn away those who can't afford treatment, so an injury can mean the end of employment, or the end of a life. There is also a lack of access to medical care and schooling.

preferred to daughters. Female infants in the countryside have fallen victim to infanticide. This means that by 2020 China will have 30 million more men than women.

URBAN AND RURAL

The migration from countryside to city is the largest movement in human history – so far, some 115 million people have relocated – and it

Exercise

On any early morning in China, millions of people, most of them elderly, gather in parks to exercise. There are several types of traditional exercise that are regarded not only as ways to take care of one's body, but also as therapy. The most common type of exercise is *t'ai chi* (Supreme Ultimate Boxing), which is in fact a martial art.

Another, perhaps less familiar to Westerners, is *qigong*, which is often translated as 'breath skill'. *Qigong*, in fact, plays a large part in the practice of *t'ai*

chi. With certain exercises, which may or may not involve conscious breathing, the patient learns to control *qi* – a person's vital energy – and to influence the course of an illness.

It is claimed that those who have mastered *qigong* can walk outdoors in sub-zero temperatures without sufficient clothing and remain oblivious to the cold. Today, an estimated 70 million people in China practise *qigong* on a daily basis, and the therapy has also developed a dedicated following in the West.

Rural life in Guizhou province

is hollowing out the rural heartland. As agriculture gives way to industry and urban sprawl, farmers are often removed from their land. Compensation is supposed to be mandatory, but the amounts can vary according to the whims of local officials. Farmers and poor rural residents have been fighting back, often by gathering in huge, hard-to-ignore protests. Sometimes the protests get violent, and sometimes, too, they get the attention of the rulers in Beijing, who generally side with the peasants. But the central government has limited power in the rural areas of China, where local party bosses often call the shots.

Thirty years ago, a city dweller's ticket to security was a job for life – the so-called 'iron rice bowl' – with the Communist Party. On the farm, it was even simpler: plant the crops, work the fields and hope the elements are on your side. However, the new ticket to success is a college degree and proficiency in English. China's youth are drawn to the bright lights of the coastal cities and don't want to work on the farms. In economic terms,

Chinese society has long since ceased to be communist. Today it is widely perceived as glorious to be rich, and cut-throat free-market capitalism has all but replaced any notions of economic equality.

GROWTH AND THE ENVIRONMENT

China's economic success has come at a considerable environmental cost. According to the World Bank, it is home to 16 of the world's 20 most polluted cities, and more than 400,000 premature deaths occur annually due to air pollution. Meanwhile, privatisation and reforms mean that the state no longer provides free healthcare, and reportedly as many as 800 million people now lack access to even basic care. These same reforms have also resulted in a largely pay-as-you-go education system that puts an enormous strain on the poor.

Since the end of 2008 the global downturn has impacted on China's economy, with yearly growth rates falling from over 10 percent to around 6 percent (still way ahead of most other economies), while domestic price inflation has risen sharply. Thus the government is faced with huge challenges: whilst ensuring that China can weather the economic storm, in the face of growing discontent it needs to ensure that the new-found prosperity is spread throughout the vast hinterland, and not limited to the southern and eastern cities.

BELIEFS AND RELIGION

The 'three teachings' of Confucianism, Daoism and Buddhism have traditionally dominated China's spiritual life. Of the two indigenous systems, Confucianism developed as a moral form of philosophy that taught ethical and pragmatic standards of behaviour, while Daoism had a religious as well as a philosophical dimension. Buddhism was imported from India in the 1st century AD, gradually evolving into a uniquely Chinese form as it was influenced by Daoism and Confucianism.

When the Communists came to power religion was deemed 'counter-revolutionary', and during the Cultural Revolution there was widespread destruction of temples, mosques and churches. After Mao's death things became less repressive, and in 1982, freedom of religious belief was guaranteed by law – although what are deemed to be 'cults', such as the Falun Gong movement, are seen as subversive and remain illegal.

Apart from the fusion of Confucianism, Daoism and Buddhism that lies at the heart of Chinese religious belief, Islam and Christianity are also practised. Beyond philosophy or theology, the age-old traditions of lucky numbers, fortune-telling and geomancy naturally survive.

FORTUNE-TELLING AND FENG SHUI

Many Chinese take superstition, as distinct from organised religion, seriously. Fortune-tellers make predictions by reading faces and palms, or doing complicated calculations based on a person's name or the time and date of birth. The Chinese zodiac of 12 animal signs divides people according to the year they were born, and also tells their fortune and future by combining philosophy and numbers.

Feng shui or 'wind and water' is a set of traditional spiritual laws, or geomancy, used to attract the best luck and prevent bad fortune. Those who

Lighting candles at Baima Si, near Luoyang

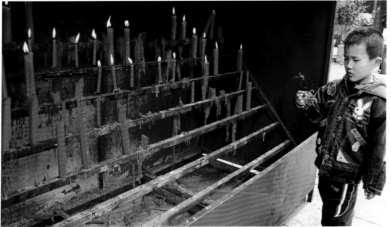

Chim fortune-telling sticks

take it seriously consult a geomancer to advise on designs of buildings, dates of important decisions, and layout of one's home and office. *Feng shui* theories are based mainly on the principle of *qi* or 'life essence' divided into *yin* and *yang*, the female-passive and male-active elements of life. The preferred orientation is north–south, with the most important structures facing south, towards the sun. A sheltered position, facing the water and away from a hillside, is also desirable.

The concept of lucky numbers persists: the number eight is considered auspicious, so the Beijing Olympics kicked off at 8.08pm on the 8th day of the 8th month of 2008. The fact that the Cantonese for the number fourteen sounds similar to the word for death means that some Hong Kong tower blocks simply progress from the 13th to the 15th floor.

ANCESTOR WORSHIP

Although the origins of ancestor worship are very ancient, it has been enhanced by Confucian notions of filial piety extending into the afterlife. By making offerings to the departed, the living show their respect and ensure that their ancestors will continue to take an interest in the fortunes of their descendants. One of the many superstitions that the revolutionary-era Communist Party attempted to banish from China, it is still a force in rural China, and Mao Zedong himself is subject to a form of ancestor worship – as the father of modern China – in public portraits and icons hanging over the dashboards of taxis and buses. Ancestor worship also manifests itself in popular holidays such as Qingming, popularly known in English as the Grave-Sweeping Festival, when traditional Chinese families go to the tombs of their ancestors, clean them up and make offerings of fruit, light incense and, particularly in Hong Kong and Taiwan, burn paper money.

CALLIGRAPHY AND PAINTING

The difficulty of learning written Chinese ensured the high social status of the scholar-gentry class. Mastery of writing and calligraphy was highly esteemed. Chinese paintings, meanwhile, are abstract and do not aim for realism. The best paintings successfully capture the spirit or essence of a subject. Furthermore, a painter is considered a master of his art when the necessary brush strokes for a bird, chrysanthemum or waterfall flow effortlessly from his hand. Chinese painting values quick execution. Indeed, the nature of the materials and brush techniques do not allow for careful sketching or repainting; mistakes cannot be hidden or painted over.

SILK AND PORCELAIN

The cultivation of the silkworm is said to go back to the 3rd century BC, and for centuries, silk held the place of currency: civil servants and officers as well as foreign envoys were frequently paid or presented with bales of silk. The precious material was transported to the Middle East and Europe along the famed Silk Road, its production a carefully guarded secret. Today's centres of silk production are concentrated around Hangzhou, Suzhou and Wuxi.

The Chinese invented porcelain sometime in the 7th century. The most widespread form was celadon, the product of a blending of iron oxide with the glaze that resulted, during firing, in a green tone. Sancai ceramics, with three-colour glazes from the Tang dynasty, became world-famous. As early as the Yuan period, a technique from the Near East was used for underglaze painting in cobalt blue, commonly known as Ming porcelain. Decorations included figures, landscapes and theatrical scenes. At the beginning of the Qing dynasty, blue-and-white porcelain attained its highest level of quality. Once patronised by imperial courts, Jingdezhen in Jiangxi province has been a centre of porcelain manufacture since the 14th century. Today, however, relatively inexpensive porcelain can be bought throughout China.

TRADITIONAL CHINESE ARCHITECTURE

The principles of traditional Chinese architecture reflect the twin philosophies of order and authority. Careful layout applies not only to residences and ceremonial buildings, but to entire cities. The longevity and universal application of this approach also mean that classical buildings across the length and breadth of China, be they temples, pagodas or imperial palaces, tend to exhibit similar characteristics.

One such hallmark is the use of curving roofs; overhanging eaves offered shelter from the rain as well as keeping out the sun in summer, and allowing it in during winter. Simple homes had plain gabled roofs. Surrounding and enclosing classical Chinese residences, temples and palaces is a wall. Cities were also surrounded by walls, their entrance gates surmounted by watchtowers. Drum and bell towers would announce the opening and closing of the city gates.

Water calligraphy on the street

Food and Drink

China has no national cuisine as such – all cuisines are regional – but certain aspects of the cookery are common throughout the country. Chinese chefs seek a balance of textures, flavours and colours within a dish, and few dishes feature any one ingredient exclusively, as captured in the phrase *se xiang wei ju quan* – which translates as colour, fragrance and taste in complete harmony. Common flavourings used across China include soy sauce, ginger, garlic, vinegar, sesame oil, soybean paste and scallions.

Most Chinese dishes are stir-fried quickly in a blazing-hot wok, with ingredients cut into bite-size pieces prior to cooking. This saves fuel and cooks meat thoroughly, while ensuring that vegetables have a crisp texture and retain their vitamins. Steaming is a technique used more in southern China than elsewhere – particularly for vegetables and fish – but it is used nationwide for cooking buns and dumplings. Braising is used for cooking pork and beef in stew-like dishes seasoned with aniseed and peppers. Few Chinese homes or restaurants have ovens, and roasting is reserved for speciality dishes, such as the famous Beijing duck.

Chinese regional cuisines combine the above techniques and flavours with ingredients and spices available in a particular area. Gourmets argue endlessly about how the regions should be divided, but generally speaking, there are four broad regional cuisines.

GUANGDONG

Food-wise, the Cantonese were ahead of their time. In the past couple of decades, the world has discovered the virtues of fresh food with simple ingredients, quickly cooked and lightly seasoned. The Cantonese have been doing this for centuries. The classic dish is steamed fish, which is lightly steamed, then doused in red-hot oil and topped with a mild sauce of coriander, ginger, pepper, sesame and soy. Other famous Cantonese dishes are too numerous to list – they include beef and broccoli with oyster sauce, diced chicken with cashew nuts, barbecue pork, steamed lobster, and the many kinds of dim sum.

Cantonese chefs like to mix fruit with meat or poultry, and lemon-roasted chicken and duck with pineapple are both typical (and excellent).

A typically fiery Sichuan dish featuring the liberal use of red chilli peppers

Another essential dish is chicken strips dipped in egg white and cooked with fresh sweet peas. This delicate dish is typically Cantonese in character: mild, lightly spiced and full of subtle flavour. The southern repertoire also includes the most expensive foods in China, including shark fin soup, bird's nest soup and sea slug, and some of the strangest, including insects, dogs and cats, reptiles, wild animals, and just about anything else that ever moved a limb or twitched a tail.

Making *xiao long bao* dumplings in Shanghai

SICHUAN

Sichuan food, with its trademark flavours of chilli pepper, Sichuan peppercorn *(ma la)*, vinegar and garlic, might be the most popular of all Chinese cuisines. In Chongqing and Sichuan, the food is volcanic and incendiary, though the hot chilli oils, peppers and peppercorns are usually combined with a complementary sweet and/ or sour flavour to provide balance. Elsewhere in China, especially the big cities, Sichuan cuisine is kinder and gentler than it is back home.

Gong bao (kung pao in the west) chicken or shrimp, cooked with a hot and sweet sauce of peanuts and chilli, is a landmark dish. Dried chilli peppers are cut into long strips and fried in oil, then removed and cooked with the meat, and at the end a rich mixture of soy sauce, wine, vinegar and sesame -seed oil is added. *Hui guo rou*, or twice-cooked meat, is pork belly that is boiled with scallions, wine and ginger, then removed and stir-fried with garlic, chilli peppers and a vegetable, usually cabbage. As with the other cuisines, there are dozens of good Sichuan dishes: *ma po dofu*, spicy bean curd with minced pork, is a staple, and so is *yin si juan*, a delicate fried bread that sometimes serves as a substitute for rice.

SHANGHAI/YANGZI DELTA

There is argument about whether Shanghai has a cuisine of its own, or whether it absorbed its food culture from surrounding territories; it is sometimes extended to include the milder and more delicate Huai Yang and Hangzhou styles. But in general, Shanghainese has come to mean a rich and sometimes oily cuisine featuring sweet, dark gravies and stews made mostly with fish, pork and freshwater swamp denizens. The Yangzi Delta is rich in fish, shrimp, crabs, snails, eels, frogs, turtles and other wetland dwellers, and the tables of Shanghai groan with those ingredients. Most are 'red cooked' in a sweet-salty sauce of sugar and soy.

Accompaniments to Beijing duck

Shanghai also gets credit for one of the most delicious of Chinese foods, the dumpling. *Xiao long bao*, the most popular type, is a mouth-watering bun containing green onion, ginger, pork and sesame oil that is a ubiquitous street food throughout China. Another delicacy is *shi zi tou*, or lion's head meatballs, which is ground pork mixed with beaten egg, scallions, ginger, minced mushrooms and bamboo shoots, then braised on a bed of cabbage. The cabbage absorbs the flavour from the meatballs, making a very tasty combination.

In Hangzhou, an exceptional dish is made from the local *longjing* tea, as thick river prawns are coated in egg white and powdered tea leaves, then steamed. The flavour is exceptional, as the mild, bitter tea and the sweet flesh of the shrimp pop with complementary flavours.

BEIJING/NORTHERN

In northern cooking, wheat flour replaces rice, and many dishes are served on delicate wheat pancakes or in sesame-seed-coated buns. The most famous northern dish is Peking (Beijing) duck, which is one of the highlights of dining in China. It is sometimes called *yi ya san chi* (one duck three ways), because the crispy skin is served first, followed by the meat, and then the bones, which arrive last in a rich soup. Peking duck takes days to prepare. The duck is boiled, brushed with wine and honey, dried for 24 hours, and then roasted and served with mild spring onion and sweet plum sauce on a thin pancake. The rich, flaky skin is the highlight, and it should be crispy and fresh, with all the fat roasted away.

The best Chinese dessert is also a northern speciality. Pieces of fruit, usually banana or apple, are deep-fried and then covered in a glaze of caramelised sugar and sesame seeds. Before they cool, the fritters are plunged into a bowl of iced water and served.

OTHER CUISINES

There are many more regional cuisines: the food of Yunnan, home to many ethnic minorities, features exotic mushrooms and mountain vegetables, goat's cheese, corn, and whole cooked beans. The Hakka people, traditionally poor and often transient, have a cuisine rich in preserved meats and vegetables, sun-dried sausage and liver, bean curd, and plenty of cabbage and pork. Chiu Chow food, from eastern Guangdong, features duck and goose meat and piquant sauces. Fujianese food, meanwhile, features local ingredients such as sweet potato and taro, and indigenous species of clam, mullet, oysters and freshwater shrimp. Hunan cuisine, the hottest of all regional styles, is a fusion of Sichuan and northern cooking, with some Muslim influences, which can be seen in skewers of lamb seasoned with cumin. Jiangxi is also considered a part of the central China spice belt, and chilli peppers and *ma la* feature heavily in local cuisine. In the Yangzi region in the north of the province, freshwater fish is more prevalent, and preparations are milder and sweeter. Xinjiang food, from the Muslim west, is popular throughout China, and features lamb, flatbread and noodles. The list could go on and on, as each small pocket of China contributes its own unique ingredients and dishes.

As a result, the variety of regional foods available in 21st-century China is astonishing. No matter how many times you eat out in China, any given meal might feature something completely original: a new dish, a new ingredient, a new preparation or even a previously undiscovered regional cuisine.

DRINKS

The Chinese almost always drink tea with their meals. In regular restaurants, it is served as a matter of course, and will generally be an inexpensive oolong. In more upscale establishments, diners are asked to choose from a selection of teas, the most popular being the quite green Longjing oolong, the somewhat darker Tieguanyin oolong, and the heavily fermented black pu'er tea from Yunnan.

Where alcohol is concerned, drinking and eating are usually combined. In cheap eateries, diners often drink beer with their noodles and *you bing* (oil pancakes), and in restaurants, they might top off their meals with *gaoliang* liquor or another spirit, sometimes brandy or Scotch whisky. Red wine is making inroads in China, and beer is common, but *gaoliang* liquor and Shaoxing *jiu* (yellow rice wine) are the key drinks.

Gaoliang, a strong and resinous-tasting distillate made from sorghum, remains popular in the north, while Shaoxing wine, comparatively sweet and mild, is more popular generally. The golden-yellow Shaoxing wine is made from glutinous rice, and has the smooth, nutty taste of a sweet sherry. It is sometimes served warm, with a dried plum added for extra sweetness.

Tea-making is a precise ritual

PHRASEBOOK

Pronunciation – *p.290* Phrases – *p.292* Menu Reader – *p.297*

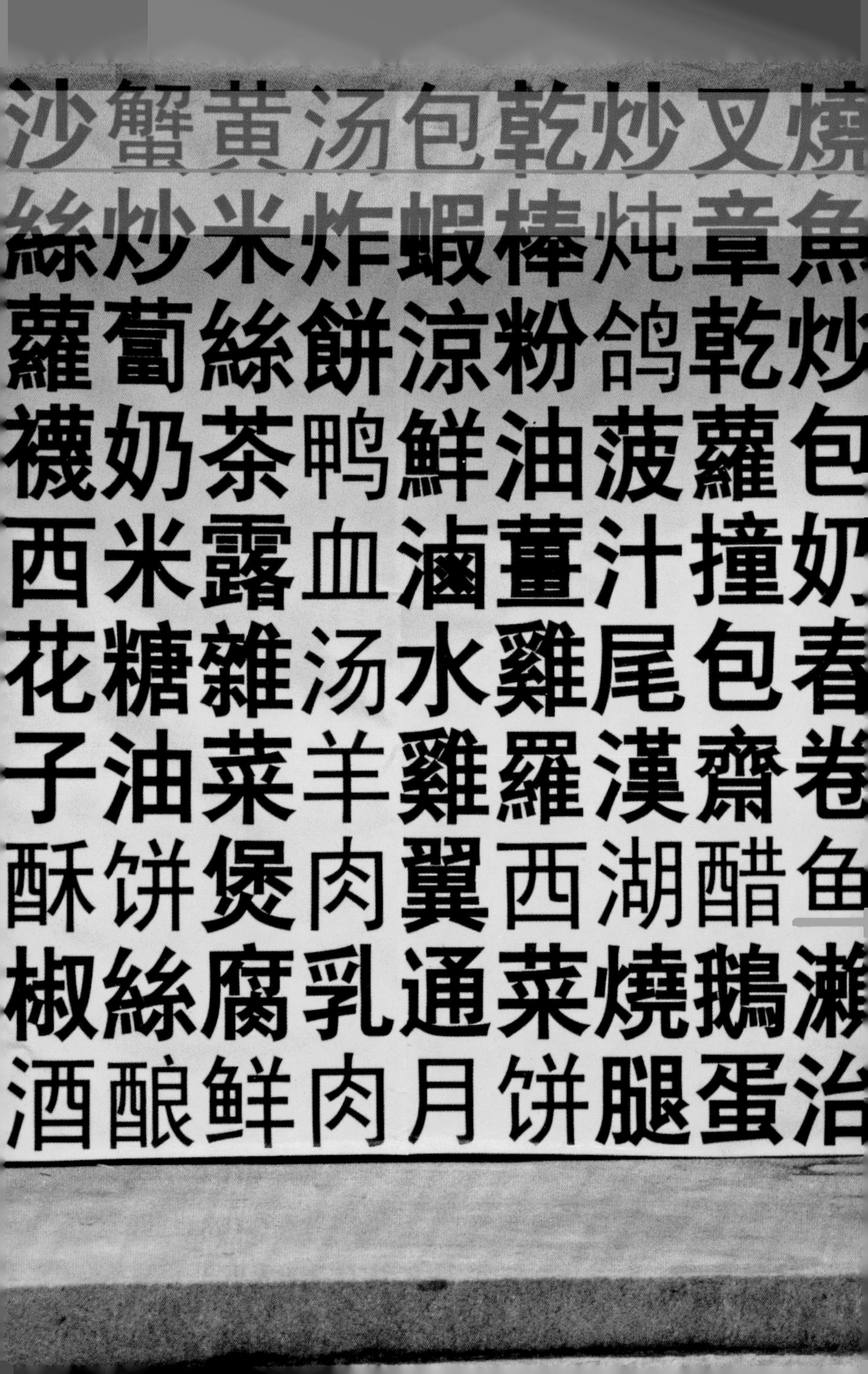

沙 蟹 黄 汤 包 乾 炒 叉 燒
絲 炒 米 炸 蝦 棒 炖 章 魚
蘿 蔔 絲 餅 涼 粉 鴿 乾 炒
襪 奶 茶 鴨 鮮 油 菠 蘿 包
西 米 露 血 滷 薑 汁 撞 奶
花 糖 雜 汤 水 雞 尾 包 春
子 油 菜 羊 雞 羅 漢 齋 卷
酥 饼 煲 肉 翼 西 湖 醋 鱼
椒 絲 腐 乳 通 菜 燒 鵝 瀨
酒 釀 鮮 肉 月 饼 腿 蛋 治

Phrase Book

Chinese is a challenging language to master, but learning a handful of essential phrases – at least in the spoken form – should not be a problem for most people. While an increasing number of Chinese in the major cities speak some English, a little phrase-book help is necessary everywhere. The official language, Mandarin (known as *putonghua)*, is spoken across much of China, although Cantonese is used in Guangdong and Hong Kong, and people in many western areas speak a range of dialects and other languages.

PRONUNCIATION

The romanised pronunciation system widely used for Chinese is called **pīnyīn**. Not all pinyin letters or letter combinations are pronounced as they normally are in English. A guide to the pronuncation of pinyin follows.

In addition to the Roman alphabet, pinyin also features tonal marks, which represent four Mandarin Chinese tones:

Tone	Mark	Description	Example	Simplified Chinese	Translation
1st	–	high and level	**mā**	妈	mother
2nd	´	starts medium, then rises to the top	**má**	麻	hemp
3rd	ˇ	starts low at level 2, dips to the bottom and then rises toward the top to level 4	**mǎ**	马	horse
4th	ˋ	starts at the top and then falls sharp and strong to the bottom	**mà**	骂	scold

Vowels without tonal marks are considered 'neutral' or 5th tone:

neutral		flat, with no emphasis	**ma**	吗	expression of mood

Initial Consonants

The following table illustrates the initial sounds in pinyin and their equivalents in English.

Symbol	Approximate Pronunciation	Example	Example in pinyin
c	like ts in pits	草	cǎo
ch	like ch in church	吃	chī
h	like ch in Scottish loch	花	huā
q	like ch in chip	旗	qí
r	like r in raw	人	rén
sh	like sh in wash	是	shì
x	like sh in she	心	xīn

| z | like ds in kids | 子 | z |
| zh | like j in judge | 中 | zhōng |

The letters b, d, f, g, j, k, l, m, n, p, s, t, w are pronounced generally as in English.

Finals

The following table illustrates the final sounds in pinyin, and their equivalents in English.

Symbol	Approximate Pronunciation	Example	Example in pinyin
a	like a in father	八	bā
e	like e in her	鹅	é
i	1. like e in me	1. 一	1. yī
	2. not pronounced after c, s, z	2. 此	2. c
	3. after ch, sh, zh and r,	3. 吃	3. chī
	with the tongue curled back, like i in bird		
o	like aw in awe	我	wǒ
u	like oo in spoon	五	wǔ
ü	pronounced with lips pursed	女	ee
ai	like ai in aisle	爱	ài
an	like an in ran	安	ān
ang	like ang in rang	昂	áng
ao	like ow in how	奥	ào
ei	like ei in eight	类	lèi
en	like en in open	恩	ēn
eng	like en in open + g	衡	héng
er	like err	二	èr
ia	like ya in yard	下	xià
ian	similar to yen	联	lián
iang	like ee-ang	两	liǎng
iao	like ee-ow	料	liào
ie	like ye in yes	列	liè
in	like in in thin	林	lín
ing	like ing in thing	龄	líng
iong	like ee-ong	雄	xióng
iu	like yo in yoga	六	liù
ou	like ou in dough	楼	lóu
ong	like oong with oo as in soon	龙	lóng
ua	like wah	华	huá
uai	similar to why	怀	huái
uan	like wahn	环	huán
uang	like wahng	黄	huáng
ue	like u + eh	学	xué
ui	similar to way	会	huì
un	like uan in truant	魂	hún
uo	similar to war	或	huò

English	Chinese	Pinyin
How much?	多少钱？	*duō shǎo qián*

The pinyin transliteration of the Chinese ideogram follows in italic Roman characters; read it according to the pronunciation guide detailed on the previous pages. Among the English phrases, you will find some words included in square brackets; these are the American English equivalents of British English expressions.

General

0	零 *líng*	100	一百 *yì bǎi*		
1	一 *yī*	500	五百 *wǔ bǎi*		
2	二 *èr*	1,000	一千 *yì qiān*		
3	三 *sān*	1,000,000	一百万 *yì bǎi wàn*		
4	四 *sì*	Monday	星期一 *xīng qī yī*		
5	五 *wǔ*	Tuesday	星期二 *xīng qī èr*		
6	六 *liù*	Wednesday	星期三 *xīng qī sān*		
7	七 *qī*	Thursday	星期四 *xīng qī sì*		
8	八 *bā*	Friday	星期五 *xīng qī wǔ*		
9	九 *jiǔ*	Saturday	星期六 *xīng qī liù*		
10	十 *shí*	Sunday	星期天 *xīng qī tiān*		

English	Chinese	Pinyin
Hello!	你好！	*nǐ hǎo*
How are you?	你好吗？	*nǐ hǎo ma*
Fine, thanks.	很好，谢谢。	*hěn hǎo, xiè xie*
Excuse me!	请问！	*qǐng wèn*
Do you speak English?	你讲英语吗？	*nǐ jiǎng yīng yǔ ma*
I don't understand.	我不明白。	*wǒ bù míng bai*
What's your name?	你叫什么名字？	*nǐ jiào shén me míng zi*
My name is…	我叫…	*wǒ jiào …*
Nice to meet you.	见到你很高兴。	*jiàn dào nǐ hěn gāo xìng*
Where are you from?	你从哪里来？	*nǐ cóng nǎ li lái*
I'm from the US/UK	我从美国/英国来。	*wǒ cóng měi guó/yīng guó lái*
What do you do?	你做什么工作？	*nǐ zuò shén me gōng zuò*
I work for…	我为…工作。	*wǒ wéi…gōng zuò*
I'm a student.	我是学生。	*wǒ shì xué shēng*
I'm retired.	我退休了。	*wǒ tuì xiū le*
I'm studying Chinese.	我在学中文。	*wǒ zài xué zhōng wén*
I'd like to go to…	我想去…	*wǒ xiǎng qù…*
Do you like…?	你想…？	*nǐ xiǎng…*
Goodbye.	再见。	*zài jiàn*

Arrival and Departure

I'm on holiday [vacation]/business.	我在度假/出差。 wǒ zài dù jià/chū chāi
I'm going to...	我要去… wǒ yào qù…
I'm staying at the... Hotel.	我住在…旅馆。 wǒ zhù zài…lǚ guǎn

Money and Banking

Where's the...?	…在哪里？ …zài nǎ li
– ATM	– 自动取款机 zì dòng qǔ kuǎn jī
– bank	– 银行 yín háng
– currency exchange office	– 货币兑换处 huò bì duì huàn chù
When does the bank open/close?	银行什么时候开门/关门？ yín háng shén me shí hou kāi mén/guān mén
I'd like to change dollars/pounds into renminbi.	我想把美元/英镑换成人民币。 wǒ xiǎng bǎ měi yuán/yīng bàng huàn chéng rén mín bì

Transport

How do I get to town?	我怎么去城里？ wǒ zěn me qù chéng lǐ
Where's the...?	…在哪里？ …zài nǎ li
– airport	– 机场 jī chǎng
– railway [train] station	– 火车站 huǒ chē zhàn
– bus station	– 汽车站 qì chē zhàn
– underground [subway] station	– 地铁站 dì tiě zhàn
How far is it?	它有多远？ tā yǒu duō yuǎn
Where do I buy a ticket?	我在哪里买票？ wǒ zài nǎ li mǎi piào
A single [one-way]/return [round-trip] ticket to...	一张到…的单程/双程票 yī zhāng dào…de dān chéng/shuāng chéng piào
How much?	多少钱？ duō shǎo qián
Which...?	哪…？ nǎ…
– gate	– 个门 ge mén
– line	– 条线 tiáo xiàn
– platform	– 个站台 ge zhàn tái
Where can I get a taxi?	我在哪里可以找到出租车？ wǒ zài nǎ li kě yǐ zhǎo dào chū zū chē
Take me to this address.	把我送到这个地址。 bǎ wǒ sòng dào zhè ge dì zhǐ

Accommodation

I have a reservation.	我有预定。 wǒ yǒu yù dìng
My name is...	我的名字是… wǒ de míng zi shì…
Do you have a room...?	有…的房间吗？ yǒu…de fáng jiān ma
– for one/two	– 一/两人 yì/liǎng rén
– with a bathroom	– 带浴室 dài yù shì

– with air conditioning	–带空调 *dài kōng tiáo*
For…	住… *zhù…*
– tonight	–今天晚上 *jīn tiān wǎn shang*
– two nights	–两个晚上 *liǎng gè wǎn shang*
– one week	–一个星期 *yí gè xīng qī*
How much?	多少钱？ *duō shǎo qián*
Is there anything cheaper?	有没有更便宜的？ *yǒu mei yǒu gèng pián yi de*

Internet and Communications

Can I access the internet/check email?	我能上网/查电子邮件吗？ *wǒ néng shàng wǎng/chá diàn zǐ yóu jiàn ma*
How much per (half-hour)?	每(半)个小时多少钱？ *měi (bàn) gè xiǎo shí duō shǎo qián*
How do I connect/log on?	我怎么上网/登录？ *wǒ zěn me shàng wǎng/dēng lù*
Hello. This is…	你好，这是… *nǐ hǎo, zhè shì…*
Can I speak to…?	我可以与…讲话吗？ *wǒ kě yǐ yǔ…jiǎng huà ma*
Can you repeat that?	你能重复一遍吗？ *nǐ néng chóng fù yí biàn ma*
I'll call back later.	我等一会再打电话。 *wǒ děng yí huì zài dǎ diàn huà*
Where's the post office?	邮局在哪里？ *yóu jú zài nǎ li*
I'd like to send this to…	我想把这个送到… *wǒ xiǎng bǎ zhè ge sòng dào…*

Sightseeing

Where's the tourist information office?	旅游信息办公室在哪里？ *l4 yóu xìn xī bàn gōng shì zài nǎ li*
What are the main attractions?	主要景点是什么？ *zhǔ yào jīng diǎn shì shén me*
Are there tours in English?	有英语导游吗？ *yǒu yīng yǔ dǎo yóu ma*
Can I have a map/guide?	我可以要一张地图/指南吗？ *wǒ kě yǐ yào yì zhāng dì tú/zhǐ nán ma*

Shopping

Where's the market/shopping centre [mall]?	市场/购物中心在哪里？ *shì chǎng/gòu wù zhōng xīn zài nǎ li*
I'm just looking.	我只是看看。 *wǒ zhǐ shì kàn kan*
Can you help me?	你能帮我吗？ *nǐ néng bāng wǒ ma*
I'm being helped.	有人帮我了。 *yǒu rén bāng wǒ le*
How much?	多少钱？ *duō shǎo qián*
Where can I pay?	我在哪里付款？ *wǒ zài nǎ li fù kuǎn*
I'll pay in cash/by credit card.	我用现金/信用卡付款。 *wǒ yòng xiàn jīn/xìn yòng kǎ fù kuǎn*
A receipt, please.	请给我收据。 *qǐng gěi wǒ shōu jù*

Culture and Nightlife

What's there to do at night?	晚上可以做什么呢？ *wǎn shang kě yǐ zuò shén me ne*
Do you have a programme of events?	你有节目表吗？ *nǐ yǒu jié mù biǎo ma*
What's playing tonight?	今晚演什么？ *jīn wǎn yǎn shén me*
Where's the…?	…在哪里？ *…zài nǎ lǐ*
– downtown area	–市中心 *shì zhōng xīn*
– bar	–酒吧 *jiǔ bā*
– dance club	–舞蹈俱乐部 *wǔ dǎo jù lè bù*
Is there a cover charge?	有没有附加费？ *yǒu mei yǒu fù jiā fèi*

Business Travel

I'm here on business.	我在这里出差。 *wǒ zài zhè li chū chāi*
Here's my business card.	这是我的名片。 *zhè shì wǒ de míng piàn*
I have a meeting with…	我和…有一个会。 *wǒ hě…yǒu yí gè huì*
Where's the…?	…在哪里？ *…zài nǎ li*
– business centre	–商业中心 *shāng yè zhōng xīn*
– convention hall	–会议厅 *huì yì tīng*
– meeting room	–会议室 *huì yì shì*

Travel with Children

Is there a discount for children?	孩子有折扣吗？ *hái zi yǒu zhé kòu ma*
Can you recommend a babysitter?	你能推荐一位保姆吗？ *nǐ néng tuī jiàn yí wèi bǎo mǔ ma*
Do you have a child's seat/highchair?	你有儿童座椅/高脚椅吗？ *nǐ yǒu ér tóng zuò yǐ/ gāo jiǎo yǐ ma*
Where can I change the baby?	我在哪里可以给孩子换尿布？ *wǒ zài nǎ li kě yǐ gěi hái zi huàn niào bù*
Can I breastfeed the baby here?	我可以在这里喂孩子吃母奶吗？ *wǒ kě yǐ zài zhè li wèi hái zi chī mǔ nǎi ma*

Disabled Travellers

Is there…?	有…吗？ *yǒu…ma*
– access for the disabled	–残疾人通道 *cán jí rén tōng dào*
– a wheelchair ramp	–轮椅坡道 *lún yǐ pō dào*
– a disabled- [handicapped-] accessible toilet	–一间残疾人可用的洗手间 *yì jiān cán jí rén kě yòng de xǐ shǒu jiān*
I need…	我需要… *wǒ xū yào…*
– assistance	–帮助 *bāng zhù*
– a lift [an elevator]	–电梯 *diàn tī*
– a ground-floor room	–一个一楼的房间 *yí gè yī lóu de fáng jiān*

Emergencies

Help!	救命！ *jiù mìng*
Go away!	走开！ *zǒu kāi*
Stop, thief!	站住，抓贼！ *zhàn zhù zhuā zéi*
Get a doctor!	找位医生！ *zhǎo wèi yī shēng*
Fire!	着火啦！ *zháo huǒ lā*
I'm lost.	我迷路了。 *wǒ mí lù le*
Can you help me?	你可以帮我吗？ *nǐ kě yǐ bāng wǒ ma*
Call the police!	给警察打电话！ *gěi jǐng chá dǎ diàn huà*
Where's the police station?	警察局在哪里？ *jǐng chá jú zài nǎ li*
There was an accident/an attack.	出事故/有人受攻击了。 *chū shì gù/yǒu rén shòu gōng jī le*
My child is missing.	我的孩子不见了。 *wǒ de hái zi bù jiàn le*
I need…	我需要… *wǒ xū yào…*
– an interpreter	–一个翻译 *yí gè fān yì*
– to contact my lawyer	–和我的律师联系 *hé wǒ de lǜ shī lián xì*
– to make a phone call	–打电话 *dǎ diàn huà*

Health

I'm ill [sick].	我病了。 *wǒ bìng le*
I need an English-speaking doctor.	我需要说英语的医生。 *wǒ xū yào shuō yīng yǔ de yī shēng*
It hurts here.	这里疼。 *zhè lǐ téng*
I have a stomach ache.	我肚子疼。 *wǒ dù zi téng*
Where's the chemist [pharmacy]?	药房在哪里？ *yào fáng zài nǎ li*
Can you make up [fill] this prescription?	你能提供这种处方药吗？ *nǐ néng tí gōng zhè zhǒng chǔ fāng yào ma*
I'm allergic to…	我对…过敏？ *wǒ duì…guò mǐn*
A receipt, please.	请给我收据。 *qǐng gěi wǒ shōu jù*

Eating Out

A table for…, please.	请给我…人的桌子。 *qǐng gěi wǒ…rén de zhuō zǐ*
Where's the toilet [restroom]?	洗手间在哪里？ *xǐ shǒu jiān zài nǎ li*
A menu, please.	请给我一份菜单。 *qǐng gěi wǒ yí fèn cài dān*
I'd like…	我想要… *wǒ xiǎng yào…*
The bill [check], please.	请给我账单。 *qǐng gěi wǒ zhàng dān*
Is service included?	包括服务费吗？ *bāo kuò fú wù fèi ma*
The wine list/drinks menu, please.	请给我酒水单/饮料单。 *qǐng gěi wǒ jiǔ shuǐ dān/yǐn liào dān*
I'd like a bottle/glass of red/white wine.	我想要瓶/杯红/白葡萄酒。 *wǒ xiǎng yào píng/bēi hóng/bái pú táo jiǔ*

aperitif	开胃酒 *kāi wèi jiǔ*	ice cream	冰淇凌 *bīng qi líng*
apple	苹果 *píng guǒ*	lamb	小羊肉 *xiǎo yáng ròu*
bass	鲈鱼 *lú yú*	lemon	柠檬 *níng méng*
bean	豆子 *dòu zi*	lobster	龙虾 *lóng xiā*
bean sprout	豆芽 *dòu yá*	mackerel	鲭鱼 *qīng yú*
beef	牛肉 *niú ròu*	mandarin orange	橘子 *jú zi*
beer	啤酒 *pí jiǔ*	mango	芒果 *máng guǒ*
bread	面包 *miàn bāo*	meat	肉 *ròu*
cabbage	圆白菜 *yuán bái cài*	milk	牛奶 *niú nǎi*
cashew	腰果 *yāo guǒ*	monkfish	扁鲨 *biǎn shā*
chicken	鸡肉 *jī ròu*	mushroom	蘑菇 *mó gū*
chilli pepper	辣椒 *là jiāo*	mussel	淡菜 *dàn cài*
Chinese liquor	白酒 *bái jiǔ*	mutton	羊肉 *yáng ròu*
chocolate	巧克力 *qiǎo kè lì*	noodle	面条 *miàn tiáo*
chopped meat	肉馅 *ròu xiàn*	orange	橙子 *chéng zi*
coriander [cilantro]	香菜 *xiāng cài*	oyster	牡蛎 *mǔ lì*
clam	蛤蜊 *gé li*	papaya	番木瓜 *fān mù guā*
coconut	椰子 *yē zi*	peanut	花生 *huā shēng*
cod	鳕鱼 *xuě yú*	pizza	比萨饼 *bǐ sà bǐng*
coffee	咖啡 *kā fēi*	pork	猪肉 *zhū ròu*
crab	螃蟹 *páng xiè*	potato	土豆 *tǔ dòu*
crucian carp	鲫鱼 *jì yú*	rice	大米 *dà mǐ*
cured pork	咸肉 *xián ròu*	salmon	三文鱼 *sān wén yú*
duck	鸭肉 *yā ròu*	scallop	扇贝 *shàn bèi*
dumpling	饺子 *jiǎo zi*	seaweed	海带 *hǎi dài*
eel	鳗鱼 *màn yú*	prawn [shrimp]	虾 *xiā*
egg	鸡蛋 *jī dàn*	soup	汤 *tāng*
fish	鱼 *yú*	soy sauce	酱油 *jiàng yóu*
French fries	炸薯条 *zhá shǔ tiáo*	soybean [soya bean]	大豆 *dà dòu*
fruit	水果 *shuǐ guǒ*	steak	牛排 *niú pái*
ginger	姜 *jiāng*	tea	茶 *chá*
grass carp	草鱼 *cǎo yú*	tofu	豆腐 *dòu fu*
guava	番石榴 *fān shí liu*	trout	鳟鱼 *zūn yú*
hake	无须鳕 *wú xū xuě*	vegetable	蔬菜 *shū cài*
hot pepper sauce	辣酱 *là jiàng*	wine	葡萄酒 *pú táo jiǔ*

297

Phrase Book

Index

Accommodation Index

Index

Credits for Berlitz Handbook China

Written by: Andrew Forbes (Minorities, Revolutionary China, The New China, Medicine, Silk Road Culture, South, Southwest, Hong Kong, Silk Road/Tibet); **Brent Hannon** (Waterways, Eating, Sacred Mountains, Wilderness, Shopping, Rail Travel, Shanghai, Yangzi); **David Drakeford** (Beijing, North, Arts, Practical Information and Contexts)
Series Editor: Alexander Knights
Commissioning Editor: Tom Le Bas
Cartography Editor: Zoë Goodwin
Map Production: Stephen Ramsay and APA Cartography department
Production: Linton Donaldson, Rebeka Ellam
Picture Manager: Steven Lawrence
Art Editors: Richard Cooke and Ian Spick
Photography: Avlxyz 284; Don Dexter Antonio 162; Courtesy Bluewaikiki.com 286; Steve Cadman 129; Henry Chen 9CL; T Chu 235; Bridget Coila 14, 89; dada2005 106; Docsdl 157; Fotolia 217, 239, 262; Courtesy Garden Hotel 176; Ginny Freeman 155/T; APA Glyn Genin 169/T, 193, 194, 197, 198, 252; Tyler Haglund 151; APA Alex Havret 7B, 18, 28, 168, 183/T, 186, 188, 191, 192, 196, 200, 202, 228, 246/247, 282, 288/289; APA David Henley 3L, 4TR, 5TL, 6BL, 7TL, 9BR, 10/11, 16, 38, 42, 43, 46, 50, 51, 145, 173, 174, 175, 205/T, 207, 208, 209, 210, 212, 213, 215, 216, 218, 219, 220, 280; Steve Hicks 41; APA lee Hin Mun 13, 55, 61T, 66, 81T, 85, 88, 110, 251, 287; Courtesy Hilton Hotels 179; Istockphoto 6BR, 22, 45, 91B, 113M/T, 161T, 170, 172, 231/T, 237, 250, 269, 270; Gustavo Jeronimo 236; Steve Jurvetson 163; Scardey Kat 199; Yusuke Kawasaki 32; Kholkute 242; Dmitry Klimenko 107; Lanchongzi 263; Jorge Lascar 87; Tom Le Bas 9TR, 241; Maria Ly 237T; APA Bruce Minnigh 2R, 5TR, 8BM/TL, 9TL, 12, 17, 23, 35, 37, 94, 95, 96, 99, 100, 101, 102, 103, 112, 146, 149, 150, 249, 253, 254, 275, 278, 279, 281; Jakob Montrasio 6TL; Michael Mooney 7MR, 244; Naturalbornstupid 44; APA Richard Nowitz 5BL, 33, 54, 61, 63, 67, 74, 77, 80, 81, 83, 248, 255, 256, 259, 283; Dmitry Perstin 233; Kevin Poh 165; Erin O'hara 111; Photolibrary.com 5CL, 6TR, 7TR, 15, 24, 34, 39, 40, 48, 49, 131, 161, 167, 222, 227, 232, 234; APA Ryan Pyle 4, 10M, 20/21, 29, 30, 31, 52, 53, 115/T, 116, 125, 137, 142, 229/T, 285; ReaMühlthau 9BL; Rex Features 276Lars Rodvaldr 5BR; Bernt Rostad 2L, 27; Jerermy Rover 187; Saebaryo 225; Mike Saechang 109; APA David Shen Kai 117, 120, 121, 122, 123, 124, 126, 127, 257, 268; Song Shan 36; APA Ming Tang Evans 4TL, 19, 56/57, 62, 64, 65, 70, 71, 72, 75, 76, 78, 79, 264/265, 266, 267; Topfoto 271, 272, 273, 274; Treasuresthouhast 240; Daniel Criz Valle 201; Mark van der Chijs 171; Willem Van Der Horst 82; Vita 84; Kong Fu Wang 93, 104; Gwydion Williams 25; Sara Yeomans166; NeilYeung 148; Mark Zastrow 8BR; Sheery Zhang 47; Chen Zhao 140
Front cover: photolibrary.com

Printed by: CTPS-China

© 2011 APA Publications GmbH & Co. Verlag KG (Singapore branch)
7030 Ang Mo Kio Ave 5
08-65 Northstar @ AMK
Singapore 569880
apasin@singnet.com.sg

First Edition 2011

Contacting Us

At Berlitz we strive to keep our guides as accurate and up to date as possible, but if you find anything that has changed, or if you have any suggestions on ways to improve this guide, then we would be delighted to hear from you. Write to Berlitz Publishing, PO Box 7910, London SE1 1WE, UK or email: berlitz@apaguide.co.uk

Worldwide: APA Publications GmbH & Co. Verlag KG (Singapore branch), 7030 Ang Mo Kio Ave 5, 08-65 Northstar @ AMK, Singapore 569880; tel: (65) 570 1051; email: apasin@singnet.com.sg
UK and Ireland: GeoCenter International Ltd, Meridian House, Churchill Way West, Basingstoke, Hampshire, RG21 6YR; tel: (44) 01256-817 987; email: sales@geocenter.co.uk
United States: Ingram Publisher Services, 1 Ingram Boulevard, PO Box 3006, La Vergne, TN 37086-1986; email: customer.service@ingrampublisherservices.com
Australia: Universal Publishers, 1 Waterloo Road, Macquarie Park, NSW 2113; tel: (61) 2-9857 3700; email: sales@universalpublishers.com.au
New Zealand: Hema Maps New Zealand Ltd (HNZ), Unit 2, 10 Cryers Road, East Tamaki, Auckland 2013; tel: (64) 9-273 6459; email: sales.hema@clear.net.nz

www.berlitzpublishing.com